THE TRUTH ABOUT CLERGY SEXUAL ABUSE

For my granddaughter, Nina Cathyrn

BILL DONOHUE

THE TRUTH
ABOUT CLERGY
SEXUAL ABUSE

Clarifying the Facts and the Causes

IGNATIUS PRESS   SAN FRANCISCO

Cover art:
Rouen Cathedral by Claude Monet

Cover design by Carl Olson

© 2021 by Ignatius Press, San Francisco
All rights reserved
ISBN 978-1-62164-485-9 (PB)
ISBN 978-1-64229-178-0 (eBook)
Library of Congress Control Number 2021932254
Printed in the United States of America ♾

CONTENTS

PREFACE

Over the past half century, the Catholic Church has experienced two scandals: the clergy sexual abuse crisis, which was caused by priests and bishops, and the exploitation of it, which was caused by strident critics of the Catholic Church and those profiting from legal cases. Both have resulted in great damage to the Church.

The clergy sexual abuse scandal, Scandal I, has to do with the internal affairs of the Catholic Church and the environment that facilitated it. It took place mostly between the mid-1960s and the mid-1980s, though the bill did not come due—in terms of the scandal's being made public—until the beginning of this century. The two parties to the scandal—the molesting priests and their enabling bishops—have done an enormous disservice to those of us who love the Church and to the Church's public image. The damage done to victims is immeasurable.

The past few decades have not been easy. Horrific stories of sexual abuse by men we respected have left us distraught, if not furious. Just as mind-boggling are those bishops who played musical chairs with these men, moving them from parish to parish.

There is another scandal, Scandal II, that also deserves our attention. It is the creation of many parties, including the media, the entertainment industry, advocacy groups, victims' activists and their lawyers, state attorneys general, and others. They are bent on promoting the false notion that no institution has a worse record of sexual abuse than the Catholic Church. Their preoccupation with the Church, which vastly outweighs their scrutiny of any other organization, appears to be a function of their animus against the Church. Quite frankly, they are playing us—they are playing the public by holding the Church to one standard and almost every other institution to another. And let's be honest, there is a lot of money to be made by doing so.

Then there are the good priests. Who are they? They are most of the priests in the Church's clergy. They have been scapegoated, pilloried, shamed, and, in some cases, left to fend for themselves. Where are their rights? There is no ACLU racing to defend them. No, the civil libertarians seem more interested in defending the rights of suspected terrorists.

Is there any good news? Yes. Great progress has been made. Indeed, among religious and secular institutions, there is no safer place for young people today than in the Catholic Church.

I have been involved in many of the events detailed in this book. It is my hope that, as a sociologist and as a Catholic leader, I am able to shatter many of the myths about the scandal. We are called to tell the truth, not shade it. That is what I have set out to do.

PART I

Separating Fact from Fiction

I

Catholics Don't Own This Problem

Branding all priests as predators has a long, ugly history in the United States. In the mid-1830s, *The Awful Disclosures of Maria Monk* became a best-selling book, second only to the Bible in American religious publishing. Although it was totally false, it promoted the notion that nuns were sexual slaves of priests; the offenders allegedly entered the convents via subterranean passages. The principal writer of this nonsense was Reverend J.J. Slocum, a Protestant minister. Having sold three hundred thousand copies before the Civil War, he succeeded in poisoning the minds of nativists who hated Catholicism.[1]

In the twentieth century, Hitler picked up where the Maria Monk tales left off. David Kertzer is the author of a well-received book on the Catholic Church. He was asked by a correspondent for National Public Radio about a comment he made, saying that Hitler threatened to disgrace the Catholic Church. Kertzer's response is jarring:

> [Hitler] was talking about pederasty and other kinds of sexual scandals. And in fact, he did create a series of what we refer to as high-profile morality trials against priests, but also against monks and nuns, in which they were charged with all sorts of depraved behavior of orgies and abusing children and so forth. And he saw this—Hitler saw this as kind of his weapon that he could use to discredit the Catholic Church.[2]

If Maria Monk and Hitler sought to discredit the Church, today's enemies seek to disable it. Instead of telling malicious lies, they prefer

---

[1] Robert P. Lockwood, "The Lie of Maria Monk Lives On", *Catalyst*, September 2001, https://www.catholicleague.org/the-lie-of-maria-monk-lives-on/.

[2] "'Pope and Mussolini' Tells the 'Secret History' of Fascism and the Church", *Fresh Air*, National Public Radio, April 24, 2015, https://www.npr.org/2015/04/24/401967360/pope-and-mussolini-tells-the-secret-history-of-fascism-and-the-church.

to convince the public that the Catholic Church has a unique problem with sexual offenders. This is patently untrue. Catholics don't own this problem.

The editorial board of the *Philadelphia Inquirer* admits that "there have been sexual-abuse scandals at other institutions, including public schools, universities, other religious organizations, the media, politics, and Hollywood. But nowhere has the abuse been as widespread and accountability so disregarded [as in the Catholic Church]."[3] The *Washington Post* agrees, saying that the Church has a "unique history as a haven for abusers".[4] As will be demonstrated, both editorials are factually incorrect.

The John Jay College of Criminal Justice in New York City, which authored two major studies on clergy sexual abuse for the United States Conference of Catholic Bishops (USCCB), came to a different conclusion. "Sexual victimization of children is a serious and pervasive issue in society. It is present in families, and it is not uncommon in institutions where adults form mentoring and nurturing relationships with adolescents, including schools and religious, sports, and social organizations."[5] The college also stated, citing its two studies, that "no organization has undertaken a study of itself in the manner of the Catholic Church"; this remains true today.[6]

It is a credit to the John Jay researchers that they offered a brief summary of many secular and religious organizations that have been beset by problems of sexual abuse.[7] Still, there were inconsistencies. Its first report noted that "few instances [of abuse] were reported to the police."[8] Yet the same report says that "approximately 24% of

[3] Editorial Board, "Another Church Scandal: Bishops Meet and Fail to Address Abuse", *Philadelphia Inquirer*, November 19, 2018, https://www.inquirer.com/philly/opinion/editorials/catholic-church-scandal-bishops-meet-baltimore-sex-abuse-editorial-20181119.html.

[4] "Fine Words, Flimsy Deeds", *Washington Post*, February 27, 2019, A20.

[5] Karen J. Terry, John Jay College of Criminal Justice (JJCCJ), and United States Conference of Catholic Bishops (USCCB), *The Causes and Context of Sexual Abuse of Minors by Catholic Priests in the United States, 1950–2010: A Report Presented to the United States Conference of Catholic Bishops by the John Jay College Research Team* (Washington, D.C.: United States Conference of Catholic Bishops, 2011), 5.

[6] Ibid., 16.

[7] Ibid., 16–23.

[8] Karen J. Terry, JJCCJ, and USCCB, *The Nature and Scope of Sexual Abuse of Minors by Catholic Priests and Deacons in the United States 1950–2002: A Research Study Conducted by the John Jay College of Criminal Justice* (Washington, D.C.: United States Conference of Catholic Bishops, 2004), 39.

priests accused of abuse were reported to the police."[9] Commenting on nationwide totals that are inclusive of every sector of society, the report says, "Only 5.7% of the incidents were reported to the police."[10] By contrast, then, the Catholic Church has done a much better job.

In 1985, a survey by the *Los Angeles Times* found that 27 percent of women and 16 percent of men said they were sexually abused as children. Just 3 percent of those alleged cases were reported to the police.[11] In 2010, Ernie Allen, the president of the National Center for Missing and Exploited Children, said, "We don't see the Catholic Church as a hotbed of this [sexual abuse of children] or a place that has a bigger problem than anyone else."[12] In 2019, it was said that "more than 60,000 children are reported to have been abused every year, outnumbering those killed by guns or cars."[13]

Sexual Abuse in Non-Catholic Religious Institutions

No other religious body collects data on its clergy, and on so many variables, the way the Catholic Church does. Most religions are decentralized and lack uniform protocols for saving records. That's a plus and a minus for the Church. It's a plus because we have a much more accurate profile of priests and deacons than we do for their counterparts in other religions. It's a minus because lawyers out to plunder the Church have a reliable and extensive source of data to ply. Even allowing for inexact comparisons, from what we know, it is obvious that the Catholic Church has no monopoly on sexual abuse.

Pastor Jimmy Hinton presides over the Church of Christ congregation in Somerset, Pennsylvania. Speaking of sexual abuse, he said, "Some people assume this is a Catholic problem. It's not, not at all.

---

[9] Ibid., 60.

[10] Ibid., 24.

[11] Jason Berry, *Lead Us Not into Temptation: Catholic Priests and the Sexual Abuse of Children* (New York: Doubleday, 1992), 278.

[12] Pat Wingert, "Priests Commit No More Abuse Than Other Males", *Newsweek*, April 7, 2010, https://www.newsweek.com/priests-commit-no-more-abuse-other-males-70625.

[13] Julie Asher, "Child Sex Abuse Called 'A Serious and Pervasive' Issue in US Society", *National Catholic Reporter*, February 11, 2019, http://www.ncronline.org/news/accountability/child-sex-abuse-called-serious-and-pervasive-issue-us-society.

There are plenty of Protestant and nondenominational churches that cover up abuse and knowingly pass abusers from church to church, or quietly dismiss a known abuser and don't bother to check up on the abuser and don't know where they settled."[14] Basyle Tchividjian, a Liberty University law professor and the grandson of Billy Graham, agrees. "Protestants can be very arrogant when pointing to Catholics", he says. "I think we are worse."[15]

In the spring of 2002, when the sexual abuse scandal in the Catholic Church was receiving unprecedented attention, the *Christian Science Monitor* reported on the results of national surveys by Christian Ministry Resources. The conclusion was an eye-opener. "Despite headlines focusing on the priest pedophile problem in the Roman Catholic Church, most American churches being hit with child sexual-abuse allegations are Protestant, and most of the alleged abusers are not clergy or staff, but church volunteers."[16] Professor Philip Jenkins, author of a book on the Catholic scandal, determined that between 0.2 and 1.7 percent of priests were pedophiles. The figure among the Protestant clergy ranged from 2 to 3 percent.[17]

In 2018, the *Fort Worth Star-Telegram* investigated sexual abuse at independent fundamentalist Baptist churches. It found that 187 had allegations of abuse made against them, involving 412 cases of sexual misconduct.[18] The churches operate independently, but some are affiliated with colleges. "You don't report to police because the pastor is the ultimate authority, not the government", said one churchgoer. Another congregant, who twice escaped being a victim of attempted sexual misconduct, said, "It's been the M.O. in fundamentalism for pastors and churches and ministries to just gloss over and sweep under the rug things of absolute epic proportion." What happens to pastors who cover up the abuse? Not only are the consequences "rare", but

[14]Peter Smith, "Victims' Advocates: Abuse Not Just a 'Catholic Problem'", *Philadelphia Inquirer*, June 25, 2018, https://www.inquirer.com/philly/news/victims-advocates-abuse-not-just-a-catholic-problem-20180625.html.

[15]Sarah Pulliam Bailey, "Billy Graham's Grandson: Evangelicals 'Worse' than Catholics on Sex Abuse", Religion News Service, September 26, 2013, https://religionnews.com/2013/09/26/billy-grahams-grandson-evangelicals-worse-catholic-church-sex-abuse/.

[16]Mark Clayton, "Sex Abuse Spans Spectrum of Churches", *Christian Science Monitor*, April 5, 2002, https://www.csmonitor.com/2002/0405/p01s01-ussc.html.

[17]Philip Jenkins, *Pedophiles and Priests* (New York: Oxford University Press, 1996), 50, 81.

[18]Sarah Smith, "Inside Star-Telegram Fundamental Baptist Abuse Investigation", *Fort Worth Star-Telegram*, December 9, 2018, 20A.

in some cases, "the abused are even forced to apologize in front of the congregation."[19]

The reporters found that three main tactics are used by these churches: "Pastors ship suspected abusers to other churches or church-affiliated schools"; "pastors recommend a suspected abuser for a new job without informing the church or school about the allegations"; "pastors pressure victims to keep quiet, telling them they'll ruin the alleged abuser's ministry or the pastors simply don't believe the accusations."[20] Some members of the Catholic clergy did exactly the same thing, but their lousy judgment has been broadcast all over the nation, and for years on end.

The Southern Baptist Convention is the largest Protestant denomination in the nation. A 1993 survey by the *Journal of Pastoral Care* found that 14 percent of Southern Baptist ministers said they had engaged in "inappropriate sexual behavior", and 70 percent said they knew of a minister who had such contact with a church member.[21]

In 2019, an investigation by the *Houston Chronicle* and the San Antonio *Express News* found that more than seven hundred people, most of them children, had been sexually abused by Southern Baptist pastors, church employees, or volunteers during the past two decades.[22] The newspapers also revealed that nearly four hundred Southern Baptist leaders have pleaded guilty to or been convicted of sex crimes. The reporters said that some of these churches use written agreements that offer legal protection to the institution and that they prohibit members from suing the church. Worse, an organized abuse-prevention company, MinistrySafe, which is supposed to be a victims' advocate, is run by legal advisers of some of the churches.[23]

Jehovah's Witnesses has had its history of sexual abuse as well. The *New York Times* found that most of the reported victims are girls

---

[19]Neil Nakahodo, Shelly Yang, and Sarah Smith, "Fundamental Baptist Church Pastors Cover Up Sex Abuse, Rape", part 1, *Fort Worth Star-Telegram*, December 9, 2018, A20–A22.

[20]Neil Nakahodo, Sarah Smith, and Steve Coffman, "Church Ties, Pastors' Friendships Allow Abusers to Escape", *Fort Worth Star-Telegram*, part 2, December 10, 2018, A1, A9–A11.

[21]Teresa Watanabe, "Sex Abuse by Clerics—A Crisis of Many Faiths", *Los Angeles Times*, March 25, 2002, A1.

[22]John Tedesco, "Abuse Survivors Urge Southern Baptists to Listen, Then Act", *Houston Chronicle*, October 5, 2019, https://www.houstonchronicle.com/news/houston-texas/houston/article/Abuse-survivors-urge-Southern-Baptists-to-listen-14495451.php.

[23]Elizabeth Dias, "Questioning Faith, and Loyalties, in Abuse Cases", *New York Times*, June 11, 2019, A1.

and that "many accusations involve incest."[24] An adult male came forward in 2019 to tell how he was sexually abused by a church elder when he was two or three years old. This went on, "approximately four to six times per week", for four years. The abuser served three and a half years in prison and then returned to ministry. A "culture of secrecy" prevented the new congregants from learning of his past.[25]

Not as much information is available about sexual abuse in the Muslim community, but matters are bad enough to have warranted the founding of Facing Abuse in Community Environments (FACE). It was created by Muslim women activists and lawyers to pursue predators.

In one case that made a media splash in 2019, an imam from Texas began counseling a thirteen-year-old girl, and five years later, he presented himself as her potential spouse. At the time he already had two wives and had no intention of marrying the girl, "Jane Doe". He began "grooming Jane to become more sexualized and to ultimately engage in illicit sexual acts with him". FACE was responsible for bringing him to justice.[26]

In 2020, the Hurma Project was launched to combat sexual abuse in the Muslim community. According to the Canadian founder, Ingrid Mattson, the term *hurma* means sacred inviolability from exploitation and abuse. Mattson, who is the first woman, first convert, and first North American–born president of the Islamic Society of North America, held a conference at the American Islamic College in 2020 to call attention to sexual abuse in the Islamic community. They were organized to bring "sex abuse by sheikhs out of the shadows".[27]

Jews have also had their problems with sexual abuse. In 2019, almost a year after an independent investigation found the executive director of the largest camping organization in North America guilty

---

[24]Laurie Goodstein, "Ousted Members Say Jehovah's Witnesses' Policy on Abuse Hides Offenses", *New York Times*, August 11, 2002, sect. 1, 26.

[25]Gabrielle Fonrouge, Alex Taylor, and Jorge Fitz-Gibbon, "Former Jehovah's Witnesses Recount Years of Sex Abuse ahead of Landmark Case", *New York Post*, August 12, 2019, https://nypost.com/2019/08/12/former-jehovahs-witnesses-recount-years-of-sex-abuse-ahead-of-landmark-case/.

[26]Aysha Khan, "Texas Imam Ordered to Pay $2.55 Million in Sexual Misconduct Case", *Religious News Service*, August 15, 2019, https://religionnews.com/2019/08/15/texas-imam-ordered-to-pay-2-55-million-in-sexual-misconduct-case/.

[27]Aysha Khan, "'A Long Time Coming': These Muslims Are Bringing Sex Abuse by Sheiks out of the Shadows", *Religious News Service*, January 15, 2020, https://religionnews.com/2020/01/15/a-long-time-coming-these-muslims-are-bringing-sex-abuse-by-sheikhs-out-of-the-shadows.

of sexual abuse or harassment, the entire board of NJY Camps, a Jewish association in New Jersey, resigned. The sixty-member board voted to disband after it became known that the top leadership knew of the sexual misconduct for years and did nothing about it.[28]

When a member of the Catholic clergy is suspected of sexual abuse, he is brought before a tribunal for investigation. If the case is deemed credible, the authorities are contacted, pending a probe. In Orthodox Jewish circles, a rabbinical court, or beth din, does the investigation, and at no time are the authorities notified. Not even the media can know. "No one shall bring to any media outlet information about any resident that could, if publicized, lead to an investigation or intensified prosecution by any law enforcement agency." That is how a beth din in Brooklyn handles matters.[29]

David Zwiebel, a noted New York lawyer who handles cases of sexual abuse for Orthodox Jews, makes it clear that under religious law, if a rabbi tells one of his followers not to go to the police, he must follow that ruling. Zwiebel, a leader with Agudath Israel, does not hesitate to condemn Orthodox dissidents who speak up about sexual abuse. He accuses them of trafficking in "malicious gossip, evil tongue and a waste of time", all of which are prohibited by the Torah.[30] The media treat such instances in passing, as if it were a human-interest story. Yet if Catholic bishops told their flocks that under Church law they may not contact civil authorities when a crime is suspected, they would be the subject of explosive headlines.

Sexual Abuse in Secular Institutions

It would take a big book to detail all the secular institutions and professions that have been plagued with sexual misconduct. Indeed, there is enough material to fill volumes. For the sake of brevity, here are

[28] Hannah Dreyfus, "NJY Camps Board Disbands, Settles with at Least One Victim", *Jewish Week*, February 10, 2019, https://jewishweek.timesofisrael.com/njy-camps-board-dis bands-settles-with-at-least-one-victim/.

[29] Simone Weichselbaum, "Rabbinical Court to Lubavitchers: Quit Yer Snitchin' about Cops, Crime to Outsiders", *Daily News*, December 10, 2010, https://www.nydaily news.com/new-york/brooklyn/rabbinical-court-lubavitchers-quit-yer-snitchin-cops-crime -outsiders-article-1.470554.

[30] Michael Powell, "De Blasio Skips His Cue to Speak Out", *New York Times*, May 29, 2014, A28.

some examples that barely get a mention in the media but are worth noting. It shows, once again, that Catholics don't own this problem.

The Family

- "Preschoolers living with one natural parent and one stepparent were 40 times more likely to become child abuse cases than were like-aged children living with two natural parents."[31]
- "About 85 percent of the offenders [of child sexual abuse] are family members, babysitters, neighbors, family friends or relatives. About one in six child molesters are other children."[32]
- "Children in households with unrelated adults were nearly 50 times as likely to die of inflicted injuries than children residing with 2 biological parents."[33]
- "Children living with their married biological parents universally had the lowest rate [of maltreatment], whereas those living with a single parent who had a cohabiting partner in the household had the highest rate in all maltreatment categories."[34]
- "An estimated 60% of perpetrators of sexual abuse are known to the child but are not family members, e.g., family friends, babysitters, child care providers, neighbors. About 30% of perpetrators of child sexual abuse are family members. Only about 10% of perpetrators of child sexual abuse are strangers to the child. Not all perpetrators are adults—an estimated 23% of reported cases of child sexual abuse are perpetrated by individuals under the age of 18."[35]

The Boy Scouts

- In February 2020, the Boy Scouts of America filed for Chapter 11 in bankruptcy court. In 1970, the Boy Scouts had five million

[31] Martin Daly and Margo Wilson, "Child Abuse and Other Risks of Not Living with Both Parents", *Ethology and Sociobiology* 6, no. 4 (1985): 197.

[32] Garth A. Rattray, "Child Month and Paedophilia", *Gleaner*, May 14, 2002.

[33] Patricia G. Schnitzer and Bernard G. Ewigman, "Child Deaths Resulting from Inflicted Injuries: Household Risk Factors and Perpetrator Characteristics", *Pediatrics* 116, no. 5 (November 2005): 687.

[34] Andrea Sedlak et al., *Fourth National Incidence Study of Child Abuse and Neglect (NIS-4): Report to Congress* (Washington, D.C.: U.S. Department of Health and Human Services, Administration for Children and Families, 2010), 12.

[35] Blue Out Penn State, "Child Sexual Abuse Information", http://sites.psu.edu/blueout/child-abuse-information.

members; by 2020, that number had been cut in half. In 2020, it had assets of $1 billion and liabilities ranging from $500 million to $1 billion. This decline was largely due to a mountain of sexual abuse lawsuits. "In recent years, an expert hired by the organization reviewed decades of records and reported that there were nearly 8,000 'perpetrators.' "[36]

- In November 2020, it was reported that the Boy Scouts will face more than 92,000 claims of sexual abuse. "The number of claims and the total payouts to settle them will easily eclipse those in the sex abuse scandal that engulfed the U.S. Catholic Church more than a decade ago, plaintiffs' lawyers say."[37]

The Military

- "More than 100,000 men have been sexually assaulted in the military in recent decades."
- "Women face a much higher rate of sexual assault in the military—about seven times that of men."[38]

Migrant Children

- "Thousands of migrant children who crossed the border into the U.S. have reported they were sexually abused while in government custody."[39]

Homes for the Disabled

- "Hundreds of pages of disciplinary records from 2015 to 2017, obtained by the [New York] Times under the state open-records law, show that more than one-third of the employees statewide found to have committed abuse-related offenses at group homes

[36] Mike Baker, "Bankruptcy for Boy Scouts as Abuse Cases Grow", *New York Times*, February 19, 2020, A1.
[37] Kim Christensen, "Boy Scouts Deluged with 92,700 Sexual Abuse Claims, Dwarfing U.S. Catholic Church's Numbers", *Los Angeles Times*, November 16, 2020, http://www.latimes.com/california/story/2020-11-16/boy-scouts-sexual-abuse-claims-top-88000-bankruptcy.
[38] Mary F. Calvert and Dave Philipps, "Six Men Tell Their Stories of Sexual Assault in the Military", *New York Times*, September 10, 2019, https://www.nytimes.com/interactive/2019/09/10/us/men-military-sexual-assault.html.
[39] Matthew Haag, "Thousands of Immigrant Children Said They Were Sexually Abused in U.S. Detention Centers, Report Says", *New York Times*, February 27, 2019, https://www.nytimes.com/2019/02/27/us/immigrant-children-sexual-abuse.html.

and other facilities were put back on the job, often after arbitration with the worker's union."

- "Recycling abuse employees has long been an endemic problem. Eight years ago, the Times reviewed thousands of pages of disciplinary files for 233 workers. In a quarter of substantiated abuse cases, employees were transferred to other homes rather than fired, including in cases involving sexual assaults."[40]

Indian Reservations

- "Federal and state officials say they have documented glaring flaws in the child welfare system at the Spirit Lake Indian Reservation in North Dakota, contending that while child abuse there is at epidemic levels, the tribe has sought to conceal it."
- "The problems uncovered by medical and social services administrators include foster children on the reservation who have been sent to homes where registered sex offenders live and a teenage female sexual-abuse victim who was placed in a tribal home was subsequently raped."
- "The tribe, according to federal officials, also hired a children's case worker who had been convicted of felony child abuse and employed another social worker who discovered a 1-year-old child covered with 100 wood ticks but did not take the child to a hospital."
- "The tribe, according to federal and state administrators, has not conducted required background checks before placing foster children, failed to make mandated monthly visits to children in foster care and illegally removed foster children from homes and placed them elsewhere without determining that the new homes would be safe."[41]

Psychiatrists

- The Citizens Commission on Human Rights says that "in its public database of criminal and disciplinary actions committed

---

[40]Benjamin Weiser and Danny Hakim, "How New York Keeps Abusers as Caregivers", *New York Times*, June 10, 2019, A1.

[41]Timothy Williams, "Officials See Child Welfare Dangers on a North Dakota Indian Reservation", *New York Times*, July 7, 2012, https://www.nytimes.com/2012/07/08/us/child-welfare-dangers-seen-on-spirit-lake-reservation.html.

by mental health industry personnel, nearly a third of criminal convictions are for sexual abuse committed by psychiatrists, psychologists, therapists and counselors including the sexual assault of children."[42]

Doctors

- The *Atlanta Journal-Constitution* conducted a national investigation of doctors and found that of "the 2,400 doctors publicly disciplined after allegations of sexual misconduct with patients, half still have active medical licenses today".
- The investigation "examined documents that described disturbing acts of physician sexual abuse in every state. Rapes by OB/GYNS, seductions by psychiatrists, fondling by anesthesiologists and ophthalmologists, and molestations by pediatricians and radiologists. Victims were babies. Adolescents. Women in their 80s. Drug addicts and jail inmates. Survivors of childhood sexual abuse."
- "Only 11 states have a law requiring medical authorities to report to the police or prosecutors when they suspect a sexual crime has been committed against an adult."[43]

Camps

- "CBS News has identified hundreds of reports of sexual abuse that occurred at children's camps across the United States. We found reports of more than 500 victims who were allegedly sexually abused at children's camps over the past 55 years."
- "More than 14 million people attend camps each year. But there are no national regulations for camps to follow. Eight states have no requirements for overnight camps to be licensed, and 18 states don't require background checks for employees."[44]

[42] CCHR International, "Sexual Abuse Epidemic in Mental Health: Psychiatrists Raping Women and Molesting Children", *Health Impact News*, November 10, 2017, https://healthimpactnews.com/2017/sexual-abuse-epidemic-in-mental-health-psychiatrists-raping-women-and-molesting-children.

[43] Carrie Teegardin, Danny Robbins, Ariel Hart, and Jeff Ernsthausen, "AJC National Investigation; Doctors & Sex Abuse; License to Betray", *Atlanta Journal-Constitution*, July 10, 2016, 1A.

[44] "Hundreds of Sexual Abuse Cases Reported at Children's Camps across U.S.", CBS News, December 10, 2018, https://www.cbsnews.com/news/hundreds-sexual-abuse-cases-childrens-camps-reported-across-us-cbs-this-morning/#:~:text=CBS%20News%20has%20identified%20hundreds,cases%20surfaced%20this%20year%20alone.

Olympics

- "More than 350 women and girls accused the USA Gymnastics national team doctor [Larry Nassar] of molesting them under the guise of medical treatment."
- "Structural flaws in the governance of both the Olympic committee and sports governing bodies have resulted in a hands-off approach that puts the priority on winning medals, not protecting athletes."[45]

Professors

- "Rates of sexual abuse and harassment in academic science are second only to the military. It's estimated that at least half of women faculty and staff face harassment and abuse and that 20 to 50 percent of women students in science, engineering, and medicine are abused by faculty."
- According to Julie Libarkin of Michigan State University, "about 30 percent of the harassers have been investigated on more than one occasion. The fact of being investigated did not deter them from harassing again."[46]

Corporations

- "For many firms, paying fines for sexual harassment has been treated as a cost of doing business. In the past seven years alone [2010–2017], U.S. companies have paid out more than $295 million in public penalties over sexual harassment claims."[47]
- "Thousands of Google employees walked off the job ... in offices spanning from California to Dublin in protest of the company's

[45] Nancy Armour, Rachel Axon, and Brent Schrotenboer, "USA Today Investigation—Banned for Sexual Misconduct but Still Coaching", *Knoxville News-Sentinel*, December 16, 2018, E3.

[46] Elsa Partan and Heather Goldstone, "Scientist Publishes a List of Known Harassers in Academia", WCAI, September 10, 2018, http://www.capeandislands.org/post/scientist-publishes-list-known-harassers-academia.

[47] Nathan Bomey and Marco della Cava, "Sexual Harassment Went Unchecked for Decades as Payouts Silenced Accusers", *USA Today*, December 1, 2017, https://www.usatoday.com/story/money/business/2017/12/01/sexual-harassment-went-unchecked-decades-payouts-silenced-accusers/881070001/.

handling of sexual harassment claims." Over 60 percent of Google's offices around the world participated in the walkout.[48]

Hollywood

- "I can tell you that the number one problem in Hollywood was, and is, and always will be pedophilia", said Corey Feldman. "There was a circle of older men that surrounded themselves around this group of kids, and they all had either their own power or connections to great power in the entertainment industry."[49]
- Feldman "addresses the 'dark side' of pal Michael Jackson that led to their estrangement, and warns of the 'growing, not shrinking' dangers of internet-era child predators in Hollywood, a place 'where adults have more direct and inappropriate connection with children than probably anywhere else in the world'".[50]
- "There are a lot of vipers in this industry", says Elijah Wood, "people who only have their own interests in mind. There is darkness in the underbelly—if you can imagine it, it's probably happened."[51]

Public Schools

- "[A] seven-month investigation [by the Associated Press] found 2,570 educators whose teaching credentials were revoked, denied, surrendered or sanctioned from 2001 through 2005 following allegations of sexual misconduct. Young people were the victims in at least 1,801 of the cases, and more than 80 percent of those were students. At least half the educators who were

[48] Taylor Telford and Elizabeth Dwoskin, "Google Employees Worldwide Walk Out over Allegations of Sexual Harassment, Inequality within Company", *Washington Post*, November 1, 2018.

[49] Kathleen Gilbert, "Recent Hollywood Pedophilia Charges Just the Tip of the Iceberg: Former Child Actors", LifeSiteNews, December 6, 2011, https://www.lifesitenews.com /news/recent-hollywood-pedophilia-charges-just-the-tip-of-the-iceberg-former-chil.

[50] Seth Abramovitch, "Corey Feldman on Elijah Wood Hollywood Pedophilia Controversy: 'I Would Love to Name Names'", *Hollywood Reporter*, May 25, 2016, http://www .hollywoodreporter.com/news/corey-feldman-elijah-wood-hollywood.

[51] Adam Carlson, "Elijah Wood Speaks Out on Child Abuse in Hollywood: 'There Are a Lot of Vipers in This Industry'", *People*, May 22, 2016, http://people.com/celebrity /elijah-wood-speaks-out-on-child-abuse-in-hollywood.

punished by their states also were convicted of crimes related to their misconduct."

- "Most of the abuse never gets reported. Those cases reported often end with no action. Cases investigated sometimes can't be proven, and many abusers have several victims."[52]

- "A year-long USA Today Network investigation found that education officials put children in harm's way by covering up evidence of abuse, keeping allegations secret and making it easy for abusive teachers to find jobs elsewhere. As a result, schoolchildren across the nation continue to be beaten, raped and harassed by their teachers while government officials at every level stand by and do nothing."

- "Congress passed a law in December 2015 requiring states to ban school districts from secretly passing problem teachers to other jurisdictions or face losing federal funds. But 45 states have not instituted the ban."[53]

- According to a 2017 report funded by the U.S. Department of Justice, "An estimated 10% of K–12 students will experience sexual misconduct by a school employee by the time they graduate from high school."[54]

- According to Terri Miller, executive director of Stop Educator Sexual Abuse, Misconduct and Exploitation, "The culpability of teacher unions in this particular issue is long, deep and as far-reaching as you can imagine, from your local school district politics to Capitol Hill. We've had unions obstruct too many good pieces of legislation on this issue at the state, local and federal level."[55]

Reading how the teacher unions have obstructed justice makes the *Washington Post* look enfeebled when it commends public schools for

[52]Martha Irvine and Robert Tanner, "AP: Sexual Misconduct Plagues US Schools", *Washington Post*, October 21, 2007, http://www.washingtonpost.com/wp-dyn/content/article/2007/10/21.

[53]Steve Reilly, "Teachers Who Sexually Abuse Students Still Find Classroom Jobs", *USA Today*, December 22, 2016.

[54]Billie-Jo Grant, Stephanie B. Wilkerson, deKoven Pelton, Anne Cosby, and Molly Henschel, *A Case Study of K–12 School Employee Sexual Misconduct: Lessons Learned from Title IX Policy Implementation* (Charlottesville, Va.: Magnolia Consulting, 2017), ii, National Criminal Justice Reference Service, https://www.ncjrs.gov/pdffiles1/nij/grants/252484.pdf.

[55]Joe Nelson and Scott Schwebke, "Battling a School Predator Epidemic; Administrative Culture Largely to Blame for Not Uprooting Teacher Sexual Misconduct, Experts Say", *Daily News of California*, November 23, 2018, AA1.

being "more accountable" than the Catholic Church in combating sexual abuse.[56]

Sexual Abuse in the Media

The media, in general, do not have a sterling record in dealing with sexual misconduct. Charlie Rose, Matt Lauer, Glenn Thrush, Mark Halperin, Leon Wieseltier, Hamilton Fish, and Michael Oreskes are just some of the big names who have been accused.

When four female journalists accused *New York Times* reporter Glenn Thrush of sexual misconduct, there was no independent investigation; the probe was done in-house. Dean Baquet, the executive editor of the *New York Times*, explained the paper's reaction: "While we believe Glenn has acted offensively, we have decided that he does not deserve to be fired."[57] Instead, Baquet allowed Thrush to undergo counseling.

This is not an indefensible position, but it smacks of hypocrisy when the same newspaper demands that bishops contact the authorities when sexual abuse allegations are made against a priest. Why is it okay for the *Times* to handle its sexual misconduct cases in-house, but not the Catholic Church? And why does the newspaper lambaste bishops for relying on counseling when the newspaper itself relied on counseling to deal with one of its own offenders?

It really gets embarrassing when we learn that the same year Glenn Thrush was plunged into hot water, three women accused Michael Oreskes of sexual harassment. Two of the alleged incidents occurred in the 1990s, when Oreskes was the Washington, D.C., bureau chief for the *New York Times*. At the time Jill Abramson, who would later become the executive editor of the *Times*, was deputy to Oreskes. She said that she knew of his alleged offenses but did nothing to stop them.[58]

---

[56] "Their Day in Court", *Washington Post* editorial, March 20, 2019, A20.

[57] Sydney Ember, "Glenn Thrush, Suspended Times Reporter, to Resume Work but Won't Cover White House", *New York Times*, December 20, 2017, https://www.nytimes.com/2017/12/20/business/media/glenn-thrush-suspension-white-house.html.

[58] Sydney Ember, "Top NPR Editor Accused of Sexual Harassment While at the New York Times", *New York Times*, October 31, 2017, https://www.nytimes.com/2017/10/31/business/npr-michael-oreskes-new-york-times.html.

The *Boston Globe* had a similar case. In March 2017, a young woman employee filed a complaint with human resources against a male journalist. She said he propositioned her to have sex with his wife. But nothing came of her complaint. A year earlier, she accused the same man of asking her to go to bed with him. He was allowed to stay on the job until more accusations were made against him from outside the office. Who was he? The *Globe* refused to say. They declared this to be a "confidential personnel matter". *Globe* editor Brian McGrory admitted he would be accused of hypocrisy, but so what? "I can live with that far more easily than I can live with the thought of sacrificing our values to slake the thirst of this moment."[59]

Whatever happened to honesty, consistency, fairness, and transparency? What about fidelity to the law? Under Massachusetts law, sexual harassment in the workplace covers both verbal and physical conduct. The law explicitly says that sexual advances and requests for sexual favors constitute sexual harassment.

While the *Globe* cut slack for itself, it was a relentless critic of the Catholic Church's handling of sexual abuse. At the time, I detailed twelve instances in which the paper's editorials hammered the Church for its "code of silence", "veil of secrecy", and "lack of transparency".[60] I criticized McGrory for this on Laura Ingraham's Fox News show, *The Ingraham Angle*.[61] In the end, he issued an apology for the way he handled this matter.[62]

In many cases of sexual misconduct in the workplace, the guilty party is at least suspected by many of his colleagues, and in some cases, virtually everyone knows what is going on. This is particularly true when the abuse is serial in nature. In such a case it is preposterous to think that only a few are aware of what is going on—this is as true for priests as it is for media executives.

[59] Mark Arsenault, "Media, Including Globe, Walk Line in Age of 'MeToo'", *Boston Globe*, December 8, 2017, A1.

[60] Bill Donohue, "Boston Globe Refuses to Name Abusers", Catholic League, December 18, 2017, https://www.catholicleague.org/boston-globe-refuses-to-name-abusers/.

[61] Bill Donohue, "Media Provide Cover for Boston Globe", Catholic League, January 3, 2018, https://www.cnsnews.com/commentary/bill-donohue/bill-donohue-media-provide-cover-boston-globe.

[62] Don Seiffert, "Globe Editor Apologizes for Coverage of Sexual Harassment by a Reporter", *Boston Business Journal*, December 22, 2017.

Les Moonves is the former CBS chief who saw his career take a nosedive once his predatory behavior became public knowledge. Journalist Kyle Smith claimed everyone around Moonves knew what he was doing: "They knew. They all knew. The men knew. The women knew. The potted plants certainly knew. Nobody said anything. They didn't want to jeopardize their next gig."[63]

A report prepared for CBS by outside lawyers verified Smith's report and found that "many of the company's employees, including high-ranking executives and even members of its board, were aware of the former chief executive Les Moonves' alleged sexual misconduct and subsequent efforts to conceal it."[64]

Why didn't *60 Minutes* turn the cameras on itself—it is very good at aiming them at the Catholic Church—and do a segment on Moonves? Maybe it is because its longtime executive producer, Jeff Fager, was himself a predator. He was fired in 2018, right after Moonves was canned.[65]

Fager may have been sacked sooner had the *Washington Post* done its job. In 2019, it ran a searing editorial against the bishops, accusing them of exercising "all but absolute" authority over investigations of abuse.[66] What makes this editorial dishonest is that it was printed at the same time that *Washington Post* editor Marty Baron was using his "all but absolute" authority to kill a story about Fager's acts of sexual harassment.

Amy Brittain, the newspaper's investigative reporter, and Irin Carmon spent four months doing a story on Fager; it was a follow-up to a November 2017 piece about Charlie Rose, who was fired from CBS after sexual harassment claims were made. The reporters spoke to several women who alleged that Fager had sexually abused them. Baron, they said, kept delaying the story and refused to speak with

[63] Kyle Smith, "Hollywood Is a Sex-Grooming Gang", *National Review*, November 30, 2018, http://www.nationalreview.com/2018/11/hollywood-sex-grooming-gang-les-moonves-harvey-weinstein.

[64] James B. Stewart, "CBS Report on Moonves Cites Failure of Oversight", *New York Times*, December 5, 2018, B1.

[65] Sara Nathan, "CBS Staffers 'Want Answers' After Year-Long Charlie Rose Investigation", *Page Six*, November 24, 2018, https://pagesix.com/2018/11/24/cbs-staffers-want-answers-after-year-long-charlie-rose-investigation.

[66] "Two Steps Forward and One Step Back Won't Cleanse the Catholic Church", *Washington Post*, May 11, 2019.

them. When the story finally ran, all the allegations against Fager were deleted; only additional allegations against Rose made it into print.[67]

Why did the *Washington Post* kill the story on Fager? According to one of the reporters, Carmon, who wrote about this sordid case in *New York* magazine, one of the reasons had to do with the ties between the newspaper and Fager's show. "The close relationship between the paper and *60 Minutes*" had something to do with it, he said.[68]

Had it not been for the exercise of Baron's "all but absolute authority", it is likely that this story would have run. Moreover, the favoritism shown to colleagues that the paper frequently accuses the bishops of practicing was also on grand display.

In 2017 NBC fired *Today* show host Matt Lauer after a detailed complaint about inappropriate sexual behavior in the workplace had been made against him. NBC then conducted an investigation of this and other allegations, which concluded that while the accusations were credible, there was no "widespread or systemic pattern" of abuse at NBC.[69] Linda Vester, a former network news anchor, blasted the investigation, saying, "They had damaging details about Lauer and others in management who allegedly protected him. Nothing happened." She said the problem is right at the top of NBC. "Why did Andy Lack, the Chairman of NBC News, not let this get out? Is it because he himself has a history of reported sexual misconduct in the workplace in the past and, so, he himself is guilty? Or is it because he just wanted to protect and—to protect other high-profile men at the company?"[70]

The *New York Times* has also protected its top people. When the head of the BBC, Mark Thompson, was slated to become the new

---

[67] Amber Athey, "Washington Post Accused of Killing Story about '60 Minutes' EP's Sexual Misconduct", *Daily Caller*, April 2, 2019, http://www.dailycaller.com/2019/04/02/washington-post-jeff-fager-harassment-story.

[68] Irin Carmon, "What Was the Washington *Post* Afraid Of?", *New York*, April 1, 2019, https://nymag.com/intelligencer/2019/04/what-was-the-washington-post-afraid-of.html.

[69] Camila Domonoske, "NBC Invesigation Finds Matt Lauer's Accusers Credible, Executives Unaware", National Public Radio, May 9, 2018, https://www.npr.org/sections/the-two-way/2018/05/09/609734430/nbc-investigation-finds-matt-lauers-accusers-credible-executives-unaware.

[70] Vester made her comments on Fox News Network's *Tucker Carlson Tonight*, November 28, 2018.

president and CEO of the New York Times Company in November 2012, he immediately came under a cloud of suspicion. A decision had been made nearly a year earlier at the BBC to kill a *Newsnight* investigation into what became the most astonishing sexual abuse scandal in the history of the United Kingdom. The person of interest was accused child rapist and serial predator Jimmy Savile, a celebrity icon who worked at the BBC from the 1960s to the mid-1990s. Thompson, who was the director general at the BBC from 2004 to 2012, denied wrongdoing.[71]

Savile was Britain's first disc jockey. He was also a television host, wrestler, dancehall manager, cyclist, marathon runner, book reviewer, Mensa member, and a child rapist. His most popular gig was hosting *Top of the Pops*, the legendary U.K. music show. His own program, *Jim'll Fix It*, lasted almost twenty years; it allowed him to make promises to kids that he tried to fulfill. Unfortunately, for a lot of these kids, Jimmy fixed them all right—by using them to fulfill his sexual appetites.[72] He preyed on minor boys and girls, both children and adolescents, and he did so in his car, in his BBC dressing room, in hospital wards, and in the bedrooms of girls at a boarding school.[73] He did this for decades, with impunity.

Thompson started working at the BBC in 1979, when Savile was raping minors on BBC property. "During my time as director general of the BBC," Thompson said, "I never heard any allegations or received any complaints about Jimmy Savile."[74] That would certainly make him unique. Bill Oddie, the former actor, said "everyone knew" within the BBC about Savile's preying on children. He spoke sarcastically about Thompson's alleged ignorance. "You worked at the BBC and you don't know anything about it? Don't

[71] Sarah Lyall, "Silence on Abuse Plunges BBC into Scandal", *New York Times*, October 14, 2012, A12.

[72] "In Bed with Jimmy", *Guardian*, April 11, 2000, 6.

[73] Sam Greenhill, Chris Greenhill, and Martin Robinson, "Ripped Out, Smashed Up and Sent in a Skip to Landfill: Jimmy Savile Headstone Removed at 1am by Family 'out of Respect for Public Opinion'—as Police Launch Hunt for BBC Child Abuse Accomplices", *Daily Mail*, October 10, 2012, https://www.dailymail.co.uk/news/article-2215324/Jimmy-Savile-gravestone-removed-family-police-launch-hunt-BBC-child-abuse-accomplices.html.

[74] Adam Taylor, "The Huge Sex Abuse Scandal Shaking the BBC Could Be a Major Headache for the New NYT CEO", *Business Insider*, October 15, 2012, https://www.business insider.com/jimmy-savile-scandal-nyt-ceo-trouble-2012-10.

be ridiculous."[75] P.D. James, the famous crime novelist, agreed: "It seems everyone knew about Jimmy Savile."[76]

No sooner had Thompson made his profession of ignorance when the BBC's own press office contradicted him. On the same day, October 7, 2012, it was reported that the previous December, Thompson was "warned by an angry senior journalist about the potential consequences of axing the Newsnight investigation". On October 24, it was reported that a respected BBC foreign correspondent, Caroline Hawley, also spoke to Thompson at a Christmas party about this issue; she says she informed him of the "broad context" of what happened. Thompson said he recalled hearing something about this but didn't ask for details.[77]

On November 16, it was reported that ten days before Thompson left the BBC in September, his lawyers wrote a letter to the *Sunday Times* in London, threatening to sue if they decided to go forward with a detailed article about the Savile issue. Unavoidably, the letter summarized the accusations against the BBC icon, thus undercutting Thompson's claim that he never heard about Savile's serial sex crimes while he was running the BBC.[78]

Then the most unbelievable defense of Thompson was raised by one of his former aides. The personal adviser said that although Thompson had personally authorized sending the letter, "it's not clear if he was shown it, but he doesn't remember reading it."[79] But if he authorized the letter, he had to have known what it was about, and that is all that counts.

The rich and powerful inside the media not only protect themselves, they also sometimes shield their rich and powerful friends. Financier and serial sexual predator Jeffrey Epstein is another case where everyone around him knew of his conduct—specifically, a sex-trafficking

[75] Gordon Rayner, "Savile Scandal Exposes Child Abuse on Unprecedented Scale", *Daily Telegraph* (national edition), October 20, 2012, 11.

[76] Tim Walker, "PD James, the Scourge of the BBC, Has Unfinished Business with Thompson", *Daily Telegraph* (national edition), October 23, 2012, 6.

[77] Raphael Satter, "BBC Scandal Raises Questions for Incoming NYT Boss", Associated Press, October 24, 2012.

[78] Matthew Purdy, "Letter Raises Questions about When BBC Ex-Chief Learned of Abuse Cases", *New York Times*, November 16, 2012, A9.

[79] Ibid.

operation involving minor girls. According to journalist Vicky Ward, who profiled Epstein, "His entire social circle knew about this and just blithely overlooked it."[80] Ward also exposed Graydon Carter, editor of *Vanity Fair*, for deleting from her story about Epstein allegations that he had sexually exploited minor girls. She said they had "cut a deal", even though the allegations were credible.[81]

Sexual Misconduct in Politics

Finally, there is no end to the politicians, both Republicans and Democrats, who have been involved in sexual misconduct or have had serious accusations made against them. I would like to share how my input brought justice to one offender.

On August 31, 2016, there was a front-page story in the *New York Post* about Anthony Weiner, the former New York Congressman who was married to Huma Abedin, a close friend of and adviser to presidential candidate Hillary Clinton. The article showed a picture of Weiner allegedly using his son as a "chick magnet" to lure sexual relations. I immediately filed a formal complaint with the New York City Administration for Children's Services (ACS), the New York branch of the New York State Office of Children and Family Services.

That same day, *Daily Mail Online*, a British media outlet, reported that an "ACS spokesman said: 'In order to protect children and their privacy, ACS does not comment on specific cases or allegations of child maltreatment, regardless of whether or not allegations have been reported, are being investigated, or have not resulted in an investigation.' It came after Bill Donohue, the president of the Catholic League, urged the New York State Office of Children and Family Service to investigate Weiner for sexually exploiting his young son."[82]

[80] Michelle Goldberg, "Jeffrey Epstein Is the Ultimate Symbol of Plutocratic Rot", *New York Times*, July 8, 2019, https://www.nytimes.com/2019/07/08/opinion/jeffrey-epstein-trump.html.

[81] Morgan Phillips, "Writer Claims Graydon Carter 'Cut a Deal' with Jeffrey Epstein to Remove Allegations from *Vanity Fair* Piece", Mediaite, July 8, 2019, http://www.mediaite.com/news/writer-accuses-graydon-carter-of-cutting-a-deal-with-jeffrey-epstein-to-remove-allegations-from-vanity-fair-piece.

[82] Bill Donohue, "Donohue's Role in FBI–Weiner Probe", Catholic League, October 31, 2016, https://www.catholicleague.org/donohues-role-in-fbi-weiner-probe/.

On September 26, I received a phone call from the ACS. I was told that my complaint had been accepted and that Weiner would be investigated. The next day, the same ACS official called to question me further. A week later, on October 3, FBI agents seized Weiner's laptop, phone, and tablet.[83]

On the laptop, which was used jointly by his wife, were e-mails between Abedin and Hillary Clinton (found on her private e-mail server). Those e-mails were disclosed by FBI director James Comey right before the November election, an event Clinton said tipped the election to Donald Trump. If it did, she had no one to blame but herself: had she not had her private server, the FBI would have had nothing to investigate. I obviously had no idea that my role in this drama would contribute to such a momentous political outcome.

Media Bias

The media occasionally do a story on sexual abuse in non-Catholic organizations, though they rarely do documentaries or a series of reports on them. Their favorite target by far is the Catholic Church. What they produce is often skewed. Here is a prime example. When newspapers, magazines, TV shows, and Internet stories cover sexual abuse by priests, they often do so in the most graphic terms. This is also true of state grand-jury and attorney-general reports. Some of the stories are incredibly salacious, though when covering sexual abuse by others, readers and viewers are usually spared the details. This is not a mistake—it is deliberate. It's called shaming.

Some media outlets have refused to sell me advertisement space in their newspapers and magazines that I wanted to use for defenses of the Catholic Church.

In 2011, when the *Kansas City Star* was relentless in its news stories on clergy sexual abuse, I sought a corrective: I offered the newspaper $25,000 to pay for an advertisement that sought to set the record straight, especially about the work of Survivors Network of those Abused by Priests (SNAP). I was denied without an explanation. Could it have been bias? It's not as though the paper could

[83] Ibid.

not have used the money: in the previous decade, it had laid off a thousand employees.[84]

In 2013, the *Philadelphia Inquirer* went on a tear against the Archdiocese of Philadelphia, spewing a lot of misleading information. On May 14, I submitted a long rejoinder to the paper's narrative. The two-page article was scheduled to run as an ad on May 20. On May 15, I was told that those "at the top" rejected it. When I asked why, I was told there would be no explanation. They turned down $58,000. Even though the newspaper had filed for bankruptcy in 2009, those "at the top" thought turning down that sum was worth it.[85]

In 2012, the *Hollywood Reporter* and *Variety* both turned down ads I wrote about a TV show that smeared nuns.

In other words, this is not an unusual occurrence. The media hold the cards: they can get their side of the story to the public, but to those who seek to rebut them—even if they offer to pay for it—good luck.

It is one thing for the media to spin a story, quite another when it totally distorts the truth. That's what happened when *CBS Evening News* did a hit job on the Catholic Church in 2003. On August 6, it reported nationwide that the Vatican issued a document in 1962, the instruction *On the Manner of Proceeding in Cases of Solicitation*, which "lays out a church policy that calls for absolute secrecy when it comes to sexual abuse by priests—anyone who speaks out could be thrown out of the church". The online version of *CBS Evening News* went further, saying that orders to cover up the sexual abuse of minors "were written in Rome at the highest levels of the Vatican".[86] None of this is true. On August 7, I appeared on CNN's *Paula Zahn Now* to discuss this matter. I held up a copy of the document on TV and charged CBS with lying about the report.

The 1962 document deals exclusively with solicitations that a priest might make toward a penitent in the confessional. Contrary to the way it was reported, the document details penalties for any priest who, "whether by words or signs or nods of the head", might convey a sexual advance to the penitent during Confession. The

[84]Bill Donohue, "Taking Aim at Bishop Finn", Catholic League, October 31, 2011.

[85]Bill Donohue, "Twin Philly Scandals", Catholic League, May 20, 2013, https://www.catholicleague.org/twin-philly-scandals/. The title of the ad was "Four Catholic Men Framed".

[86]Bill Donohue, "CBS: Catholic Bashing System," *Catalyst*, September 2003, https://www.catholicleague.org/cbs-catholic-bashing-system/.

ultimate penalty—being bounced from the priesthood—was a possibility. In other words, not only was this document not a "cover-up" scheme—it was just the opposite: it was designed to deter sexual misconduct by spelling out penalties for any priest engaged in sexual solicitation in the confessional.[87]

Here is something else the document made clear that CBS did not report. If the penitent were to tell someone (perhaps another priest) about a sexual solicitation in the confessional, the penitent had thirty days to report the incident to the bishop or face excommunication. If anything, this proves how utterly serious the Vatican was about such an offense—it threatened to punish the penitent *for not turning in the guilty priest.*[88]

It is striking that most media outlets, including the *New York Times*, did not say a word about the 1962 Vatican document. How, then, did CBS get it so wrong? Because it took its cues from some lawyers involved in cases against the Church. Indeed, I identified three of them. They were the first out of the box blasting the Catholic Church with their false allegations, and CBS took their bait.[89] Because it was a bogus story, it died quickly, but much damage had been done.

CNN issued a documentary in 2010 that was strewn with unsubstantiated allegations against Pope Benedict XVI. "For decades before he became pope," said host Gary Tuchman, "Joseph Ratzinger was a high-ranking Vatican official who, more than anyone else besides Pope John Paul, could have taken decisive action to stem the sexual abuse crisis." This was patently untrue. Not only was Ratzinger not in charge of this issue "for decades", but he wasn't given the authority to police the sexual abuse problem until 2001 (astonishingly, later in the program, Tuchman concedes as much).[90]

The most serious accusation against Ratzinger was his alleged handling of Father Lawrence Murphy, who is believed to have molested two hundred deaf boys in Wisconsin in the 1950s. CNN did not say

[87]Bill Donohue, "CBS Takes the Bait of Victims' Lawyers", August 8, 2003, https://www.catholicleague.org/cbs-takes-the-bait-of-victims-lawyers/.

[88]Bill Donohue, "CBS Guilty of Unfairly Maligning Vatican", August 7, 2003, https://www.catholicleague.org/cbs-guilty-of-unfairly-maligning-vatican/.

[89]Ibid. See also "CBS Takes the Bait of Victims' Lawyers".

[90]Bill Donohue, "Response to CNN Documentary on the Pope", Catholic League, September 28, 2010, https://www.catholicleague.org/response-to-cnn-documentary-on-the-pope-2/.

that the crimes alleged against Murphy extended to the 1950s, that the authorities were not formally asked to investigate until the mid-1970s, and that following a probe, the police dropped the case. Fast-forward to 1996, the first time the Vatican was notified. The Vatican didn't care that the statute of limitations had expired: it ordered a trial.

Father Thomas Brundage was the judicial vicar, the one who presided over the case between 1996 and 1998. When asked about Ratzinger's role, he said, "At no time in the case, at meetings that I had at the Vatican, in Washington, D.C. and in Milwaukee, was Cardinal Ratzinger's name ever mentioned." He said he was "shocked" when the media tried to tie Ratzinger to the Murphy case.[91]

Why didn't CNN report any of these facts? Perhaps it was willing to accept without question the innuendo-laden commentary of attorney Jeff Anderson, who, according to his website, "pioneered the use of civil litigation to seek justice for the survivors of child sexual abuse". Had CNN been doing right by the story, it would have dug deeper and told the truth about Cardinal Ratzinger.

The *Boston Globe* is the newspaper that broke the sexual abuse scandal in the Church wide open. It hammered the Church for lacking transparency, yet years later it proved it had a hard time with transparency itself in a manner that appeared to me as proof of bias against the Church. On November 4, 2018, there was a front-page story in the *Boston Globe* alleging more than 130 bishops, or about a third of those still living, had been accused of "failing to adequately respond to sexual misconduct in their dioceses".[92] The news story, which was based on a study by reporters from the *Globe* and the *Philadelphia Inquirer*, garnered national headlines; it was released prior to a conference of United States bishops who were meeting in Baltimore to discuss the sexual abuse scandal.

As a sociologist, I had some serious problems with the methodology of the study, and so I e-mailed the *Globe* about them. They were cordial but would not budge on my request to see the data. That's right, the same newspaper that insists on total transparency on the

[91] Ibid.

[92] Jenn Abelson and Thomas Farragher, "In Abuse Scandal, Spotlight Squarely on Bishops: A Joint Review by the Globe and the Philadelphia Inquirer Finds Misdeeds Rife in the Church Hierarchy but Accountability Largely Absent Despite 2002 Vows", *Boston Globe*, November 4, 2018, A1.

part of the bishops—demanding that they fully disclose their internal data—would not make public its data on the bishops.

What made the data suspect was the statement from the two newspapers that they had examined "court records, media reports, and interviews with church officials, victims, and attorneys".[93] What made me most suspicious were the interviews with "church officials, victims, and attorneys". Based on past experience, I doubted the trustworthiness of certain defense attorneys, victims' watchdog groups, and media outlets. I wanted to read who the reporters chose to interview and what they said. But the beacons of transparency slammed the door in my face.

Because I kept pressing Brian McGrory, the editor of the *Boston Globe*, asking if he would allow me to verify the story, he pitched my request to Scott Allen, assistant managing editor for projects. When he denied me access to the raw data, I asked for permission to at least read the transcripts of the interviews that were conducted. Again, I was turned down. Allen said, "We don't circulate our interviews unless we plan to publish them." That's understandable, but the effect of this policy in my case was the suppression of potential criticism.

It cannot be said too strongly that although many in the media have been unfair to the Church and hypocritical in their censure, there would have been no Scandal II without Scandal I: molesting priests and their enabling bishops. That can never be slighted. Many of the bishops lacked fortitude, one of the cardinal virtues. They should have had the courage to do what was right, not what was expedient.

Scandal I and Scandal II are both the outcome of people violating another cardinal virtue—justice. The injustice committed by molesting priests (who violated the cardinal virtue of temperance) and their enabling bishops (who violated the cardinal virtue of prudence) has left a big scar on the victims and on the Church, and they need to be held accountable.

The Catholic Church, however, is a force for great good, which is why those bent on damaging it—from the inside and the outside— need to be held accountable too. There is too much at stake not to.

---

[93] Ibid.

2

The Church Confronts the Scandal

The first molesting priest to capture public attention was a Louisiana cleric, Gilbert Gauthe. That was in 1985. Ironically, it was at a time when clergy sexual abuse was subsiding, though few knew it then. Gauthe pleaded guilty to eleven counts of molestation and was sent to prison. Another priest, James Porter, made big news when his predatory behavior in Fall River, Massachusetts, was revealed in the early 1990s. In the late 1990s, Rudolph Kos became a public figure when the Dallas Diocese was ordered to pay more than $31 million to his victims. Immediately following this disclosure was the indictment of Boston's John Geoghan, a serial child rapist who was murdered in prison.

Gauthe was sentenced to twenty years in prison for the sexual abuse of more than three dozen boys; his victims ranged in age from seven to fifteen. As Mary Eberstadt put it, he was "a sexually active gay man with a taste for children and adolescents too".[1] How was it possible for a serial molester to go unnoticed by other priests, nuns, laypeople, and his bishop? It wasn't. Gauthe's superiors knew for ten years what he was doing. After he molested his first victim, he quickly learned that nothing would be done to him. His bishop told him to confess his sins. That was it. The bishop never mentioned it again. After Gauthe was moved to another parish, the abuse continued, and so did the complaints.[2]

This is the kind of response that enrages Catholics. Bad as Gauthe was, it is even worse that his bishop allowed him to continue his

---

[1] Mary Eberstadt, "The Elephant in the Sacristy", *Weekly Standard*, June 17, 2002. See also Eberstadt's article "The Elephant in the Sacristy, Revisited", *Weekly Standard*, September 24, 2018.

[2] *60 Minutes II*, CBS News transcripts, June 12, 2002.

crimes against children with impunity. Did the Vatican know what was going on? Not while he was preying on his victims. But by 1984, news about Gauthe had reached the Vatican Embassy, and it assigned one of its canon lawyers, Father Thomas Doyle, to deal with his case. Father Doyle issued a series of reports, providing evidence that Gauthe was not the only predator priest in active ministry.

In 1985, Pope John Paul II assigned Bishop A.J. Quinn of Cleveland to investigate the scandal in Louisiana. According to Doyle, besides a press conference announcing a committee to study the situation, nothing was done about it. Indeed, the committee was never established.[3]

Doyle and Gauthe's attorney, Ray Mouton, prepared a report on priestly sexual abuse and sought to present it to the bishops in the spring of 1985. They warned of more scandals, but their efforts, too, went nowhere. Bishop William Levada of Los Angeles showed support for Doyle and Mouton, but in the end, he told Doyle that their work would not be given to the bishops at their upcoming meeting in Collegeville, Minnesota. After the bishops' meeting, a pastoral letter was issued, but it was not on clergy sexual abuse: it was on poverty. It was written by Milwaukee Archbishop Rembert Weakland, who would later be forced to resign over sexual and financial misconduct.[4]

For the next thirty-plus years Father Doyle worked on clergy sexual abuse cases, helping those making accusations against Catholic priests and the lawyers defending them, and it appears that this role has taken a toll—both on him and on the Church. In 2019 he said, "Most of my adult life has been involved with this issue. It's changed me dramatically. It's changed my belief system. I no longer have any trust in the institutional church."[5] It could also be said that the feeling is mutual. He was removed in 2003 from his assignment as a chaplain in the Archdiocese of Military Services, a post he had held since 1986. The head of the archdiocese, Archbishop Edwin F. O'Brien, accused

[3] Ibid.

[4] Michael D'Antonio, *Mortal Sins: Sex, Crime, and the Era of Catholic Scandal* (New York: St. Martin's Press, 2013), 37–39.

[5] Jeremy Rogalski and Tina Macias, "Catholic Priest Shuns Collar to Fight for Survivors of Clergy Abuse", WUSA9, January 10, 2019, https://www.wusa9.com/article/news/inves tigations/unforgivable/catholic-priest-shuns-collar-to-fight-for-survivors-of-clergy-sexual -abuse/285-1d16e66d-5a17-4f14-a074-7793c8cac10d.

Doyle of not following orders, such as the requirement to offer daily Mass for Catholics on military bases.[6] Doyle is now known as an "inactive priest and former member of the Dominican order".[7]

The Boston Globe Unloads

Barely a week into 2002, the *Boston Globe* rolled out its series on the sexual abuse of minors in the Catholic Church. It stunned the nation and outraged Catholics. At that time, it was not apparent that the media would exploit the scandal to sell headlines and perhaps to undermine an institution whose teachings they reject.

> It was a rare event in 2002 to read a newspaper account of the scandal that was patently unfair, much less anti-Catholic. The *Boston Globe*, the *Boston Herald*, and the *New York Times* covered the story carefully and with professionalism. The evening news anchors on television similarly did what they are supposed to do—report, not editorialize. Peter Jennings did a one-hour special on the scandal that was handled with distinction. The problems we had with the media were mostly limited to pundits, cartoonists and script writers for TV shows.[8]

I wrote that in the Catholic League's *2002 Annual Report on Anti-Catholicism*.

The anger and fury that rocked Catholics was directed at the Church, not the media. A front-page story in the Sunday *New York Times* in March 2002 quoted me as saying, "I am not the church's water boy. I am not here to defend the indefensible."[9] It was not

---

[6]Daniel J. Wakin, "Catholic Priest Who Aids Church Sexual Abuse Victims Loses Job", *New York Times*, April 29, 2004, https://www.nytimes.com/2004/04/29/us/catholic-priest-who-aids-church-sexual-abuse-victims-loses-job-military-chaplain.html.

[7]Tom Roberts, "Thomas Doyle Traces the Disintegration of Clerical/Hierarchical Culture", *National Catholic Reporter*, November 27, 2018, http://www.ncronline.org/news/accountability/ncr-connections/thomas-doyle-traces-disintegration-clericalhierarchical-culture.

[8]My remarks can be found on the Catholic League website, http://www.catholicleague.org, in the executive summary of the 2002 annual report.

[9]Dan Barry and Robin Toner, "U.S. Catholics, Sad and Angry, Still Keeping Faith", *New York Times*, March 24, 2002, A1.

something I wanted to say—I am known for vigorously defending the Church—but intellectual dishonesty is something I despise.

The *Times* story accurately described my position: "He also sounded what has become a dominant theme in the conservative reaction to the scandal: that the victims of sexual abuse were primarily adolescent boys—not younger children—and that there is a link between the abuse and the number of gay men in the priesthood." I told the newspaper that the priesthood had "gone soft", allowing for an "open rebellion against the church's sexual ethics". I also noted that "a certain unmanliness has taken place."[10] This was not received well by so-called progressive Catholics.

In April 2002, Pope John Paul II summoned American cardinals and the leaders of the bishops' conference to meet with him in what was known as the "Vatican summit". The Holy Father said that there is "no place in religious life for abusers".[11] Not only did his words carry the weight of the leader of the Catholic Church, but they came just two months before the annual meeting of the U.S. bishops, who convened that year in Dallas.

What the pope said was much appreciated by Catholics. Still, when asked at the time what I thought about the state of the Church, I could not admit to being mollified. "I don't know of a single Catholic priest or layman who isn't furious about the sex abuse scandal in terms of the tolerance they [the hierarchy] have had for intolerable behavior, and the way they've played musical chairs with these miscreant priests. I've never seen such anger."[12]

As the Dallas conference approached, Catholics were cautious. I said as much when asked by the *New York Times* about my faith in the Church's hierarchy to rectify matters: "I don't know if they can set it straight. It has to do with what has been lacking in these men all along—common sense and courage. There's an impatience now. American Catholics are not going to wait ad infinitum for this church to change."[13] I was not alone in feeling uneasy. Liberals such

---

[10] Ibid.

[11] Victor L. Simpson, "Pope: Abuse in Sex Scandal is a Crime", Associated Press, April 23, 2002.

[12] The Investigative Staff of the *Boston Globe*, *Betrayal: The Crisis in the Catholic Church* (Boston: Little Brown and Company, 2002), 112.

[13] Laurie Goodstein, "Scandal in the Church: The Cardinals; On a Mission to Restore Credibility", *New York Times*, April 21, 2002, A1.

as Father Richard McBrien and conservatives such as Phil Lawler both cited the need for the bishops to reestablish the trust of Catholics; they were skeptical about the prospects.[14]

Days before the meeting, the U.S. bishops' Ad Hoc Committee on Sexual Abuse released a draft of the proposed document that would be voted on at the conference. I was relieved and said at the time, "The draft is a reasonable document that should allay the worst fears of a skeptical laity. It is thoughtful, pointed and fair to all parties."[15]

Three days later, I warned about a new problem on the horizon: the exploitation of the scandal by "steeple-chasing lawyers". Whether motivated by the potential for huge monetary gains, contempt for the Catholic Church, or both, such lawyers could do serious harm to the Church's mission. At the time, I questioned why only Catholic priests were being targeted by lawyers, while ministers, rabbis, teachers, social workers, and therapists were given a pass. These lawyers, along with victims' groups, wanted the statute of limitations lifted in cases of priestly sexual abuse but showed no interest in having this apply across the board to others. "No wrongdoing by the Church justifies attempts to plunder its resources by rewriting the law", I said. "This is the work of bandits disguised as attorneys."[16]

On June 7, 2002, the *New York Times* published an op-ed ad I had written, "All Eyes Are on Dallas". I expressed my concern that "not even the best-written guidelines will end the scandal." What was needed, I said, was what Pope John Paul II called for at the "Vatican summit" in April—namely, "the Pastors of the Church need clearly to promote the correct moral teaching of the Church and publicly to reprimand individuals who spread dissent." To which I added, "It does not exaggerate to say that nothing enables behavioral deviance more than theological dissidence."[17]

The run-up to Dallas ended on an ominous note. It was on the eve of the bishops' conference that the CBS show *60 Minutes* introduced

[14] Matt Stearns and Scott Canon, "Bishops to Address 'Crisis of Leadership' at Conference", Knight Ridder/Tribune News Service, June 9, 2002.

[15] Bill Donohue, "Bishops Draft Reasonable Document", June 4, 2002, http://www.catholicleague.org.

[16] Bill Donohue, "Rule of Law Applies—Even to the Church," June 7, 2002, https://www.catholicleague.org/rule-of-law-applies-even-to-the-church-2/.

[17] Bill Donohue, "All Eyes Are on Dallas", *New York Times*, op-ed page ad, June 7, 2002, A27, posted on Catholic League, http://70.40.202.97/wp-content/uploads/2011/09/ALL-EYES-ARE-ON-DALLAS.pdf.

Americans to Gilbert Gauthe's horrific acts and to the equally horrific
delinquency of Church officials. The bishops had their backs to the
wall. The *60 Minutes* segment on Gauthe set the stage for what was
about to happen.

The Dallas Reforms and Accused Priests

The Dallas Charter (*Charter for the Protection of Children and Young
People*) was a comprehensive list of reforms that did much to quell
the anger of most Catholics. It established a National Review Board
to conduct an annual review of the way dioceses and eparchies are
addressing clergy sexual abuse. The Office of Child and Youth Protection was formed to keep tabs on this issue as well. It developed
norms for the dioceses and the eparchies, including review boards
that would investigate claims of abuse at the local level. Importantly,
confidentiality clauses in settlements with victims were prohibited
(unless requested by victims).

The Catholic Church does not get enough credit for prohibiting confidentiality agreements. It stands in stark contrast to common
practice elsewhere. For example, Hollywood celebrities accused of
sexual misconduct routinely avail themselves of confidentiality agreements. Such secret agreements allowed Bill Cosby and Harvey Weinstein to get away with their predatory behavior for decades.[18] One of
the persons who helped Weinstein negotiate secret settlements was
feminist attorney Gloria Allred.[19] It seems that for years many professional women who consider themselves feminists were silent about or
even complicit in sexual misconduct at the highest levels of society,
that is, until the Me Too movement got rolling.

Perhaps the most controversial reform made at the Dallas conference was the adoption of a "zero tolerance" policy: it allowed for the
permanent removal of a priest or deacon from ministry if he admits
to sexual abuse or is found guilty of it. However, the policy did not

[18]"Secret Settlements Protect Sexual Predators", *USA Today*, November 12, 2017, http://
www.usatoday.com/story/opinion/2017/11/12/secret-settlements-protect-sexual-predators
-weinstein-assault/833861001/.

[19]Alexandra Alter, "New Weinstein Book Names Previously Unknown Sources", *New
York Times*, September 10, 2019, B4.

apply to the bishops (the Vatican subsequently made it applicable). Having "zero tolerance" for anyone who sexually abuses a minor sounds, on the face of it, as a wholly justified response to a horrendous crime. There was, however, the prospect of swinging the pendulum too far, and this gave some Catholics pause. "But there is a problem regarding the rights of the accused", I said. "It appears that the charter may short-circuit some due process rights."[20]

No one was more forceful in his criticism of the lack of due process for accused priests than Cardinal Avery Dulles. The bishops' document, he said, "puts a very adversarial relationship between the bishop and the priest. The priest can no longer go to his bishop in confidence with a problem that he has. He has to be very careful what he says to the bishop because the bishop can throw him out of ministry for his entire life."[21]

Dulles outlined his concerns about the Dallas Charter in the pages of America, the influential Jesuit magazine. Referring to the "zero tolerance rule" he wrote, "The bishops adopted the very principles that they themselves had condemned in their critique of the secular judicial system." He was distressed at the prospect of having an accused priest removed from ministry without regard to his due-process rights; in addition to the injustice done to the priest, this move would leave the faithful to believe he was guilty, without his being proven as such. Dulles was also alarmed at the ambiguity in the language of the charter and of its failure to distinguish between minor offenses and more serious ones. Then there was the question of adjudicating old cases. This is not easy to do when one considers that "memories fade or become distorted, witnesses die or leave the area, and physical evidence becomes more difficult to obtain." He was particularly incensed that the bishops did not include in the charter something the pope implored them to consider: the "power of Christian conversion".[22]

[20]Bill Donohue, "Bishops Make Progress but Much Work Remains", June 14, 2002, http://www.catholicleague.org.

[21]Laurie Goodstein and Sam Dillon, "Scandals in the Church: The Bishops' Conference; Bishops Set Policy to Remove Priests in Sex Abuse Cases", New York Times, June 15, 2002, A1.

[22]Avery Dulles, "Rights of Accused Priests: Toward a Revision of the Dallas Charter and the Essential Norms", America, June 21, 2004, https://www.americamagazine.org/issue/488/article/rights-accused-priests.

Dulles was not alone in expressing reservations about the "zero tolerance" policy. In fact, four months before the Dallas Charter was issued, the Vatican's Pontifical Academy for Life published a report by non-Catholic psychiatrists and psychologists who said a "zero tolerance" policy was mistaken.[23] Even the *New York Times* admitted that while it embraced "zero tolerance", it nonetheless cautioned against overreacting. "We do not favor defrocking one-time offenders who have rehabilitated themselves", said an editorial. "Like the bishops, we believe in recovery and redemption." The newspaper's position was published just before the Dallas conference convened.[24]

In October 2002, the Vatican appointed a joint commission of bishops, four from the United States and four from the Holy See, to revise certain provisions of the Dallas Charter; the changes were submitted to the United States bishops at their next meeting, in November. The Vatican rightfully objected to some of the ambiguity in the charter and its lack of due-process rights for accused priests. Some were critical of the joint commission, but none more than Father Andrew Greeley. Without any evidence he said that the cardinals reviewing the charter were "convinced that the sex-abuse crisis was created by Jewish-controlled media to punish the church for its support for a Palestinian state".[25]

Father Thomas G. Guarino, a professor of theology at Seton Hall University, is a brilliant champion of the rights of priests. He argues that "almost every accusation is deemed 'credible' unless the accused can prove that thirty years ago (and most accusations are from decades long past) he was on a different continent when the alleged abuse occurred. In other words, 'credible' has come to mean 'not entirely impossible.' "[26] Looking back at what happened in Dallas, Guarino is not pleased. "The bishops were sold a bill of goods in the Charter, concocted by PR agents and lawyers but without solid Catholic theology. And now they are too frightened—by attorneys general,

---

[23] Nicole Winfield, "Vatican Issues a Report Critical of Policy", Associated Press, February 23, 2004.

[24] "Bishops at the Crossroads", *New York Times*, June 9, 2002, A14.

[25] Andrew Greeley, "Clueless Curia Isn't Listening to U.S. Anger", *Chicago Sun-Times*, October 25, 2002, 47.

[26] Thomas G. Guarino, "Betsy DeVos and the Bishops", *First Things*, December 8, 2017, https://www.firstthings.com/web-exclusives/2017/12/betsy-devos-and-the-bishops.

the media, lawyers, advocacy groups, and disgruntled laity—to seek justice."[27]

It is distressing to note that almost two decades after the scandal became known, Cardinal Daniel DiNardo, who was president of the bishops' conference at the time, admitted that lawyers were still working on what it means to be "credibly accused".[28] Even more worrisome is that the onus of proof has been reversed: instead of a priest being innocent until proven guilty, he is guilty until he is proven innocent. No one knows this better than Cardinal George Pell, who was imprisoned for a crime he did not commit. Although he was finally exonerated, for years he had endured the condemnation of activists, jurists, and pundits who accepted the accusations against him without evidence as they worked their way through the Australian justice system.[29]

The situation is ominous. I receive correspondence from priests, including bishops, alarmed over the way determinations of guilt are being made—it takes very little in some dioceses to award compensation to alleged victims, even those with very shaky stories. An eighty-five-year-old priest contacted me because he is being accused by a known drug addict of an alleged offense that took place forty years ago and his plea of innocence means nothing—his name was posted in the diocesan newspaper as an accused priest. This man is being deprived of his presumption of innocence; his reputation is being destroyed before his guilt has been proven. Even if he is guilty, this treatment is a violation of our country's principles of justice. If he is innocent, this is a travesty. And he is not alone. Even priests who have been accused and found not guilty still have their names posted on diocesan websites among the accused.

The emotional damage done in cases like this is not confined to priests. "My uncle's name appeared on the list of priests accused of sexual abuse issued last week by the Archdiocese of Baltimore. I would like to call him and ask him what I should think about this,

[27] Thomas G. Guarino, "The Dark Side of the Dallas Charter", *First Things*, October 2, 2019, https://www.firstthings.com/web-exclusives/2019/10/the-dark-side-of-the-dallas-charter.

[28] Christopher White, "Two Decades into Crisis, No Consensus on What 'Credibly Accused' Means", *Crux*, December 19, 2018, https://cruxnow.com/church-in-the-usa/2018/12/two-decades-into-crisis-no-consensus-on-what-credibly-accused-means/.

[29] George Pell, *Prison Journal: The Cardinal Makes His Appeal* (San Francisco: Ignatius Press, 2020).

but he died in 1981. Where is the fairness in defaming men who are not here to defend themselves?" This statement was published in a letter to the *Washington Post* in 2019.[30]

Even more distressing are public demands that priests are entitled to no due-process rights. Some want priests immediately removed from ministry as soon as an accusation is made. "We understand that it is a violation of the priest's due process—you're innocent until proven guilty—but we're talking about the most vulnerable people in our society and those are children."[31] If this were just the musings of a blogger, it wouldn't mean much. But this is the position of Anne Burke, who served as the head of the first National Review Board commissioned by the bishops to deal with clergy sexual abuse. At the time, she was an Illinois Appellate Court justice; she was later elevated to chief justice of the court.

In an interview I had in my office with a female reporter from CNN, she became quite critical of the Church for not posting the names of accused priests on its diocesan websites. I picked up the phone and, holding it in my hand, asked her for the name and phone number of her boss. When she asked why, I said I was going to accuse her of sexual harassment. I added that I wanted to see if CNN would post her name on its website. She said, "I get it." I put down the phone.

No organization in the United States is expected to post the names of employees accused of sexual misconduct, except for the Catholic Church. This expectation is absurd and unfair and wins no one over. The Church should not do this. Instead, it should insist on a level playing field and protect the rights of accused priests, just as every other institution in the nation protects its employees.

The Extent of the Scandal

In February 2004, researchers at the John Jay College of Criminal Justice issued *The Nature and Scope of Sexual Abuse of Minors by Catholic Priests and Deacons in the United States 1950–2002*. According to

[30] Maureen Loftus Hogel, "The Dead Can't Defend Themselves", *Washington Post*, April 29, 2019, A20.

[31] Cathleen Falsani and Stefano Esposito, "Cops Wanted to Charge Priest Sooner: Archdiocese Advised McCormick to Remain Silent, Source Says", *Chicago Sun-Times*, January 25, 2006, 3.

this report, approximately 4 percent of the Catholic clergy during the period studied had been accused of sexually abusing a youth under the age of eighteen. It was found that 75 percent of abuse occurred between 1960 and 1984.[32] Others who examined the data, such as the *New York Times*, concluded that "most of the abuse occurred in the 1970s and 1980s" and that the number of accused priests "declined sharply by the 1990s".[33] Everyone agrees that the 1970s was the worst decade.

How many minors were allegedly abused? In 1993, Father Andrew Greeley, a sociologist, speculated that there were "well in excess of 100,000" victims.[34] The John Jay social scientists, however, put the figure at 10,667.[35] Why was Greeley so far off? Because he *assumed* that on average there were fifty victims for every abusing priest.[36] The correct number is one.[37]

Who were the victims? "The majority of victims (81 percent) were male, in contrast to the distribution by victim gender for sexual crimes in the United States." Importantly, the John Jay study found that pedophilia was not the problem, even though the media constantly refer to "pedophile priests". Indeed, it found that 78 percent of the victims were postpubescent.[38] About half of the victims who made allegations of abuse socialized with the priests outside of church, and the priests were typically invited to their families' homes.[39]

How many of the accusations were substantiated? A draft report of the John Jay study that was given to the bishops estimated that 61 percent of the accusations had been substantiated.[40] For some

[32] Karen J. Terry, John Jay College of Criminal Justice (JJCCJ), and United States Conference of Catholic Bishops (USCCB), *The Nature and Scope of Sexual Abuse of Minors by Catholic Priests and Deacons in the United States 1950–2002: A Research Study Conducted by the John Jay College of Criminal Justice* (Washington, D.C.: United States Conference of Catholic Bishops, 2004), 27.

[33] Laurie Goodstein, "Decades of Damage; Trail of Pain in Church Crisis Leads to Nearly Every Diocese", *New York Times*, January 12, 2003, 1.

[34] Andrew Greeley, "How Serious Is the Problem of Sexual Abuse by Clergy?", *America*, March 20, 1993. 7.

[35] Terry, JJCCJ, and USCCB, *Nature and Scope*, 4.

[36] Greeley, "How Serious Is the Problem?", 7.

[37] Terry, JJCCJ, and USCCB, *Nature and Scope*, 6.

[38] Ibid., 9–10.

[39] Ibid., 7.

[40] Michael Paulson, "Abuse Study Says 4% of Priests in US Accused", *Boston Globe*, February 17, 2004, http://archive.boston.com/news/nation/articles/2004/02/17/abuse_study_says_4_of_priests_in_us_accused/.

unexplained reason, when the report was published, the figure jumped to 80 percent.[41] The impression given to the public was that virtually all of the accused priests were guilty.

According to a survey by the *Washington Post* published in 2002, less than 1.5 percent of the estimated sixty thousand or more men who served in the Catholic clergy were accused of child sexual abuse.[42] A *New York Times* survey reported that 1.8 percent of all priests ordained between 1950 and 2001 were accused of sexually abusing minors.[43] Thomas Kane, author of *Priests Are People Too*, estimated in 2002 that between 1 and 1.5 percent of priests had charges made against them.[44] Also in 2002, the Associated Press (AP) found that approximately 0.67 percent of contemporary priests had charges pending against them.[45]

Everyone agrees that *no priest* should ever be involved in sexually abusing a minor. But it must also be stressed that the evidence shows that *almost all priests have never been accused of abusing a young person*. This fact does not get the kind of coverage it deserves. Why? Because it doesn't fit the narrative that so many in the media have adopted. Father Greeley was so upset with the media for not emphasizing that most priests are "reasonably mature, happy men" that he concluded, "The sexual abuse crisis has become an occasion for Catholic-bashing and celibate-bashing." He was most incensed with the *New York Times* for its negative coverage, saying it had "crossed the border into hostility and ventured on to the stomping grounds of virulent anti-Catholicism".[46]

The most common act that priests were accused of was touching over a victim's clothing (52.6 percent). Relatively few priests, however, were alleged to have committed only this act.[47] On the other hand, most abusers did not have hundreds of victims, as some have alleged.

[41] Terry, JJCCJ, and USCCB, *Nature and Scope*, 94.

[42] Alan Cooperman, "Hundreds of Priests Removed Since '60s; Survey Shows Scope Wider Than Disclosed", *Washington Post*, June 9, 2002, A1.

[43] Goodstein, "Decades of Damage".

[44] Interview with Bill O'Reilly, *The O'Reilly Factor*, aired May 3, 2002, on Fox News.

[45] Bob von Sternberg, "Insurance Falls Short in Church Abuse Cases; Catholic Dioceses Are Forced to Find Other Sources to Pay Settlements", *Star Tribune*, July 27, 2002, 1A.

[46] Andrew M. Greeley, "The Times and Sexual Abuse by Priests", *America*, February 10, 2003, 17.

[47] Terry, JJCCJ, and USCCB, *Nature and Scope*, 6.

"The majority of priests (56%) were alleged to have abused one victim, nearly 27% were alleged to have abused two or three victims, nearly 14% were alleged to have abused four to nine victims and 3.4% were alleged to have abused more than ten victims." This next statistic is rarely reported: "The 149 priests (3.5%) who had more than ten allegations of abuse were allegedly responsible for abusing 2,960 victims, thus accounting for 26% of allegations. Therefore, *a very small percentage of accused priests are responsible for a substantial percentage of the allegations*" (my italics).[48]

This is astonishing. Of the 4,393 priests who had an accusation made against them between 1950 and 2002 (not all of which were substantiated), a mere 149 of them accounted for more than a quarter of the allegations. Data like this disprove the conventional wisdom that most priests are predators. It is a malicious lie.

Did the Reforms Work?

Another great lie about the Catholic Church is that the sexual abuse scandal continues unabated. This is utter nonsense. To be sure, there are still serious issues—such as the failure of the Vatican to explain in a timely fashion who knew what and when about Theodore McCarrick, the disgraced former cardinal—but in terms of the scope of the scandal, it has long ceased to be a crisis.

According to Georgetown University's Center for Applied Research in the Apostolate, the average number of allegations made against current clergy members in any given year has dropped precipitously. In the 1970s, there were 6,155; the figure for the 1980s was 3,594; there were 777 in the 1990s and 351 in the 2000s. We are now down to single digits.[49]

Here is a chart on the number of credible allegations made since the National Review Board began compiling the data.[50]

---

[48] Ibid.

[49] Bart Jones and Craig Schneider, "Catholic Church at a 'Turning Point'", *Newsday*, March 7, 2019, https://www.newsday.com/long-island/catholic-church-sex-abuse-scandal -1.28150439.

[50] The figures are from the National Review Board audits in its *Annual Report on the Implementation of the Charter for the Protection of Children and Young People*, found on the website of the United States Conference of Catholic Bishops (USCCB). Following are the page numbers

2004	22	2012	6
2005	9	2013	7
2006	14	2014	6
2007	4	2015	7
2008	10	2016	2
2009	8	2017	6
2010	7	2018	3
2011	7	2019	8

The National Review Board has done excellent work compiling the data. It has done a poor job touting the good news. Those responsible for the reports always remind us that one victim is too many, which, of course, is true. But that should not prevent them from doing a little arithmetic. For example, take the 2018 report. It detailed twenty-six new allegations involving current minors, three of which were substantiated (the three men were removed from ministry). This means that 0.006 percent of the 50,648 members of the clergy had a substantiated accusation made against them in that one-year period. The 2019 report found thirty-seven new allegations, only eight of which, or 0.016 percent (out of 49,972 clergy members), could be substantiated.

It should not take the Catholic League to do the math and hail the incredible progress. But it does. When it was revealed that there were only three substantiated cases made, the chairman of the National Review Board, Francesco C. Cesareo, took the opportunity to say, "These current allegations point to the reality that sexual abuse of minors by the clergy should not be considered by the bishops as a thing of the past or a distant memory."[51] That is a pitiful reaction. Anne Burke, who led the first National Review Board, has consistently denied that there has been any progress, and at the end of 2019, she said that the problem of clergy sexual abuse was "worse" than it

---

for each year cited: 2004, 7; 2005, 29; 2006, 8; 2007, 28; 2008, 28; 2009, 35; 2010, 35; 2011, 3; 2012, 4; 2013, 9; 2014, vii; 2015, vii; 2016, vii; 2017, vii; 2018, vi; 2019, 28. Note: the audits for years 2004–2010 list the number of credible allegations; the figures for 2011–2012 are the number deemed credible by law enforcement; the figures for 2013–2019 are the number of substantiated allegation.

[51] Francesco C. Cesareo, letter to Daniel Cardinal DiNardo, February 27, 2019. See page vi of the 2018 annual report found on the USCCB website.

had been before.[52] She cited no evidence. There isn't any. No one is calling for a victory lap, but not to acknowledge the incredible progress that has been made is unfair. Moreover, it does nothing to stop the false assumption that many priests continue to abuse minors.

No other institution, religious or secular, has a more impressive record of combating the sexual abuse of minors today than the Catholic Church (much more about this later). Is the progress wholly a function of the Dallas reforms? No, but much of it is. The fact that the number of allegations was declining before the reforms is proof that the progress cannot be attributed to the new norms alone. For one, the sexual revolution began to wane. It is also true that many of the bishops began to step up, some out of duty and others out of fear. No matter, the naysayers are still with us, refusing to acknowledge the progress.

Dr. Mary Gail Frawley-O'Dea, a psychologist, was invited to address the bishops in Dallas. In January 2003, she predicted that the crisis would soon reappear. "You will see some kind of a bubble in 2005, when the people who were abused in the 1990s come forward."[53] She was wrong. It never happened. More accurate were Gregory Erlandson and Matthew Bunson, who noted in 2010 that "the United States Church, which was for several years at the epicenter of the scandals, is now leading the way in establishing norms and providing guidelines for dealing with priests abusers, assisting the victims, and preventing further crimes."[54]

Good news about the progress that has been made is not well received by those who wallow in bad news. They can be found on the far right as well as the far left. The right says that Vatican II made too many reforms; the Left says it didn't make enough. Both sides love it when bad news emerges—they go into self-congratulatory mode.

When New York Archbishop Timothy Dolan was interviewed on *60 Minutes* in 2011, he said the sexual abuse scandal was "over with". That sent Jamie Manson of the *National Catholic Reporter* into orbit.

[52] Claudia Lauer and Meghan Hoyer (AP), "Hundreds of Accused Clergy Left Off Church's Sex Abuse Lists", *Time, Salt Lake Tribune*, December 30, 2019, https://www.sltrib.com/news/nation-world/2019/12/28/hundreds-accused-clergy/.

[53] Goodstein, "Decades of Damage".

[54] Gregory Erlandson and Matthew Bunson, *Pope Benedict XVI and the Sexual Abuse Crisis: Working for Redemption and Renewal* (Huntington, Ind.: Our Sunday Visitor, 2010), 13.

She attacked Dolan for his remark, offering no evidence that he was wrong.[55] He wasn't. One year later, on the tenth anniversary of the *Boston Globe*'s series on the scandal, the best the newspaper could do was publish one throwaway sentence.[56] If matters had deteriorated in the Church, it would have run a lengthy front-page story; but given the good news, it simply wasn't worth saying much about it.

Wild accusations that the Church has not changed are made all the time, and from prominent sources. In October 2019, there was an angry editorial in the *Washington Post* about the failure of the Vatican to deal squarely with former cardinal Theodore McCarrick. The editorial was right about that—a full accounting should have been made by then—but those at the newspaper let their emotions color their thinking on matters closer to home. The editorial referred to "fresh allegations ... of rape, assault, molestation and other outrages".[57] It made the reader think that the scandal is still ongoing. This is simply untrue.

Monsignor Stephen Rossetti, who knows this subject well, noted in 2018 that the first John Jay study found that 4 percent of priests were accused of abusing minors. "This number has plummeted and is now estimated to be less than 1 percent."[58] Further proof that great progress has been made can be found by reading the various reports issued by dioceses and state attorneys general.

In March 2019, Church-suing attorney Jeff Anderson issued a report on accused priests in Illinois over the past half century. There were many media stories about the 395 priests named in the report, but most of them were incomplete. Not all were priests: the report included deacons, seminarians, brothers, and nuns. Some priests were from religious orders, not under the jurisdiction of a bishop. In other cases, the order priests were not from Illinois, and their alleged offenses, if they happened at all, may not have taken place there. Moreover, these were only allegations, most of which were never

[55]Jamie Manson, "Dolan on 60 Minutes: 'Charmer' or 'Shrill Scold'?", *National Catholic Reporter*, March 22, 2011, http://www.ncronline.org/blogs/grace-margins/dolan-60-minutes-charmer-or-shrill-scold.

[56]"This Day in History", *Boston Globe* editorial, June 13, 2012, G34.

[57]"The 'Untouchable' Mr. McCarrick", *Washington Post*, October 26, 2019, A16.

[58]Stephen Rossetti, "Five Ways to Safeguard Children Everywhere", *America*, September 20, 2018, http://www.americamagazine.org/politics-society/2018/09/20/five-ways-safeguard-children-everywhere.

substantiated in a court of law. Here is what really counts: of the 395 persons mentioned, 394 were either dead or out of ministry![59] That left one guy. Does this not suggest that the scandal is no longer a crisis in the United States?

In April 2019, the Diocese of Sacramento released a report on 1,500 clergy members who served in the diocese over the past seventy years. There were 44 accused priests, roughly 3 percent of the total. Importantly, 3 priests committed roughly half of the abuse.[60] In other words, almost all the priests were never involved in sexually molesting minors.

In September 2019, Missouri attorney general Eric Schmitt issued a report on sexual abuse committed by priests, deacons, seminarians, and nuns. It was determined that 163 priests out of more than 2,000 who worked in Missouri since World War II had an accusation made against them. More than half were dead. Of the 154 priests for which a date was provided, all but 15 of the accusations occurred before 1990 (only three in the 2010s); 117 occurred during the 1960s, 1970s, and 1980s.[61] In short, the crisis no longer exists.

In October 2019, the Colorado attorney general released a report on sexual abuse in the Catholic Church over the past seventy years. It found that of the 166 priests named, 5 abused 102 of the minors, or 61 percent of the total. In fact, 2 were responsible for 82 of the cases. Fully 84 percent of the victims were boys, and most were postpubescent, meaning that their victimizers were homosexuals.[62] Again, we find that a few bad priests accounted for most of the offenses.

The situation was similar in New York. In 2019, Cardinal Timothy Dolan, the archbishop of New York, announced that almost all

[59] Corky Siemaszko, "About 390 Catholic Priests, 6 Nuns in Ill. Named as Alleged Sexual Abusers on Massive List", NBC News, March 20, 2019, https://www.nbcnews.com/news/us-news/about-390-catholic-priests-6-nuns-ill-named-alleged-sexual-n985581.

[60] Marcus Bretón and Alexandra Yoon-Hendricks, "Identities Revealed of Over 40 Sacramento-Area Priests Accused of Sexual Abuse", Sacramento Bee, April 30, 2019, https://www.sacbee.com/news/local/article229815334.html.

[61] Eric Schmitt, Catholic Church Clergy Abuse Investigation Report, September 13, 2019, Missouri Attorney General, https://ago.mo.gov/docs/default-source/press-releases/2019/catholicchurchclergyabuseinvestigationreport.pdf.

[62] Roman Catholic Clergy Sexual Abuse of Children in Colorado from 1950 to 2019, Special Master's Report, October 22, 2019, Colorado Attorney General, https://coag.gov/app/uploads/2019/10/Special-Masters-Report_10.22.19_FINAL.pdf.

of the abuse occurred in the last century and that, of the 120 priests named in a report, many were dead and none were in ministry.[63]

Public Perceptions Are Flawed

"There are not over a hundred people in the United States who hate the Catholic Church. There are millions, however, who hate what they wrongly believe to be the Catholic Church—which is, of course, quite a different thing." Those words are as true today as they were in 1938, when Fulton J. Sheen, then a monsignor, wrote them.[64]

When the scandal hit the front pages of newspapers in 2002, a *Wall Street Journal*–NBC News poll found that 64 percent believed that Catholic priests "frequently" abused children.[65] Ten years later, it was found that only 21 percent of Catholics could correctly identify that the abuse cases were more common before 1985 than since.[66] Bishops and pastors share much of the blame for this ignorance; it is their job to educate the faithful, but few give homilies that mention anything about the progress that has been made.

In 2018, a CBS poll asked respondents about the seriousness of priestly sexual abuse. Here are the results: very serious, 69 percent; somewhat serious, 21 percent; not that serious, 7 percent; don't know or no answer, 4 percent.[67] If this question had been asked between the mid-1960s and the mid-1980s, the results would likely have been the reverse: we would expect that approximately 7 percent would say

[63] Jennifer Peltz, "New York Archdiocese Names 120 Priests Accused of Sex Abuse", Associated Press, April 26, 2019, https://apnews.com/c2d572976fdc4e1fb2aa2e9903cb3a2f.

[64] Tod Worner, "Father Fulton Sheen and the Millions Who Hate the Catholic Church", Aleteia, June 20, 2016, https://aleteia.org/2016/06/20/father-fulton-sheen-the-millions-who-hate-the-catholic-church/.

[65] Pat Wingert, "Priests Commit No More Abuse Than Other Males", *Newsweek*, April 7, 2010, https://www.newsweek.com/priests-commit-no-more-abuse-other-males-70625.

[66] Mark M. Gray, "Pain Never Disappears from Unhealed Wounds," *1964* (blog), August 8, 2018, http://nineteensixty-four.blogspot.com/2018/08/pain-never-disappears-from-unhealed.html.

[67] Fred Backus and Jennifer De Pinto, "Catholic Americans Give Pope Poor Marks on Handling Sex Abuse Scandal—CBS News Poll", CBS News, October 17, 2018, http://www.cbsnews.com/news/catholic-americans-give-pope-poor-marks-on-handling-sex-abuse-scandal-cbs-news-poll.

there is a "very serious" problem, and roughly 69 percent would say that the problem is "not that serious". Here is the paradox: the timeline just cited is exactly the period when most of the sexual abuse of minors took place, but few were aware of it. Today, there is almost no abuse taking place, yet the alarms are going off.

In the spring of 2019, a Pew Research Center survey found that eight in ten Americans believed that Catholic clergy sexual abuse was an "ongoing problem", while only 12 percent said these problems "happened in the past and mostly don't happen anymore"; a quarter of Catholics, 24 percent, held to the latter interpretation.[68]

As disturbing as this misperception is, even worse is the fact that many prominent Catholic leaders refuse to challenge this distorted view. At a lay-leadership conference held in 2019 at Georgetown University, the Pew data were discussed, but no one bothered to correct the record: the data dispute the invidious perception that the scandal is ongoing.

In November 2019, NBC released an interesting survey of Catholics who work for the Church in one capacity or another. It found that almost four in ten (39 percent) said the sexual abuse scandal is "still a major problem"; 14 percent said it "is no longer a major problem"; and 46 percent said this was never more of a problem for the Catholic Church than it has been for other institutions involved in the care of minors. Nuns were the most alarmed, and the most uninformed, with 56 percent believing that it is still a major problem today.

In the televised documentary on this survey, NBC gave me an opportunity to set the record straight. "This is a result of the poisoning of the public mind", I said. "Most of the bad guys, most of the priests who molested, are either dead or out of ministry. That's not an opinion. That's a fact."[69]

---

[68] "Americans See Catholic Clergy Sex Abuse as an Ongoing Problem", Pew Research Center, June 11, 2019, https://www.pewforum.org/2019/06/11/americans-see-catholic-clergy-sex-abuse-as-an-ongoing-problem/.

[69] Chris Glorioso and Evan Stulberger, "Survey Reveals Employees of Catholic Church Divided on Clergy Abuse and Reforms", NBC, updated December 6, 2019, https://www.nbcsandiego.com/news/national-international/survey-reveals-employees-of-catholic-church-divided-on-clergy-abuse-and-reforms/2194308/.

3

The Poisoning of the Public Mind

In 2018, I did a radio interview with John Steigerwald, a well-known Pittsburgh personality, about clergy sexual abuse. He said that in all his years in Catholic schools, he never heard of any case of priestly molestation. That is hardly unusual; the number of offending priests is very small. Yet he received a barrage of criticism for what he said.[1] This is telling. It shows that many people believe, despite the facts, that the number of offending priests is large.

What accounts for this poisoning of the public mind? Four factors explain why the public perception of the scandal is distorted: the role of the media, the role of Hollywood, the role of the Pennsylvania grand-jury report, and the role of victims' lawyers and advocates.

The Role of the Media

When it comes to the Church, some in the media never seem to give credit where credit is due. Take, for example, a remarkable 2019 editorial in the *Washington Post* accusing the Church of failing to report molesters. It said that "past predations and coverups are often revealed by journalists, government authorities or victims and their advocates, but rarely by the church itself."[2] It gave, by way of example, news that former cardinal Theodore McCarrick was a molester. It was a lousy example.

It was Cardinal Timothy Dolan who outed McCarrick—not the media. It was his Independent Reconciliation and Compensation

[1]Bill Donohue, "Former U.S. Attorney Indicts Priests", Catholic League, November 30, 2018, https://www.catholicleague.org/former-u-s-attorney-indicts-priests/.
[2]"The 'Untouchable' Mr. McCarrick", *Washington Post*, October 26, 2019, A16.

Program that secured information from a McCarrick victim, and it was Dolan who made it public.[3] How many rapists who work in the media—think of CBS and NBC—have had one of their senior officials turn them in? None.

The media are aware that the number of molesting priests is miniscule compared with what it was decades ago, but instead of acknowledging this, many reporters and commentators seek new ways to besmirch the Church. Here's how the games are played.

In 2019 a law firm, Seeger Weiss, tallied the amount of money the Church spent on lobbyists in the states,[4] and the findings were picked up by the media. The most egregious story of them all was in *USA Today*. According to the two reporters who wrote this piece, it is callous, if not cruel, for the bishops to fight legislation that singles out the Catholic Church under a law that suspends the statute of limitations in sexual abuse cases.[5]

Whenever an organization is under attack, the leaders bring in public relations experts, lawyers, and lobbyists to minimize the damage— this is doubly true when the attack is unfair. It would be shocking if they did not. The media certainly do this when they are hit with a scandal. Why, then, do they act in horror when they learn that the Catholic Church employs these same people? The unmistakable message is that the Church has no business acting in self-defense.

What made the *USA Today* article also astonishing is that, as recently as December 2016, it did a really good job of exposing sexual abuse in public schools, yet it never once mentioned public schools in its story on the Catholic Church. If it were fair, it would have said that changes in the statute of limitations *almost never apply to public schools*.

Just think what would happen if the reverse were true. What if public schools were being singled out for scrutiny and religious institutions were given a pass? The public schools would pull out all the

[3] "Statement on Cardinal McCarrick, by Cardinal Dolan," Zenit, June 20, 2018, http://www.zenit.org/articles/statement-on-cardinal-mccarrick-by-cardinal-dolan.

[4] Seeger Weiss, *Church Influencing State: How the Catholic Church Spent Millions against Survivors of Clergy Abuse*, Williams Cedar, June 2019, https://www.williamscedar.com/wp-content/uploads/2020/09/ChurchInfluencingStateCatholic.pdf.

[5] Marisa Kwiatkowski and John Kelly, "The Catholic Church and Boy Scouts Are Lobbying against Child Abuse Statutes", *USA Today*, October 2, 2019, https://www.usatoday.com/in-depth/news/investigations/2019/10/02/catholic-church-boy-scouts-fight-child-sex-abuse-statutes/2345778001/.

stops, and who would blame them? This raises a related question: Why are public schools exempt when statutes of limitations are extended?

Unless explicitly stated otherwise, the public sector is protected by what is known as the doctrine of sovereign immunity. This means that an alleged victim of sexual abuse in the public schools has just ninety days to file a claim. After that, there is no means of redress. This rule resulted from the power exercised by the public school unions and their friendly lawmakers in the state capitols. Guess who gets the union money at election time?

When the statute of limitations is revised to allow for a "look back" period—allowing alleged victims to file suit for offenses that happened decades ago—this provision does not apply to the public sector. In other words, the law intentionally discriminates against the private sector, and more often than not against the Catholic Church alone.

Even when the "look back" provision includes public schools, making them vulnerable to lawsuits, as happened in New York with the Child Victims Act, most of the suits are still filed against the Catholic Church. Why? Because teachers' records usually do not state why a problem teacher was moved to another school district or terminated. Moreover, the multiple layers of the public school bureaucracy that attorneys must traverse in pursuit of damaging information make the Catholic Church a much easier target. Add to this the ideological factor—anti-Catholic bias is the last socially acceptable prejudice.

The media have a tendency to tell old stories of abuse while giving the impression that the abuse is ongoing. Wisconsin Public Radio did this in November 2019.[6] The next month, so did CNN. Neither Wisconsin Public Radio nor CNN mentioned that the number of substantiated current cases against the clergy is almost nonexistent; that would get in the way of its condemnation of the Church. The CNN story was so inaccurate that it provoked me to raise a question: "Why does CNN hate the Catholic Church?"[7]

Of course, news outlets could run scores of stories about sexual abuse in other institutions, but they rarely do. *USA Today* came close

[6]Bill Donohue, "Wisconsin Public Radio's Hit Job on the Church", Catholic League, November 18, 2019, https://www.catholicleague.org/wisconsin-public-radios-hit-job-on-the-church/.

[7]Bill Donohue, "Why Does CNN Hate the Catholic Church?", Catholic League, December 2, 2019, https://www.catholicleague.org/why-does-cnn-hate-the-catholic-church/.

when it gave Wisconsin public schools an F for the way they share information about abusive teachers who are released to another school, but it failed to run a separate story about the teachers themselves.[8] The next month CNN followed with a story of its own on old cases in the Catholic Church.

The public does not think too highly of the media. One reason for this is the tendency of reporters to write sensationalized or one-sided stories. In 2019 the AP interviewed Catholics who appeared before one of the diocesan review boards tasked with assessing claims of sexual abuse. Every person interviewed had something negative to say. Moreover, there were no summary data; the entire article was based on anecdotes. Also, the article tried to make victims out of the accusers, simply because they were grilled by lawyers representing the Church. Accusers *should* be grilled. When someone makes a serious charge about a priest (who may not even be alive) or anyone else, the burden is on the accuser to make a credible case. That demands vigorous questioning. Naturally, the AP never indicated that accused priests have due-process rights that need to be respected.[9]

In addition to condemning the Church for defending itself, the media also condemns the Church for not policing priests it has kicked out. No other institution is held to this standard. Yet in the last quarter of 2019, there were several such stories.

The AP led off in October with the results of its nine-month investigation of former priests who were credibly accused of sexual misconduct. It concluded that when a priest is released from ministry, the Church does not keep tabs on him.[10] True. Neither does any other institution: no organization monitors employees let go for sexual misconduct.

---

[8]John Kelly, "How USA TODAY Graded the States on Teacher Background Checks", *USA Today*, February 14, 2016, http://www.usatoday.com/story/news/2016/02/14/how-we-graded-states-teacher-background-checks/80214540/. See the chart for the states.

[9]Reese Dunklin, Matt Sedensky, and Mitch Weiss, "AP: Catholic Church Boards Reviewing Sex Abuse Fail Victims", 660 News, November 20, 2019, https://www.660citynews.com/2019/11/20/ap-catholic-church-boards-reviewing-sex-abuse-fail-victims/.

[10]Many newspapers and TV stations picked up this story. See Claudia Lauer and Meghan Hoyer, "AP: Hundreds of Priests Accused of Child Sexual Abuse Living with No Oversight," WFAA-TV, October 4, 2019, https://www.wfaa.com/article/news/nation-world/priests-accused-sex-abuse-living-no-oversight/507-230fb190-d880-4057-a293-91f2b4b8375f.

The AP also found fault with the Church because some priests who were defrocked took jobs in public schools or in other professions working with young people. Why is this the Church's fault? Shouldn't the fault lie with those doing the hiring? Are they not responsible for performing background checks? The most astonishing criticism was to hammer the Church for not listing as sex offenders priests who have been released from ministry for alleged but not proven misconduct.[11] Are the reporters aware that *no accused person is listed as a sex offender unless he has been convicted*? It is not certain whether this was sheer ignorance or anti-Catholic bias.

In November 2019, *USA Today* published the results of its nine-month investigation on the same topic.[12] It employed thirty-nine reporters to write about an eighty-five-year-old priest who was accused of abuse in the 1970s. Was there any more to this story? No, that was it. The story also quoted someone who was disturbed to learn that an accused priest who lives near him in Florida was not on the sex-offender registry. Apparently it never occurred to the reporters that since he was never found guilty, he doesn't have to register as a sex offender. As with the AP reporters, it is not clear whether ignorance or bigotry was operative.

When WCPO-TV Cincinnati (an ABC affiliate) did a story on the Church's failure to "supervise" former priests accused of sexual misconduct, I addressed it, pointing out its shortcomings.[13] Fortunately, a resident of Cincinnati read what I said and alerted me to something I did not know. WCPO fired one of its investigative reporters, Stephen Hill, for sexual misconduct. My own investigation found that when he was released from prison in 2009, the general manager at the time refused to talk to the *Cincinnati Enquirer* about any potential employment opportunities Hill might have.[14] The station did nothing to "supervise" him.

[11] Ibid.

[12] Lindsay Schnell and Sam Ruland, "Thousands of Catholic Priests Were Accused of Sexual Abuse, Then What Happened? An Investigation Reveals Most Have Become the Priest Next Door", *USA Today*, updated November 13, 2019, https://www.usatoday.com/in-depth/news/nation/2019/11/11/catholic-sexual-abuse-accused-priests-arent-sex-offender-registry/4012206002/.

[13] Bill Donohue, "WCPO Church Probe Smacks of Bias", Catholic League, November 19, 2019, https://www.catholicleague.org/wcpo-church-probe-smacks-of-bias/.

[14] Bill Donohue, "WCPO Cincinnati Is a Proven Fraud", Catholic League, November 21, 2019, https://www.catholicleague.org/wcpo-cincinnati-is-a-proven-fraud/.

In 2020, ProPublica, a liberal, nonprofit investigative Internet outlet funded by prominent foundations, teamed up with the *Houston Chronicle* to do another one of those stories on accused priests who have left the Church. Do these media outlets expect that the Catholic Church should put a tracking device on former accused priests so the media can monitor them? ProPublica even boasted that it developed an interactive database to search for accused priests.[15] It did not tell us why it did not develop one for former accused public school employees.

Not all reporters are as bad as referenced here, but unfortunately there are too many who are either incompetent or biased, or both. These journalists contribute to the perception that the scandal is still ongoing, thereby distorting the truth.

The Role of Hollywood

In 2013, after two Muslim brothers bombed Boston, everyone from Boston archbishop Seán O'Malley to secretary of state John Kerry implored Americans not to blame all Muslims. It was good advice. Others went further, saying that Islam had nothing to do with it. The Southern Poverty Law Center ridiculed the idea that radical Muslims had anything to do with the carnage, accusing those who made such observations as blaming the "bogeyman".[16] Moreover, there were no jokes or snide remarks made about Muslims on any of the late-night talk shows. Everyone followed the lead established by President George W. Bush after 9/11: do not make wild generalizations blaming Muslims for the behavior of a few terrorists.

This kind of reaction stands in stark contrast to the way priests are spoken about in the wake of the scandal. The vilest jokes are made

---

[15]Katie Zavadski, Topher Sanders, ProPublica, and Nicole Hensley, *Houston Chronicle*, "Dozens of Catholic Priests Credibly Accused of Abuse Found Work Abroad, Some with Church's Blessing", ProPublica, March 6, 2020, https://www.propublica.org/article/dozens-of-catholic-priests-credibly-accused-of-abuse-found-work-abroad-some-with-the-churchs-blessing.

[16]Bill Donohue, "If Only Priests Were Terrorists", Catholic League, June 7, 2013, https://www.catholicleague.org/if-only-priests-were-terrorists-2/. The Southern Poverty Law Center statement was issued the same day. See Marilyn Elias, "Extremists Blame Favorite Bogeymen for Boston Bombings", Southern Poverty Law Center, April 17, 2013, https://www.splcenter.org/hatewatch/2013/04/17/extremists-blame-favorite-bogeymen-boston-bombings.

about *priests in general*, blaming the clergy as a whole for the offenses of a few. Not surprisingly, this leaves the public with the perception that nothing has changed. The perception is flawed, but as sociologist W. I. Thomas said, "If men define situations as real, they are real in their consequences."[17]

Hollywood has certainly contributed to the most vicious portrayals and stereotypes of the Catholic Church. Much of that has to do with the entertainment industry's animus against Christianity in general. Michael Medved has tracked the hostility better than anyone, and he fingers a secular "bubble" in Hollywood. "The problem here is that the media reflects the lives of a tiny portion of Americans, and then broadcasts that reflection to everybody", he says. Bringing Christianity to Hollywood is like bringing it to "the most remote reaches of Ecuador, where people have never, ever encountered anything like this before".[18]

It has been like this for a long time. In 1997, John Dart wrote a piece for the *Los Angeles Times* saying that "Hollywood and organized religion have regarded each other with deep suspicion, and sometimes open hostility, since the days of flickering silents."[19] Actress Jennifer O'Neill put it succinctly when she said, "If you mention Jesus Christ in Hollywood, all hell breaks loose."[20] In 2021, actor Kevin Sorbo noted that "being a Christian and a conservative in Hollywood, that's kind of like being a double-leper."[21] Mel Gibson learned this lesson when he tried to find a studio for *The Passion of the Christ*.

Television producers are very careful not to stereotype minorities and homosexuals, but when it comes to priests, they relentlessly

[17] William I. Thomas and Dorothy Thomas, *The Child in America*, 2nd ed. (New York: Knopf, 1929), 572.

[18] Erik Tryggestad, "The Christian Chronicle Interviews Michael Medved", *Christian Chronicle*, April 21, 2005, http://www.christianchronicle.org/the-christian-chronicle-interviews-michael-medved.

[19] John Dart, "Lights! Camera! Spirituality! Expressing Religious Beliefs Is No Longer Taboo in Hollywood, Resulting in More Movies with Morally Uplifting Themes", *Toronto Star*, April 4, 1997, D1.

[20] James Hirson, "Hollywood Celebs Prefer Castro to Christ", *Newsmax*, July 14, 2003, http://www.newsmax.com.

[21] Craig Bannister, "Kevin Sorbo: 'Being a Christian and a Conservative in Hollywood' Is 'Like Being a Double-Leper'", *CNSNews*, February 19, 2021, www.cnsnews.com/blog/craig-bannister/kevin-sorbo-being-christian-and-conservative-hollywood-being-double-leper.

promote the most obscene portrayals. *South Park* can be fun to watch, but when it depicts priests as predators, it shows its dark side. For many years, the women on *The View*, especially Joy Behar, Whoopi Goldberg, and Elisabeth Hasselbeck, ripped the Church with abandon, all under the approving eye of coproducer Barbara Walters. For decades, David Letterman, Jay Leno, Jon Stewart, and Trevor Noah used their late-night talk shows to smear priests. But none can top Bill Maher, whose filthy remarks are legendary.[22]

Among filmmakers, Harvey Weinstein and his brother Bob are some of Hollywood's biggest Catholic bashers. *Priest*, *Dogma*, *40 Days and 40 Nights*, *The Magdalene Sisters*, and *Philomena*—these films all stereotyped priests or religious and ridiculed Catholicism.

The Magdalene Sisters deliberately misrepresented the Magdalene laundries in Ireland, which were homes run by nuns for dispossessed, often wayward, girls and women. Most of the residents were well treated: no one was murdered, imprisoned, or forced to stay. There was no slave labor. Not a single woman was sexually abused by a nun. The harsh treatment portrayed in *The Magdalene Sisters* is a lie. How do we know? Because the evidence is fully documented in what is known as the *McAleese Report*, a government effort to get at the truth.[23]

Similarly, the movie *Philomena* is a fabrication. The film maintains that Philomena Lee was forced to give up her son by greedy nuns and that she eventually found him in the United States. In fact, she voluntarily gave up her son when neither she nor her family could provide for him, and she signed a contract granting custody to the nuns when she was twenty-two. She never found her son: he died in 1995 and was buried on the grounds of the very convent that welcomed her when she was in need. She did not look frantically for him for fifty years, as the film claims. Indeed, the first time she set foot in the United States was in November 2013, when she went to Los Angeles to hawk her movie.[24]

---

[22] Type their names in the search engine on the Catholic League website to read several examples of their remarks.

[23] Bill Donohue, "Myths of the Magdalene Laundries", Catholic League, 2013, https:// www.catholicleague.org/myths-of-the-magdalene-laundries/.

[24] Bill Donohue, "Debunking 'Philomena'", Catholic League, 2014, https://www.catholic league.org/wp-content/uploads/2014/01/DEBUNKING-PHILOMENA-cover.pdf.

What is perhaps most infuriating about Hollywood's depictions of predatory priests is its refusal to offer a movie like *Spotlight* on sexual abuse in Tinseltown. Boston producer Matthew Valentinas wanted to draw attention to the pedophilia rings that dot Hollywood, and to that end he enlisted Amy Berg to do the film. She is a veteran: she was nominated for an Oscar for her documentary about molesting priests, *Deliver Us from Evil.*

Berg's film *An Open Secret* is a devastating look at the way Hollywood predators manipulated, intimidated, and raped aspiring child actors. The rapists were not strangers—they were mentors. To be specific, they were managers, publicists, and agents, men who were held in high esteem by everyone, including the child actors and models whom they molested.

Valentinas assumed it would not be hard to find distributors interested in his film. He was wrong. "We approached most studios and everyone passed. We thought, we have a great director, everything was cleared and legally vetted—why would it be a risk for a company to take it?"[25] No one would. This went on for years; finally, the movie opened in a few cities, but it never was given a wide release. The resistance was strong and across the board. The Hollywood elite has no interest in spotlighting its own decadence.[26]

The Role of the Pennsylvania Grand Jury

The findings of the Pennsylvania grand-jury report in 2018 received unprecedented attention, and the report did more to advance the false perception that nothing has changed than any single factor in recent times. It is hard for the truth to surface amid all the negative chatter.

On August 14, 2018, Pennsylvania attorney general Josh Shapiro released a grand-jury report on six of the eight Catholic dioceses in the state. News stories said he found evidence of 301 priests who abused more than 1,000 children over a period of seventy years. As I said at the time, those stories were thrice false: (1) not all the alleged

[25] Peter Keough, "A Hollywood Problem Out in the Open", *Boston Globe*, May 31, 2015, N9.

[26] Bill Donohue, "Movie on Child Rape in Hollywood Overlooked", Newsmax, November 6, 2015, https://www.newsmax.com/billdonohue/hollywood/2015/11/06/id/700940/.

offenders were priests; (2) most of the alleged victims were adolescents, not children; and (3) the report was not evidentiary—it was investigative—meaning that the accused priests were never given the opportunity to rebut the charges. Moreover, roughly 3 percent of the allegations took place after the 2002 Dallas reforms were adopted.[27] So much for the scandal being ongoing.

Importantly, nothing could be done about most of those who were actually guilty. Almost all the accused were either dead or had been thrown out of the priesthood, as I noted at the time.[28] This was rarely acknowledged. No wonder Shapiro was able to prosecute only two priests.[29] He knew this from the get-go, but he used the report to push for a suspension of the statute of limitations. Never once did he insist that public schools be treated in the same way.

The narrow focus on the Catholic Church in Pennsylvania began more than a decade before Shapiro's effort. It started when Philadelphia district attorney Lynne M. Abraham became the first prosecutor in Pennsylvania to use the grand-jury system to expose decades-old clergy sex abuse. She started her probe in 2001 and issued a report in 2005. She was given a specific charge to investigate the sexual abuse of minors in *all* religious organizations, yet she probed only the Catholic Church.

On March 31, 2011, I sent Abraham a letter via overnight mail. I was quite specific: "In the Grand Jury report of September 26, 2001 (First Judicial District, Criminal Trial Division), it says that the Grand Jury was charged 'to investigate the sexual abuse of minors by individuals associated with religious organizations and denominations.' You were the District Attorney at that time. Could you identify which 'religious organizations and denominations' you pursued, other than the Roman Catholic Church? It is important to the process that we ascertain accurate information."[30] She never replied.

[27] "Statistical Analysis Seeks Context for Pa. Grand Jury Report", Catholic News Agency, December 6, 2018, https://www.catholicnewsagency.com/news/philadelphia-archdiocese -commissions-analysis-of-grand-jury-report-98000.

[28] Bill Donohue, "Pennsylvania Grand Jury Report Debunked", *Catalyst*, September 2018, https://www.catholicleague.org/pennsylvania-grand-jury-report-debunked-3/.

[29] Jacey Fortin, "Victim of Clergy Abuse Gets $2 Million in a Settlement", *New York Times*, March 27, 2019, A15.

[30] The letter is cited in a news release I wrote, "Rolling Stone Gets Ugly: Vile Hit on Philly Archdiocese", Catholic League, September 20, 2011, https://www.catholicleague.org /rolling-stone-gets-ugly-vile-hit-on-philly-archdiocese/.

Abraham never prosecuted a single priest. She knew from the beginning that she was constrained by the statute of limitations, but she was able to use her grand-jury report to smear the Church in the press (much to the applause of the *Philadelphia Inquirer*), giving all other religions a pass, in clear violation of her mandate.

In 2011, Abraham's successor, Seth Williams, picked up where she left off, trying to bring down the archbishop of Philadelphia. He too failed to nail the Church. But the courts did not fail to nail him. In 2017, he was sentenced to five years in prison for accepting a bribe.[31]

More important is the damage he did to innocent men by relying on the bogus tales of Danny Gallagher, aka "Billy Doe", who claimed victim status. Journalist Ralph Cipriano described Gallagher as "a former drug addict, heroin dealer, habitual liar, third-rate conman and thief [who] made the whole story up. And all four men who went to jail—including a priest who died there—were innocent."[32] Cipriano was telling the truth. In fact, he deserved a Pulitzer Prize for his yeoman's work.

One of the most outrageous aspects of the media's coverage of the 2018 grand-jury report was its failure to explain what triggered the report in the first place. It was not law enforcement that found a guilty party: it was a bishop who started it all.

In November 2011, Bishop Mark Bartchak, who headed the Diocese of Altoona-Johnstown, learned of offenses committed by Brother Stephen Baker in the 1990s at Bishop McCort Catholic High School in Johnstown. He immediately notified the authorities. The police never contacted Cambria County district attorney Kathleen Callihan. But once she learned of this case, she decided not to start a grand-jury probe. Instead, she asked for a state investigation, handing the matter over to Attorney General Kathleen Kane.

Now imagine for a moment if a public school superintendent in central Pennsylvania were to turn in a teacher believed to have sexually abused a student. Imagine further that the local district attorney decides to contact the state attorney general—instead of conducting

---

[31] Associated Press, "Ex-Philadelphia District Attorney Seth Williams Sentenced to Five Years in Prison", Action News, https://6abc.com/philadelphia-seth-williams-district-attorney /2561107/.

[32] Ralph Cipriano, "The Legacy of 'Billy Doe'", *Catalyst* (January/February 2019), https://www.catholicleague.org/the-legacy-of-billy-doe/.

his own probe—and this leads to an investigation of every school district in the state. And that, in turn, triggers state investigations of the public schools throughout the nation. It wouldn't happen, not in a million years. It should be noted that Shapiro stepped in after Kane was sentenced to prison in 2016 for leaking sealed, confidential grand-jury documents, unrelated to the Catholic Church, to the media and then lying under oath.[33]

What did Shapiro get for his efforts? He knew that the statute of limitations stopped him from prosecuting most of those who were guilty, but his goal seemed to be more about shaming the Church,[34] especially since he let every other institution off the hook.

The reaction of many conservatives who are otherwise thoughtful writers to the grand-jury report was astounding. George Will began his tirade against the Catholic Church by making false charges: " 'Horseplay,' a term to denote child rape, is, says Pennsylvania Attorney General Josh Shapiro, part of a sinister glossary of euphemisms by which the Catholic Church's bureaucracy obfuscates the church's 'pattern of abuse' and conspiracy of silence."[35] But most of the alleged victims were not children, and most were not raped: inappropriate touching—which is indefensible—was the typical offense. Also, the word "horseplay" was not part of the lexicon of Church officials: it appears once in more than 1,300 pages of the report, and it was used to describe the behavior of a seminarian.[36]

Making a distinction between minor sexual infractions and rape is fairly standard practice in the media. CBS journalist Leslie Stahl insists on it, arguing that those guilty of minor offenses should not have their lives destroyed as a result.[37] Yet when I drew that distinction,

[33] Max Blau and Darran Simon, "Former PA Attorney General Kathleen Kane Gets Prison Term", CNN, October 24, 2016, https://www.cnn.com/2016/10/24/politics/pennsylvania -attorney-general-sentencing/index.html.

[34] Fortin, "Victim of Clergy Abuse".

[35] George Will, "Has the Catholic Church Committed the Worst Crime in American History?", TribLIVE, March 13, 2019, http://www.triblive.com/opinion/george-will-has -catholic-church-committed-worst-crime-in-american-history/?.

[36] Bill Donohue, "The Gullible George Will", Catalyst (April 2019), https://www.catholic league.org/the-gullible-george-will-2/.

[37] Dawn C. Chmielewski, " '60 Minutes' Lesley Stahl on CBS' Sexual Harassment Scandal", Deadline, October 3, 2018, https://deadline.com/2018/10/60-minutes-lesley-stahl-on-cbs -sexual-harassment-scandal-it-has-been-very-painful.

noting that most of the alleged victims were not raped, journalist Andrew Ferguson was incensed, claiming that the grand-jury report was "piled high with factual claims".[38] In fact, none of what is in a grand-jury report should be assumed to be factual.

Former Harvard Law professor Alan Dershowitz knows better: "The grand jury has a specific function. It's supposed to only indict or not indict. Indeed, prosecutors generally don't issue reports for that reason because they only hear one side of the case. They don't hear the other side. There's no cross examination of witnesses. That's why it is regarded as wrong for prosecutors to issue reports."[39]

It is precisely because grand-jury reports are not factual that the Catholic League filed an amicus brief challenging the right of the Pennsylvania grand-jury report to make public the names of eleven priests who claimed that doing so would violate their reputational rights as guaranteed by the state constitution. On December 3, 2018, our case, handled by Pittsburgh lawyers from Jones Day, won: the Pennsylvania Supreme Court ruled 6-1 in our favor.[40] In November 2019, a Pennsylvania Supreme Court task force, which had been empaneled two years earlier, vindicated our effort: it recommended abolishing grand-jury reports.[41]

Even some Catholics of a more liberal bent saw through the grand-jury report. Former *New York Times* religion reporter Peter Steinfels took it apart, piece by piece. To declare, as the report said, that "all victims were brushed aside, in every part of the state, by church officials who preferred to protect the abusers and their institutions above all" was unconscionable. He called it "grossly misleading, irresponsible, inaccurate, and unjust". He also referred to the report "as a weapon in the debate over this issue", citing its "ugly, indiscriminate, and inflammatory" rhetoric and unsubstantiated charges, "to say nothing of the evidence the report ignores".

[38] Andrew Ferguson, "With Friends Like Bill Donohue", *Washington Examiner*, August 21, 2018 www.washingtonexaminer.com/weekly-standard/with-friends-like-bill-donohue.

[39] Alan Dershowitz, *Tucker Carlson Tonight*, Fox News Network, December 7, 2018.

[40] Rice v. Diocese of Altoona-Johnstown et al. (No. 325 WAL 2019). See also Bill Donohue, "Victory for Priests' Rights; Amicus Brief Prevails", *Catalyst* (January/February 2019), https://www.catholicleague.org/victory-for-priests-rights-amicus-brief-prevails/.

[41] Julie Shaw, "Pa. Supreme Court Task Force Suggests Abolishing Grand Jury Reports", *Philadelphia Inquirer*, updated November 24, 2019, https://fusion.inquirer.com/news/investigating-grand-juries-supreme-court-task-force-report-20191122.html.

He concluded that this was "truly unworthy of a judicial body" that is "responsible for impartial justice".[42]

Steinfels aptly saw that the use of the grand jury as a weapon was picked up by several states, some of which went beyond revising the statute of limitations: they sought to break the seal of the confessional. Lawmakers in Kentucky, Maryland, Kansas, Nevada, and Mississippi pursued attempts to end the priest-penitent privilege, all in the name of learning about cases of sexual abuse. Hypocrisy was shown glaringly in New Hampshire, when the state assembly voted to end the priest-penitent privilege while expressly keeping the protections for the attorney-client privilege.[43]

The most protracted confrontation occurred when the California legislature sought to break the seal of the confessional. The effort to stop the bill was led by Los Angeles archbishop José Gomez. The Catholic League also played a role by mobilizing tens of thousands of Catholics to e-mail state lawmakers. I personally asked California state senator Jerry Hill, who sponsored the bill, to "provide my office with documentation to support [the] claim" that the "clergy-penitent privilege has been abused on a large scale, resulting in underreported and systemic abuse of children across multiple denominations and faiths." He could not, and in the end, he gave up and withdrew his bill.[44]

The Role of Victims' Lawyers

A major force distorting public perception of the Church is the professional victims' advocates and the Church-suing lawyers who work with them. Some of the latter write checks to some of these outfits, which supply them with clients. Victims have rights, of course, but many of those who professionally advocate on their

---

[42]Peter Steinfels, "The PA Grand Jury Report: Not What It Seems", *Commonweal*, January 25, 2019, https://www.commonwealmagazine.org/pa-grand-jury-report-not-what-it-seems.

[43]Ellen K. Boegel, "The Seal of Confession and Mandatory Reporting: A Survey of State Laws", *America*, July 1, 2019, americamagazine.org/2019/07/01/mandatory-reporting -seal-confession-state-laws.

[44]Bill Donohue, "Victory in California; Confessional Bill Withdrawn", *Catalyst* (September 2019), https://www.catholicleague.org/victory-in-california-confessional-bill-withdrawn/.

behalf seem to have an agenda, or at least an interest, that transcends the victims' welfare.

Most sexual abuse of minors takes place in the home; boyfriends of their mothers and stepfathers are most often the perpetrators of this crime. But they do not have deep pockets, so many lawyers who pursue civil cases have no interest in them. Why bother with them when frying the big fish—the Catholic Church—promises to be more lucrative?

When the Child Victims Act was passed in New York in 2019, it established a one-year "look back" provision that allowed victims to file suit regardless of how long ago the offense allegedly occurred. Although the law applied to the private and public sectors alike, it was clear from the marketing copy on various lawyers' and law firms' websites that many were trying to attract those victimized by Catholic priests. No one was more anxious to focus on them than the law firm of Jeff Anderson.

Anderson has become incredibly rich "suing the [expletive]" out of the Catholic Church, as he likes to put it.[45] He has thrice sued the Vatican, losing every round. Seemingly full of hatred for the Church, he is known for publishing the names of accused priests whose cases have never been evaluated and in which no details are given. This led Ed Forbes, senior director for news and engagement for the USA Today Network Northeast, to condemn him for "traffic[king] in accusations that lack any obvious standard for being made public". The journalist said he would not publish the names listed by Anderson.[46]

When Anderson, who once called himself a "dedicated atheist",[47] issued his report on the dioceses in Illinois, he accused them of keeping secret files on accused priests. But as the special counsel to the Archdiocese of Chicago said, this was false. All the names were reported to the authorities.[48] The lawyer, John O'Malley, was

[45]David Schimke, "True Believer", *Citypages* (Minneapolis–Saint Paul), April 16, 2003, posted on BishopAccountability.org, http://www.bishop-accountability.org/news2003_01_06/2003_04_16_Schimke_TrueBeliever.htm.

[46]Ed Forbes, "Why We Didn't Publish Names on Sex Abuse Claims List", *The Record* (Bergen County, New Jersey), May 7, 2019, L8.

[47]Monica Davey, "A Frenzied Pace for Lawyer Behind Vatican Suits", *New York Times*, April 28, 2010, https://www.nytimes.com/2010/04/28/us/28lawyer.html.

[48]"Lawyers Release List of Illinois Catholic Clergy Accused of Sexual Misconduct", ABC7 Chicago, March 20, 2019, https://abc7chicago.com/religion/lawyers-release-list-of-illinois-catholic-clergy-accused-of-sexual-misconduct/5208420/.

further incensed with Anderson for portraying as perpetrators those who have been investigated and cleared. Citing one case, O'Malley said, "Police didn't decide he was a perpetrator. The archdiocese did not. Jeff Anderson did. People are entitled to their reputations until proven otherwise."[49] Lawyers for other dioceses made similar criticisms of the way Anderson proceeded.[50]

Anderson is hardly alone in showing contempt for the reputation of priests who have been accused but never found guilty. Mitchell Garabedian, who was featured in the movie *Spotlight*, about the Archdiocese of Boston, was ripped by Brian McGrory of the *Boston Globe* for what he did to Father Charles Murphy, a priest whom Garabedian twice sued.

In 2006, Father Murphy was sued for improperly touching a minor; it was a woman who claimed that the incident had occurred twenty-five years earlier. The priest maintained his innocence, and on the eve of the trial, the woman dropped her suit. In 2010, Father Murphy was sued by a man who alleged that the priest had fondled him forty years earlier. As it turned out, the accuser was deep in debt, and his credibility was challenged by his own family members. The priest was exonerated after an archdiocesan review board took six months to examine the charges. Father Murphy died in 2011, a broken man. McGrory said that what Garabedian did was "a disgrace".[51]

When I read this story, I called Garabedian to question him about it. I simply asked if he had any regrets for pressing charges against Father Murphy. The famed lawyer went ballistic, screaming at the top of his lungs. He bellowed that he lost the case because of the archdiocese's "kangaroo court". I asked him to calm down and to speak rationally, but instead he made sweeping condemnations of Boston priests.[52]

In 2013, a Missouri man made allegations against a priest who allegedly molested him and three other altar boys in the early 1980s.

[49] Nader Issa and Mitch Dudek, "Report Shines Light on 395 Catholic Priests, Church Staff Accused of Sex Abuse", *Chicago Sun-Times*, March 21, 2019, chicago.suntimes.com /2019/3/21/18425127/report-shines-light-on-395-catholic-priests-church-staff-accused-of-sex -abuse.

[50] Bill Donohue, "Assessing the Abuse Report on Illinois Priests", Catholic League, March 22, 2019, https://www.catholicleague.org/assessing-the-abuse-report-on-illinois-priests/.

[51] Brian McGrory, "Collateral Damage", *Boston Globe*, June 15, 2011, 1.

[52] Bill Donohue, "Boston Priest-Suing Lawyer Goes Bonkers", Catholic League, June 15, 2011, https://www.catholicleague.org/boston-priest-suing-lawyer-goes-bonkers/.

Two of the three other altar boys were dead, and the one still living said that none of the abuse ever occurred. I investigated the accuser and found that he had been implicated in a murder. Although another man was convicted, it was public record that the priest's accuser had "motive to commit the murder and the opportunity to do so". I took this information from court records found on the Internet, yet the accuser acquired the services of Church-suing attorney Rebecca Randles (she often works with Jeff Anderson) and sued me for defamation.

Four years later, after the case wound its way through the courts, the Eighth Circuit United States Court of Appeals ruled in favor of me and the Catholic League by dismissing all claims in the lawsuit, including the defamation claim.[53] It was a harassment lawsuit from the beginning; I never defamed anyone. I was ably represented by Erin Mersino, who worked at the time for the Thomas More Law Center and now serves on the board of directors of the Catholic League.

The Role of Victims' Advocates

BishopAccountability.org tracks clergy sexual abuse by aggregating news articles and published reports. In August 2019, it posted four stories on Father Joe Townsend of Tulsa, Oklahoma; it posted another one in October. Father Townsend had been put on administrative leave in July when it was alleged that he had acted improperly while an associate pastor at St. Pius X Catholic Church from 1988 to 1991. He denied the accusation of sexual misconduct, and no criminal charges were ever brought. In December, the diocese cleared him altogether. After the media published reports that Father Townsend had been exonerated, BishopAccountability.org did also, although not before the Catholic League. But the damage had already been done to the priest's reputation.

BishopAccountability.org says that it simply publishes the names of accused priests whose cases are being examined and does not confirm the veracity of allegations.[54] But where is the accountability for

---

[53] "Closing Chapter in Lawsuit Ends in Final Victory for Bill Donohue", Thomas More Law Center, August 17, 2017, http://www.thomasmore.org/news/closing-chapter-lawsuit-ends-final-victory-bill-donohue.

[54] See http://www.bishop-accountability.org/db_overview.

the harm done to innocent clergy? The group also condemns dioceses that do not publish the names of accused priests (even though no institution lists accused employees)[55] and demands the names of accused deceased priests.[56] What is it trying to accomplish?

One can only guess when BishopAccountability.org criticized the second of the two John Jay reports on clergy sexual abuse *before it was issued.*[57] Worse, Terence McKiernan, founder and president of BishopAcccountability.org, accused Cardinal Timothy Dolan of "keeping the lid" on fifty-five names of predator priests without providing proof. My e-mails to McKiernan asking him to identify the priests have all gone unanswered.[58]

In December 2013, Father Michael O'Connell stepped down after allegations that he had abused a minor twenty years earlier were made. The Chicago priest said he had never even met the accuser. In April 2014, a police investigation could not substantiate the accusation, and Father O'Connell was reinstated. Both the Cook County sheriff police and the Archdiocese of Chicago's independent review board concluded that the charge against him was unfounded. Everyone was happy for Father O'Connell except for the Survivors Network of those Abused by Priests (SNAP). "We have met this victim and find him very credible", said the professional victims' advocates. Barbara Blaine, founder and president, said that "it leaves children at risk" to have Father O'Connell back in ministry.[59] She had no evidence that the police or the review board were wrong. She relied wholly on her impressions of the accuser.

[55]Keith Kountz, "Abuse Victims Confront Bridgeport Archdiocese", WTNH News 8, March 28, 2011, posted on BishopAccountability.org, http://www.bishop-accountability.org/news2011/03_04/2011_03_29_Kountz_AbuseVictims.htm.

[56]"Letter to Dr. Mary Jane Doherty, Chairperson of the Archdiocese of Boston Review Board", July 27, 2011, posted on BishopAccountability.org, http://www.bishop-accountability.org/BA_Letters/2011_07_27_Letter_to_Dr_Mary_Jane_Doherty.htm.

[57]Laurie Goodstein, "1960s Culture Cited as Cause of Priest Abuse", *New York Times*, May 18, 2011, A1.

[58]Bill Donohue, "SNAP Exposed: Unmasking the Survivors Network of those Abused by Priests", special report, Catholic League, August 22, 2011, https://www.catholicleague.org/snap-exposed-unmasking-the-survivors-network-of-those-abused-by-priests-2/. One of my e-mails is dated March 7, 2014.

[59]Michelle Manchir, "Cleared of Misconduct, Priest Set to Rejoin Parish", *Chicago Tribune*, April 16, 2014, C7.

This is standard operating procedure for this loose association of victims' advocates. For them apparently, accused priests do not deserve to be presumed innocent until proven guilty, as are others suspected of a crime, if the accuser seems to be telling the truth. They seem to fail to consider what would happen to our system of justice if the presumption of innocence were removed from everyone and people were punished on the basis of accusations only.

No one can know for certain what motivates another person, but it appears that some victims' advocates are hurt and confused people who are not simply concerned with bringing abusers to justice. Until he was discredited, David Clohessy was the face of SNAP. While in that role he was an unrelenting critic of the Church's handling of clergy sexual abuse, yet he refused to turn in one particular accused priest to the authorities: his brother, Kevin Clohessy.

"From early on," Clohessy said, "the raging debate within me was: he's my brother; he's an abuser. Do I treat him like my brother? Do I treat him like an abuser?"[60] He seems unaware that some bishops might have been similarly torn when confronted with an accusation against one of their brother priests. Of course, this can also be an example of in-group favoritism, a common phenomenon.

Father Clohessy was ordained in 1985, and it didn't take long before stories about his conduct made the rounds in the Diocese of Jefferson City, Missouri. He developed a reputation for plying adolescent males with booze and molesting them. David Clohessy was alerted to his brother's homosexual predations early on but kept them to himself. A reporter for the *Boston Globe* asked him if he knew of any whistleblowers, and he identified Donna Cox. This was risky. After all, as a youth minister in the late 1980s and early 1990s where his brother worked, she had learned of Father Clohessy's conduct. So David Clohessy told the reporter that Cox might mention his brother and asked that he not be named. The reporter said it was unlikely that his name would be published; but a month later, when the diocese named Father Clohessy, the *Globe* did too, in another story.

[60] Frank Bruni, "Am I My Brother's Keeper?", *New York Times Magazine*, May 12, 2002, sect. 6, 42.

David Clohessy's own travails with the Church began in 1991 when he filed a lawsuit against the Diocese of Jefferson City, claiming he was sexually abused by a priest between 1969 and 1973, from the ages twelve to sixteen (the suit was dismissed because it fell outside the statute of limitations). What took him so long to file suit? He said he had no memory of what happened until 1988. What happened then? He said he and his fiancée were watching a Barbra Streisand movie, *Nuts*, when his memory was jarred.[61]

After tracking SNAP for years, and having serious doubts about its veracity, I decided to do some investigating. In 2011, I asked an ex-CIA agent and her husband to attend a SNAP conference held near Reagan National Airport in Washington, D.C. I have written about her account, and it is riveting.[62]

There were approximately 110 to 130 people in attendance. All were white, and most were women in their fifties and sixties. The recurring theme of the conference was the evil nature of the Catholic Church. The word "evil" was used repeatedly to describe "the institution". Garabedian said, "This immoral entity, the Catholic Church, should be defeated. We must stand up and defeat this evil." Father Thomas Doyle, the canon lawyer who has been involved in multiple clergy abuse cases, said the Catholic Church was founded by Constantine, not Jesus. He said that "the Mass equals magic words" and called priestly vestments "dresses".

Then came the shakedown. Although Anderson said that the lawsuits against the Church have not been about the money, he conducted a fundraising appeal for SNAP, matching dollar for dollar any donation. But he drew the line when an attorney offered to donate $10,000.

David Clohessy instructed the crowd on how to manipulate the media. He told attendees that if they sue the Church, they should hold a press conference outside a chancery or a police station. Holding it outside a chancery makes it easy for reporters because they need only go to one location to interview both the claimant and the diocesan public relations person.

61 Ibid.
62 Donohue, "SNAP Exposed".

But talk is not enough, Clohessy added. "Display holy childhood photos!" he said. "If you don't have compelling childhood photos, we can provide you with photos of other kids that can be held up for the cameras." In interviews, "use feeling words" such as "I was scared. I was suicidal" and "use the word 'kids' as often as possible." He advised, "Be sad and not mad."[63]

Clohessy succeeded at the helm of SNAP for a long time, because what he said was music to the ears of the Church's critics and many people, including many Catholics, thought he was the victims' best friend.

SNAP started its descent in 2012; five years later, it imploded. At the end of 2011, a Missouri judge ordered Clohessy to be deposed in a case involving Father Michael Tierney, a priest in the Diocese of Kansas City–St. Joseph, Missouri. He was accused in 2010 of sexually abusing a male in 1971. His lawyers asked for SNAP's internal documents, and the judge ordered Clohessy to produce twenty-three years' worth of them. The lawyers wanted to see if SNAP had been coaching alleged victims and plaintiffs to say that they had repressed their memories of abuse. The judge said that Clohessy "almost certainly" had knowledge that was relevant to Father Tierney's case.[64] The lawyer for the accuser was Rebecca Randles.

On January 2, 2012, Clohessy took the stand.[65] When asked if he identified himself as a rape crisis counselor, he said, "I don't know." When asked if he has had any training as a rape crisis counselor, he said he did not. Yet he had been counseling alleged victims for a living, even though he lacked a degree in counseling and never had any formal classes in this field. When asked if his colleague Barbara Blaine was a licensed counselor, he said he did not know (she has a master's degree in social work). In fact, no one at SNAP was a licensed

[63] Ibid.

[64] "Judge Orders SNAP to Turn Over Abuse Records", Catholic News Agency, April 25, 2012, https://www.catholicnewsagency.com/news/judge-orders-snap-to-turn-over-abuse-records.

[65] All of the testimony can be found in "Circuit Court of Appeals of Jackson County, State of Missouri, *John Doe, B.P. vs. Father Michael Tierney, et al.*", January 2, 2012, Case No. 1016-CV-29995. See my analysis, which lists the page numbers of the testimony cited herein: Bill Donohue, "SNAP Unravels", *Catalyst* (April 2012), https://www.catholicleague.org/snap-unravels-catalyst/.

counselor, yet that is the service they offered. When asked where the counseling took place, Clohessy said, "We meet people wherever they want to meet, in Starbucks, at, you know—wherever people feel comfortable, that's where we meet." When asked how much of their $3 million budget is spent on counseling, he said he did not know.

Clohessy said that SNAP had a business address but that he didn't know the zip code. Having no office—he worked out of his home in the Saint Louis area—he personally fielded phone calls from alleged victims. "Individuals call me and they share their pain with me", he said. "I console them and I may be on the phone with them for an hour."

Then the lawyers asked Clohessy, "You won't tell us the sources of your funding; isn't that correct?" Clohessy agreed that was correct. The question was asked because SNAP had been accused of being greased by lawyers such as Anderson and Garabedian for years. What does SNAP do with its money? In 2007, it spent a total of $593 for "survivor support". The following year it spent $92,000 on travel.

Apparently, Clohessy knew next to nothing about his staff. Besides Blaine, he said, "we have an administrative person who is new." He said he could remember only her first name. He also said he has a fundraising person but confessed, "I don't know the spelling of her last name." When asked who is responsible for SNAP's website, he said, "I don't know."

The most revealing comment Clohessy made was in response to the following question: "Has SNAP to your knowledge ever issued a press release that contained false information?" He answered: "Sure."

Two months after Clohessy was deposed, Laurie Goodstein of the *New York Times* called me to ask about his comments. I honed in on his admission that he lies to the media. She said she was unaware of that. I asked if she had a copy of the deposition handy, and she did. When I pointed out the page number and where to find his remark, she sounded surprised, as if the remark was a regrettable mistake. In her article, she mentioned that Clohessy had been asked about falsehoods in SNAP releases and that his answer was "sure". But then she allowed him to walk it back. She had called him about this, and "he said his response had been an acknowledgment that there must have been some errors in the thousands of news releases and alerts that the group had sent out over the years." She quoted him as saying, "But never intentionally, and never mistakes of substance."[66]

But the question was not about "errors" or "mistakes"; it was about information he released to the media that he knew to be false. I doubt Goodstein would allow a defender of the Church to walk back a comment that made him look bad. Further proof that she is not a nonpartisan in this matter was given later that year when HBO released the documentary *Mea Maxima Culpa: Silence in the House of God*. Goodstein not only appeared in the film, which is at the very least unfair to the Church, but also was an associate producer along with Jeff Anderson.[67]

After commending Goodstein's article in which she quoted Clohessy, the *New York Times* portrayed him as a victim of "aggressive legal tactics", saying it was the duty of the judge to "reject unfairly burdensome discovery requests". The brazenness of the newspaper is astounding. It never accused Church-suing lawyers such as Anderson, Randles, or Garabedian of using "aggressive legal tactics".

In January 2017 a former SNAP employee, transgender Gretchen Rachel Hammond, sued Clohessy, Blaine, and Barbara Dorris (the outreach director), offering testimony that, if true, proved everything I had been saying about the outfit's corruption and dishonesty for decades.[68] Indeed, when Hammond met with Bernadette Brady-Egan, the Catholic League's vice president, and policy analyst Don Lauer at our New York City headquarters (I wasn't sure if she had some other agenda, so I declined to meet with her), she said she was aware of my criticisms of SNAP when she took the job but was not persuaded. She changed her mind after seeing their operations firsthand.

Hammond, who had been SNAP's director of development, claimed in the lawsuit that "SNAP routinely accepts financial kickbacks from attorneys in the form of 'donations'", and in return

---

[66] Laurie Goodstein, "Church Using Priests' Cases to Pressure Victims' Network", *New York Times*, March 13, 2012, A1.

[67] Justin Chang, "Mea Maxima Culpa: Silence in the House of God", *Daily Variety*, September 14, 2012, 55.

[68] All of the evidence cited in this section can be found in the lawsuit in the Circuit Court of Cook County, Illinois, *Gretchen Rachel Hammond v. Survivors Network of those Abused by Priests*, January 17, 2017. See also my article "SNAP Implodes", Catholic League, January 30, 2017, https://www.catholicleague.org/snap-implodes/.

SNAP "refers survivors as potential clients to attorneys, who then file lawsuits on behalf of the survivors against the Catholic Church. The cases often settle to the financial benefit of the attorneys and, at times, to the financial health of SNAP, which has received direct payments from survivors' settlements."

The suit listed one "donation" after another made by plaintiff attorneys to SNAP, which made up the lion's share of funds collected by Clohessy and company in any given year. For example, in 2008, "a Minnesota lawyer", possibly Anderson, contributed 55 percent—$414,140—of SNAP's total donations for the year; three years later, he contributed over 40 percent of its total revenue.

The lawsuit also claimed that SNAP funneled money to itself via dummy organizations. "Tellingly, at one time during 2011 and 2012", it said, "SNAP even concocted a scheme to have attorneys make donations to a front foundation, styled the 'Minnesota Center for Philanthropy,' and then have the Minnesota Center for Philanthropy make a grant to SNAP in order to provide a subterfuge for, and to otherwise conceal, the plaintiff's attorneys' kickbacks to SNAP."

Hammond claimed that SNAP officials were more concerned about raking in the dough than in serving the interests of their clients. The lawsuit cites an e-mail exchange between SNAP officials discussing a subpoena that was issued to them. One of them asked if he should mention the subpoena in their newsletter. It "may prompt more donations", said the person who replied, even though "on the other hand, it'll also upset more survivors." Blaine responded, "My initial response is that we err on the side of using it to raise money."

Hammond's suit alleged that "SNAP does not focus on protecting or helping survivors—it exploits them." It further claimed that SNAP "callously disregards the real interests of survivors, using them instead as props and tools in furtherance of SNAP's own commercial fundraising goals. Instead of recommending that survivors pursue what is in their best personal, emotional, and financial interests, SNAP pressures survivors to pursue costly and stressful litigation against the Catholic Church, all in order to further SNAP's own publicity and fundraising interests."

According to the lawsuit, the people involved with SNAP are motivated by hostility toward the Catholic Church. "While SNAP claims it is motivated by the interests of survivors," the lawsuit says, "in fact, SNAP is motivated largely by the personal animus of its directors and officers against the Catholic Church. For example, Clohessy recommended that an alleged victim pursue a claim against the Archdiocese of Milwaukee, saying every nickel it doesn't have is money that can't be spent on 'defense lawyers, PR staff, gay-bashing, contraceptive-battling, etc.'"

Hammond said that when she confronted SNAP officials about its activities, she was subjected to retaliatory action, which caused her stress and depression, resulting in health problems. That is the reason she sued, she said, and also for a loss of wages after SNAP fired her in 2013.

Hammond named Clohessy in the lawsuit, and he resigned as SNAP's director. In an interview with the *National Catholic Reporter*, he said that he had informed the organization's board of his decision months before the lawsuit was filed, implying that the two events were unrelated, but SNAP announced his departure only afterward.[69] Blaine, the founder of SNAP, also resigned.

Road to Recovery is another victim's group that ran into problems. In the summer of 2019, Catholic News Agency (CNA) ran a two-part series on a man they chose to identify as "Michael" (that is not his real name; the middle-aged man chose to remain anonymous).[70] He told a story about being abused and about his dealings with both SNAP and Road to Recovery.

In the fall of 2019, I met with him, along with Bernadette Brady-Egan and Rick Hinshaw, our communications director at the time, and asked him about a number of issues. He is a well-educated man and a professional success. What he experienced is incredible. I invited him to share his story by publishing it in the Catholic League journal,

[69] Brian Roewe, "SNAP's New Year Starts with Departure, Lawsuit", National Catholic Register, January 30, 2017, https://www.ncronline.org/news/accountability/snaps-new-year-starts-departure-lawsuit.

[70] Ed Condon, "'Freedom to Forgive'—How One Man Abused by a Priest Found Healing", Catholic News Agency, August 1, 2019, https://www.catholicnewsagency.com/news/freedom-to-forgive---how-one-man-abused-by-a-priest-found-healing-46867; Ed Condon, "Abuse Survivor: Some 'Victim Advocacy' Groups 'Have Their Own Agendas'", Catholic News Agency, August 2, 2019, https://www.catholicnewsagency.com/news/abuse-survivor-some-victim-advocacy-groups-have-their-own-agendas-70588.

Catalyst, which he did.[71] What follows is taken from that story, the CNA series, and my interview with him.

Michael's problems began when he was fifteen years old when, he claimed, he was sexually abused by Father James Rapp at his Catholic high school. Seven years later, he said, when he was twenty-two, he told a priest in Confession that he had been molested. "The problem was that I didn't know that the priest behind the confessional screen was an active homosexual. So, when I confessed to him, and he offered to help me, I didn't know I was being solicited." For eighteen months, the priest counseled him, but also subjected Michael to "lewd homosexual conversation and harassment". He admits that his situation was complicated: the priest's counseling did help, and since he was preparing for medical school, he thought he could weather the solicitations.

"I became dialed into my faith like never before," Michael said, "attending Mass and praying on my knees every night. I seemed to be recovering. But that all ended one night when he phoned me, ostensibly drunk, blurting out the most appalling sexual propositions. It was truly devastating. After that night I could no longer sit through a Mass. I left the Church, vowing I would never speak about my abuse again." Decades later, he received professional counseling. He had post-traumatic stress disorder and was suffering from severe anxiety. The good news is that he improved and returned to the Church.

In 2010, when Michael was in his forties, he learned about SNAP and Road to Recovery and sought to learn more about the priest who abused him. He reached out to Robert Hoatson, the former priest and founder of Road to Recovery. When they corresponded by e-mail, the first thing Hoatson asked him was whether he needed an attorney. Michael was taken aback, but the two of them hit it off, and, under Hoatson's influence, Michael filed suit against the Church and was able to recoup some of the money he had spent on counseling. He also left the Church for the second time. "I drew the line when Hoatson encouraged me to get my children out of the Church," he said.

[71] Bill Donohue, "Victims' Lawyers and Advocates Exposed", *Catalyst* (April 2020), http://www.catholicleague.org.

Hoatson introduced Michael to Garabedian at a SNAP conference in Chicago. When Michael asked about their relationship, Hoatson said, "Mitch takes good care of me." That was one among many revelatory moments Michael would encounter at the conference. He shared one that put a smile on my face. He said that he learned at the conference how much I was hated by the SNAP crowd.

"SNAP proclaims to be a support group for survivors," Michael said, "but what I experienced was anything but support for survivors. SNAP invited the shark attorney, used the victims like chum, and watched the frenzy unfold. I saw Jeff Anderson, the mega sex abuse plaintiff attorney, giggly and excitedly prance around the conference to funnel money to SNAP." He also met Patrick Wall, another ex-priest who pledged to help victims. He told Michael he was an attorney working for Anderson. "My heart sank," Michael said, "my eyes welled up in tears. I went to the SNAP conference to get better, and I had hoped they would help, but all I saw was SNAP aligning victims with attorneys for money and to weaponize victims against the Church."

Michael met Clohessy in the hotel lobby. He knew that Clohessy had authored an article about his abuser and wanted to know more about him. "When asked," Michael wrote, "he couldn't remember writing the article. He couldn't give me any information about my abuser. I thought, 'How can someone write an article and not remember a single thing about it?'" Clohessy apologized but never offered to help him.

After the conference, Gretchen Rachel Hammond successfully sued SNAP, and Michael was delighted. He was further emboldened when, on December 23, 2017, he experienced a remarkable and unexpected reversion to the Catholic faith. One might have thought everyone would be happy with that, but Hoatson wasn't. This was not a surprise given that the priest had previously told Michael that it would be good for his whole family to quit the Church.

The two did not communicate much after that, but there was an important exchange that took place once the Pennsylvania grand-jury report was released in August 2018. Hoatson sent Michael his press release on the subject. It said that "homosexuals don't rape minors, predators rape minors." He then went on to say that Catholics should "embrace homosexual and transgender priests". This didn't sit well with Michael, given his experience. He came to the conclusion that "there is an ongoing agenda to cover up the homosexual nature of the abuse crisis." As we shall see, his observation is supported by the evidence.

4

Myths of the Scandal's Origins Debunked

There are many myths about the origins of clergy sexual abuse that need to be debunked. Before doing so, it would be helpful to discuss what an accurate conception of this subject entails.

No one has understood why the clergy sexual abuse scandal took place better than Pope Emeritus Benedict XVI. His lengthy 2019 essay on the roots of clergy sexual abuse was illuminating and courageous.[1] He showed how forces inside and outside the Church came together to create the problem, and he bravely spoke the truth about matters that few would dare speak.

He started by placing the scandal in a social context. He noted that it is impossible to understand why the scandal took place without referencing the effects of the sexual revolution, which hit the dominant culture *and the Catholic Church* like a hurricane. It is not a coincidence that sexual abuse flourished inside the Church when celebrations of sexual libertinism flourished outside the Church. The latter helped set the stage for the former. It was the triumph of moral relativism—the denial of moral absolutes—that helped to cripple the Church.

Benedict put his finger on a harsh reality: dissent in the Church peaked at the same time the scandal unfolded. Catholic moral theology, which is grounded in natural law, was abandoned in exchange for a more relativistic approach, one that denied the existence of intrinsic evil. This was taught in seminaries at the time. Not only that, but books by Benedict were censored.

When pornographic films were shown to seminarians, and a gay subculture was not simply tolerated but encouraged, Benedict notes,

---

[1] Benedict XVI, "Full Text of Benedict XVI: The Church and the Scandal of Sexual Abuse", Catholic News Agency, April 10, 2019, https://www.catholicnewsagency.com /news/full-text-of-benedict-xvi-the-church-and-the-scandal-of-sexual-abuse-59639.

it is hardly surprising to learn that sexual misconduct grew by leaps and bounds. "In various seminaries homosexual cliques were established," he writes, "which acted more or less openly and significantly changed the climate in the seminaries."[2] The climate that emerged was toxic.

At bottom, Benedict stresses, the scandal is rooted in a crisis in faith. When the very existence of God is questioned, and when moral certainty dissipates—even with regard to foundational principles— then mere opinion becomes the new norm. This is a dangerous slope; it resulted in many sins, including priestly sexual abuse.

Benedict recognizes that the Church is a much better place today than it was at the height of the scandal. Reforms can and should be made, but he cautions us not to engage in the folly of trying to reinvent the Church. Indeed, he sees such proposals as the work of the devil. "The idea of a better Church, created by ourselves", he says, "is in fact a proposal of the devil, with which he wants to take us away from the living God."[3]

What we need, Benedict argues, is greater respect for the Eucharist and the establishment of "habitats of Faith".[4] The appropriate corrective to sexual abuse, or any other plague in the Church, cannot be achieved absent a renewal of faith, grounded in eternal moral truths. Anything less will miss the mark.

This was not the first time that Benedict spoke about threats to the Church coming from within. On May 11, 2010, after a flight to Fatima, he told accompanying journalists something that must have startled them:

The Lord told us that the Church would constantly be suffering, in different ways, until the end of the world.... As for the new things which we can find in this message [of Fatima] today, there is also the fact that attacks on the Pope and the Church come not only from without, but the sufferings of the Church come precisely from within the Church, from the sin existing within the Church. This too is something that we have always known, but today we are seeing it in a really terrifying way: that the greatest persecution of the Church

[2] Ibid.
[3] Ibid.
[4] Ibid.

comes not from her enemies without, but arises from sin within the
Church, and that the Church thus has a deep need to relearn penance,
to accept purification, to learn forgiveness on the one hand, but also
the need for justice. Forgiveness does not replace justice. In a word,
we need to relearn precisely this essential: conversion, prayer, penance
and the theological virtues.[5]

Pope Benedict XVI resigned on December 17, 2012, the day he
received a three-hundred-page, two-volume dossier that was "an exact
map of the mischief and the bad fish" inside the Holy See. Blackmail,
corruption, and gay sex at the Vatican were detailed in the report, the
culmination of a nine-month investigation by Spanish cardinal Julián
Herranz, with the assistance of Cardinal Salvatore De Giorgi, former
archbishop of Palermo, and Slovak cardinal Jozef Tomko.[6]

Myths about Molesting Priests

No analysis of the causes of the scandal should neglect the interpretation of it proffered by molesting priests themselves.

David Finkelhor is a respected student of the sexual abuse of minors.
He says many of the abusers experience "cognitive dissonance", a
phenomenon in which conflicting thoughts create an uncomfortable
condition: it demands an outcome that alleviates the tension, one
way or another. For example, some molesting priests, knowing that
what they are doing is wrong, may stop. Others may rationalize their
behavior, convincing themselves that they are showing affection, if
not love, for their victims.[7] In effect, abusers neutralize their predatory

[5] Interview of Benedict XVI with Journalists during the Flight to Portugal, May 11, 2010,
Vatican website, http://www.vatican.va/content/benedict-xvi/en/speeches/2010/may/docu
ments/hf_ben-xvi_spe_20100511_portogallo-interview.html.

[6] Doug Stanglin, "Report: Pope Resigned in Wake of Gay Priest Scandal", USA Today,
February 22, 2103, https://www.usatoday.com/story/news/world/2013/02/22/pope-leaks
-fallout/1938321/.

[7] Karen J. Terry, John Jay College of Criminal Justice (JJCCJ), and United States Conference of Catholic Bishops (USCCB), The Causes and Context of Sexual Abuse of Minors by
Catholic Priests in the United States, 1950–2010: A Report Presented to the United States Conference
of Catholic Bishops by the John Jay College Research Team (Washington, D.C.: United States
Conference of Catholic Bishops, 2011), 68–69.

behavior with excuses and justifications that allow them to continue.[8] Finkelhor is convinced that many abusers "have massive denial systems" that make treatment difficult. He recommends jailing them.[9]

The John Jay researchers, in their second study of clergy sexual abuse, found that abusive priests rationalized their behavior by saying they were involved in a "relationship", not a sexual encounter. "They viewed the sexual behavior as consensual, not harmful, and they viewed any behavior short of intercourse as not wrong because it was not sex."[10] Some molesters said their victims were "willing" or "precocious", thus deflecting culpability. Others considered themselves to be the victims because of accusations of indecency.[11] I have known such priests, and they leave quite an impression.

Abusers also like to blame their behavior on developmental disorders. They cite their sexual immaturity as a causative agent.[12] As we shall see later, they are not incorrect in making this observation; it's just that it cannot be invoked as an excuse for their behavior. Similarly, citing alcohol and drug abuse is another ploy; these twin problems have bedeviled many molesting priests, but they are not exculpatory.[13] Another popular way of ending cognitive dissonance is to indict the Church hierarchy—to say that the leaders failed to socialize them adequately. But this also dodges personal responsibility for sexual abuse.[14]

The Celibate, Male Priesthood

Many people both inside and outside the Church blame the problem of clergy sexual abuse on celibacy. If celibacy were responsible, why are most priests not molesters? Father Greeley picked up on

[8] Ibid., 115.

[9] Jason Berry, Lead Us Not into Temptation (New York: Doubleday, 1992), 71.

[10] Terry, JJCCJ, and USCCB, Causes and Context, 112–113.

[11] Ibid., 107.

[12] Ibid., 105.

[13] Karen J. Terry, JJCCJ, and USCCB, The Nature and Scope of Sexual Abuse of Minors by Catholic Priests and Deacons in the United States 1950–2002: A Research Study Conducted by the John Jay College of Criminal Justice (Washington, D.C.: United States Conference of Catholic Bishops, 2004), 47, 76–77, 105.

[14] Terry, JJCCJ, and USCCB, Causes and Context, 113.

this, saying that if 4 percent of priests are driven to sexual abuse because of celibacy, why are the other 96 percent not affected by this Church rule?[15] The John Jay researchers also saw the hole in the celibacy argument. "From the eleventh century to the present, men ordained in the Roman Catholic priesthood have forgone marriage and abstained from any sexual contact with others." Given that this requirement is not new, the researchers ask, why should celibacy be seen as a cause of sexual abuse during the years when it flourished?[16]

Those who favor the celibacy explanation believe that if priests could marry, there would be less sexual abuse. Maggie Gallagher, an astute student of marriage and the family, bluntly seized on the weakness of this position. "As if wives are the answer to the sexual urges of men who get their kicks from adolescent boys."[17] She is right. Moreover, heterosexual priests are also expected to abide by the celibacy restriction, yet their role in the scandal is minimal compared with that of homosexual priests.

A related thesis holds that the exclusion of women from the priesthood explains the problem. Why, then, are most priests not abusers? Jamie Manson, a Catholic dissident and gay activist, took Pope Benedict XVI to task for criticizing the gay subculture in seminaries, saying that "it never occurred to him that his radical exclusion of women from ministry and his radically homophobic theology might have contributed to that phenomenon."[18] In other words, the Church's prohibition (it is not Benedict's) of women priests and the Church's teachings on homosexuality created a gay subculture in seminaries. Then why did the gay subculture flourish when sexual norms were not enforced? Why was it not noticeable in the 1950s? And why has it subsided now that the norms are observed again? The absence of women priests has nothing

[15] Andrew Greeley, "For Priests, Celibacy Is Not the Problem", *New York Times*, March 3, 2004, https://www.nytimes.com/2004/03/03/opinion/for-priests-celibacy-is-not-the-problem.html.

[16] Terry, JJCCJ, and USCCB, *Causes and Context*, 34–35.

[17] Quoted in Mary Eberstadt, "The Elephant in the Sacristy", *Weekly Standard*, June 17, 2002, 22.

[18] Jamie Manson, "Pope Benedict Explains Things to Me", *National Catholic Reporter*, April 12, 2019, http://www.ncronline.org/print/news/accountability/grace-margins/pope-benedict-explains-things-me.

to do with why gay men surfaced in the priesthood during the sexual revolution.

Moreover, there are many religions that have an all-male clergy—the Mormons, the Orthodox churches, Orthodox Judaism, the Missouri Synod of the Lutheran Church, Islam, and the Southern Baptist Convention—yet no one blames whatever problems they have on their ordination strictures.

The conversation about the alleged role of celibacy in creating the scandal has the unfortunate effect of downplaying its raison d'être. Cardinal Robert Sarah reminds us why the Church adopted it. "By his celibacy", he writes, "a priest renounces the human fulfillment of his ability to be a spouse and father according to the flesh. Out of love, he chooses to give up that in order to live exclusively as the spouse of the Church, offered entirely to the Father." He adds how it pains him to see celibacy disdained these days. The priesthood, he says, is not an office: it is a state of life.[19]

Opportunity and Poor Formation

Cardinal Blase Cupich, archbishop of Chicago, was asked in 2019 about the role of homosexuality in the scandal. He admitted that a high percentage of the abuse involved "male on male sex abuse", but he said that "homosexuality itself is not a cause." He got around this by saying it was a matter of "opportunity and also a matter of poor training on the part of people".[20]

It is undeniably true that adults who regularly interact with minors have greater opportunities to abuse them. But the opportunity thesis, when applied to priests, typically contends that because priests have traditionally had more access to boys than girls—altar boys being the prime example—that accounts for why more boys have been victims of abuse than girls. The institution of altar boys, however, existed

---

[19]Robert Cardinal Sarah, *The Day Is Now Far Spent* (San Francisco: Ignatius Press, 2019), 64.

[20]Courtney Grogan, "Ahead of Summit, Cupich Discusses Sex Abuse, Homosexuality, Priestly Formation", Catholic News Agency, February 18, 2019, https://www.catholic newsagency.com/news/ahead-of-summit-cupich-discusses-sex-abuse-homosexuality -priestly-formation-36025.

before the scandal took off in the 1960s, yet before that time relatively few priests abused boys. Moreover, if this thesis had validity, we should have seen a spike in priests molesting girls in recent years, but we haven't. Girl altar servers date back to 1983, after canon law was changed. They became even more common in 1994, when Pope John Paul II ruled that girls may be altar servers.[21] Yet the data show that in the last decade, eight in ten victims of priestly sexual abuse were boys, the same ratio previously found by the John Jay researchers.

There is something perverse about the "opportunity thesis" that must be addressed. I spent five years in Catholic summer camp with boys, four years in a Catholic military boarding high school, and four years in the U.S. Air Force. I never heard of heterosexual men having sex with other men because they didn't have access to females. Such an idea suggests that heterosexual men are so sexually wired that they will seize any opportunity to have sex with whomever is available. Perhaps this is true about some men, but it is a sexist and slanderous accusation to make about men in general.

Psychiatrist Richard Fitzgibbons, who has treated many priests, and author Dale O'Leary question the opportunity thesis: "Opportunity and availability", they write, "only affect the behavior if the temptation is already felt. If the thing or person that is available does not tempt a person, availability is irrelevant. A man who finds homosexual acts repulsive will not be tempted by the availability of vulnerable adolescent males. Priest offenders with adolescent boys were obviously experiencing homosexual temptations."[22]

And what about the "poor training" thesis? To be sure, courses on human formation in the seminaries have helped, and they were not common until more recent times. But it remains true that almost all of those priests who sexually abused minors went through the same "poor training" that their nonabusing cohorts experienced. Why, then, did the "poor training" not affect the 96 percent of priests who never had an accusation made against them?

Blaming the Church's teachings on sexuality for the scandal is a common explanation offered by dissident Catholics. This is like

---

[21] Charles W. Hall, "Diocese Limits Most Altar Servers to Boys; Arlington Made Decision Despite Papal Ruling Opening Role to Girls", *Washington Post*, December 1, 1994, A1.

[22] Richard Fitzgibbons and Dale O'Leary, "Sexual Abuse of Minors by Catholic Clergy", *Linacre Quarterly*, 78, no. 3 (August 2011): 266.

blaming teachers who insist on honesty for their cheating students. How can it be that the Church's sexual ethics, which proscribes promiscuity, is responsible for promiscuous priests? That would suggest that the remedy can be found in either changing the teachings or relaxing their enforcement. The latter is what happened, and that is what fueled the scandal. In other words, the teaching thesis has it backward: it was during a time when teachings on sexual morality were undermined, both inside and outside the Church, that priests with impulse-control problems got the message and acted accordingly. Hence, the scandal. But don't tell that to those who reject Catholic sexual morality.

Catholic Sexual Morality

Father Thomas Doyle, among others, has claimed that "extreme judgmentalism in matters of sex" has contributed to the clergy sexual abuse scandal.[23] Catholicism takes its teachings on sexuality from Christ, who built upon the foundation of Judaism's Ten Commandments, which forbid adultery (Mt 5:27–28). For those who might say that applies only to the married, Jesus also condemned fornication (Mt 15:19). And then there is Christ's warning to those who seduce children: "Whoever causes one of these little ones who believe in me to sin, it would be better for him to have a great millstone fastened round his neck and to be drowned in the depth of the sea" (Mt 18:6).

Instead of the Church, who does Doyle think has the answer? Dr. Ruth. After listening to Dr. Ruth Westheimer, the celebrity sexologist, Doyle said, "She made more sense in five minutes than a hundred bishops talking for an hour."[24]

Villanova University theologian Massimo Faggioli believes that "the appointment of a generation of conservative bishops" often led to "double lives in some seminaries, religious orders, and ecclesial movements". He blames what he calls the "rigorism" of conservative bishops for the scandal.[25] Yet if we were to interview priests who are

[23] Michael D'Antonio, *Mortal Sins* (New York: St. Martin's Press, 2013), 43.
[24] Ibid., 46.
[25] Massimo Faggioli, "Benedict's Untimely Meditation", *Commonweal*, April 12, 2019, https://www.commonwealmagazine.org/benedicts-untimely-meditation.

chaste, would we not find that the Church's teachings abetted their chastity? Priests who live a double life do so because they have failed to order their behavior according to the vows they voluntarily took.

In many seminaries in the 1970s and the 1980s, students were assigned a book by Father Anthony Kosnik that had more in common with Dr. Ruth than with the pope. "Inadvertently," Kosnik gently writes, "Catholic pastoral practice has promoted the incidence of promiscuity among homosexuals precisely by advising them against forming intimate or exclusive friendships."[26] Let's see how this works if applied to heterosexuals: priests who hit on women might not have done so had they been advised to have close, exclusive relationships with their female friends. Does anyone believe this to be true?

Father Edward Beck is a champion of gay rights and a commentator on CNN. He shares Kosnik's view, holding that "the church rarely has dealt well with issues of human sexuality." So what should we do? "Priests, like everyone else, want to have sex. We want to be touched. We want to be desired. In order to forgo these natural impulses, we employ coping mechanisms to offset the sexual urges. We do so for the sake of a 'higher good,' but let's not delude ourselves that it is natural or easy—or that sometimes we don't fail."[27]

No doubt celibacy does not come easy. But if it is too heavy a burden for a man, perhaps it is best for him to leave the priesthood or not to join it in the first place. Moreover, it is nonsense to maintain that the Church's sexual reticence caused sexual abuse. If that were the case, then the heyday of clergy sexual abuse would have been in the 1950s, when stricter norms were followed. Yet little in the way of sexual misconduct was reported at that time.

Before good approaches to priestly formation in chastity can be discussed, however, we first must see the beauty of Christ's teaching, which has been entrusted to the Church. Pope John Paul II's Theology of the Body can help us to do that. His interpretation of Catholic sexual morality is a positive one: it embraces self-giving. In contrast

---

[26] Anthony Kosnik, et al., *Human Sexuality: New Directions in American Catholic Thought* (New York: Paulist Press, 1977), 215.

[27] Father Edward Beck, "The Catholic Church Can Root Out Sexual Abuse. But Does It Have the Will to Act?", CNN, February 10, 2019, https://www.cnn.com/2019/02/10/opinions/catholic-church-sex-abuse-reform-father-beck/index.html.

to the hedonistic strain in the dominant culture of the West, Pope John Paul II maintained that the only sexual expression worthy of man is one based on self-giving love, not self-indulgence.

Aspiring to follow such a teaching, in imitation of Christ, cannot be blamed for the sex scandal. In 2002, just months after the *Boston Globe* series appeared, and prior to the Dallas conference, Michael Novak debunked the myth that orthodox Church teachings were to blame for the scandal. He noted that "orthodoxy has been vindicated and progressivism found utterly bankrupt. No priests faithful to the traditional sexual teaching of the Church, and to their own maturely and voluntarily taken vows, caused any of the scandals aired in 2002. Traditional teaching did not fail. Had it been followed to the letter and in a full loving spirit, there would have been no scandals. Far from it."[28]

Homophobia

It is amusing to read how some strident critics of the Church's sexual ethics manage to come clean about the role of homosexuality in the scandal yet blame homosexual predatory behavior on homophobia, not on the homosexuals who committed the crimes. In 2018, Robert Mickens published a piece in the *Washington Post* admitting that homosexuals, not pedophiles, were responsible for the clergy sexual abuse scandal. He also noted that "psychologically healthy gay men do not rape boys or force themselves on other men over whom they wield some measure of power or authority."[29] But then he argued that "homophobia" caused gay men to become predators.

Mickens blamed the Church for adopting policies that "actually punish seminarians and priests who seek to deal openly, honestly and healthily with their sexual orientation". It is "homophobia" that is driving the problem, because it "keeps gay men in the closet".[30]

---

[28] Michael Novak, "The Fall of the Progressive Church", *National Review*, May 1, 2002.

[29] Robert Mickens, "The Catholic Church Is Enabling the Sex Abuse Crisis by Forcing Gay Priests to Stay in the Closet", *Washington Post*, July 23, 2018, https://www.washington post.com/news/acts-of-faith/wp/2018/07/23/the-catholic-churchs-sex-abuse-scandals -show-it-has-a-gay-priest-problem-theyre-trapped-in-the-closet/.

[30] Ibid.

His logic is deeply flawed and does not square with the evidence. It was when homosexuals were in the closet—in the 1940s and the 1950s, for example—that they did the least damage. Gays surfaced in the 1960s, when norms were relaxed. Blaming "homophobia" is a dodge. It is employed as justification for re-creating the very milieu that created the problem in the first place (more about this soon). We should never want to return to a time when heterosexual men left the seminaries because they were surrounded by gay men acting out with impunity.

Clericalism

Clericalism is another reason given for the clergy sexual abuse. In fact, it has become so popular that it is now accepted by the Vatican. If by "clericalism" is meant elitism, a sense of superiority born of arrogance, then this is a useful way to describe some enabling bishops who failed to listen to complaints about sexual misconduct or do anything meaningful about it. The term is also useful for understanding the way clerics get away with abusing their authority—by intimidating into silence anyone who would question their behavior.

But clericalism alone offers no explanatory value in understanding why molesting priests acted out in the first place. There are plenty of obnoxious clerics who put themselves on a pedestal, and who are known to abuse their power, yet never engage in sexual abuse. George Weigel is correct: "Clericalism is a facilitator of abusive behavior; it is not a cause."[31]

The clericalism argument matches nicely with vintage left-wing ideology, whose origins are Marxist. The Left sees the world through the lens of power. As Marx taught, society consists of superordinates and subordinates and is held together by coercion, not consensus. This vision has proven useful in analyzing the scandal because it concentrates on the bishops, the superordinates who abused their power. The Left always blames the power holders, giving a pass to everyone else, no matter how irresponsible he may be. If the subjects acted badly, they reason, it is only because of conditions created by their

---

[31] George Weigel, "This Catholic Moment", *First Things* (October 2019): 24.

masters. In other words, the scandal can be laid squarely at the door-step of the bishops, not the molesting priests.

To reduce the clergy sexual abuse scandal to clericalism is intellec-tually shallow. After all, there would be no enabling bishops had it not been for molesting priests.

Why Bishops Enabled the Molesters

To assess more accurately why some bishops enabled molesting priests, we need to consider some causes that are not part of the conventional wisdom on this subject. There are several reasons why this happened: fear of scandalizing the Church, in-group favoritism, elitism, ineptitude, the role of therapists, and the failure to follow Vatican norms. These factors are explanations, not excuses. Unfortu-nately, they are not widely acknowledged.

Pope Francis, in a 2014 homily, repeated Jesus' strong words about the "millstone" in store for those who sin against children. The Holy Father warned us that "scandals destroy faith" and that all Christians are "capable of scandalizing" others with their actions.[32]

It was fear of scandalizing the faithful that motivated some bishops to cover up the behavior of their molesting priests. It is a cruel irony that their refusal to come clean—even with the best of motives—resulted in scandal: once the truth was revealed, it caused some Cath-olics to question their faith. Pope Benedict XVI understood what happened. He cited "misplaced concern for the reputation of the Church and the avoidance of scandal" as a prime motivating force behind the cover-ups.[33]

In-group favoritism is perhaps the single most common reason why cover-ups are so ordinary. Do not the father and the mother of a street-fighting teenage son try to protect him from being sanc-tioned by law enforcement, fearing the consequences that a record of his conduct will have? Employers who are friends with miscreant

---

[32] Junno Arocho Esteves, "Pope's Morning Homily: 'Scandal Destroys Faith!' ", Zenit, Nov-ember 10, 2014, http://www.zenit.org/articles/pope-s-morning-homily-scandal-destroys-faith.

[33] Gregory Erlandson and Matthew Bunson, *Pope Benedict XVI and the Sexual Abuse Crisis* (Huntington, Ind.: Our Sunday Visitor, 2010), 113.

colleagues cover up for them all the time. They do it in the corporate world. Cops do it. Doctors do it. Lawyers do it. The clergy do it. Who doesn't try to shield a friend or a loved one from being permanently blacklisted? Wanting to keep bad news stories out of the media is a natural impulse. To put it differently, there is nothing significant about a "significant other" who conceals dirt about his friend or lover.

Of course, when the conduct is a criminal offense, in-group favoritism cannot be used as an excuse. Nonetheless, we need to acknowledge what social scientists have long known: showing favoritism for our in-group is a universal characteristic; there is no society in which it does not exist.[34] To put it differently, sporting a prejudice toward our in-group is expressive of the human condition. It is therefore hardly surprising that many bishops were naturally inclined to protect their offending priests from public rebuke. Their mistake was in seeing their behavior as purely a sinful act, when, in reality, the more serious infractions were crimes. Their other mistake was to underestimate the pain and the suffering experienced by the victims and their parents, who when given the chance would go after the Church with a vengeance.

Some bishops exhibited rank elitism in dealing with the problem. The "bishop-knows-best" attitude got many of them into trouble. When Bishop Thomas V. Daily was working in the Archdiocese of Boston (he had been chief deputy to Cardinal Humberto Medeiros and Cardinal Bernard Law), he routinely brushed aside credible accusations against molesting priests. "I am not a policeman. I am a shepherd." That was his stunning reply to a woman who said her sons and nephews were abused by the notorious Father John Geoghan.[35] When Jackie Gauvreau, an active parishioner at Saint Jean Church in Newton, persistently called the archdiocese to complain about a serial homosexual abuser, Father Paul Shanley, Daily told the receptionist to put her on hold; he advised her to let her hang for hours until she gave up.[36] Boston Bishop John McCormack, deputy to Cardinal

[34] Donald E. Brown, *Human Universals* (New York: McGraw-Hill, 1991), chap. 6.

[35] The Investigative Staff of *The Boston Globe*, *Betrayal: The Crisis in the Catholic Church* (Boston: Little, Brown and Company, 2002), 24.

[36] Leon J. Podles, *Sacrilege: Sexual Abuse in the Catholic Church* (Baltimore, Md.: Crossland Press, 2008), 163.

Law, was just as arrogant. In the 1990s, a nun had detailed accusations against more than a hundred Boston priests, but he consistently rebuffed her pleas to do something about it.[37]

The fear of giving scandal and in-group favoritism help to explain why good bishops made some bad decisions, but those who sported the elitist "bishop-knows-best" attitude were not acting in good faith. They were delinquent in their duties. It was not just in Boston where bishops exuded this disposition, but no other diocese was worse.

Sometimes the reason for not acting diligently is ineptitude. This is the case when red flags are ignored or when an "I do not want to get involved" sentiment is operative. This is one of the most salient reasons why bishops enabled their molesting priests. It is too easy, however, to put the entire blame on the bishops.

From reading the accounts of priestly sexual abuse, it is evident that, in many instances, there were several—sometimes scores—of people who either knew that a priest was abusing a minor or had good reason to believe that he might have been and most did nothing about it. This includes deacons, nuns, brothers, and laypeople. Regarding the latter, it makes the suggestion that more lay involvement is needed to prevent clergy sexual spurious, if not risible. The failure of the laity to step up and get involved is almost never cited, though it should be.

From my own experience, I can attest to the reluctance of several authority figures to get involved. In the mid-1970s, one of my third-grade students at St. Lucy's, a now defunct Catholic elementary school in Spanish Harlem, came to me first thing in the morning crying her eyes out. She said her mother had been beating her. Though I did not see any visible marks on her, I believed she was telling the truth. I thought about reporting it to the principal but felt certain that he would do nothing about it. He was a good man, an ex-brother, but he was so discouraged by the horrible conditions that existed in this inner-city ghetto that I knew he would just throw up his hands, saying this is the way life is in Spanish Harlem. So I went past him and contacted the New York City agency that handled cases of abused children.

[37]David France, *Our Fathers: The Secret Life of the Catholic Church in an Age of Scandal* (New York: Broadway Books, 2004), 236–37.

Shortly thereafter, I was summoned to the principal's office. Standing there was the principal, the mother, the case worker, and the guidance counselor. The mother asked, "What is this all about?" The three authority figures said nothing and looked down at the floor. I said to the mother, "Your daughter says you don't love her." The mother paused and then broke down. She was given help by a Catholic agency, and matters improved at home. The principal was not happy that I went over his head, but he was also relieved that my instincts were right and that help was afforded.

Ten years later, when I was a professor, one of my colleagues, who was a homosexual and also my friend, started showing signs of a breakdown. He was drinking much more heavily than usual, was no longer living in his apartment, and was coming on to male students. When I learned that he was selling his model trains, a prized possession of his, I knew matters were deteriorating rapidly, so I met with the president and the academic dean, two ardent feminists; the president was a nun. When I told them about the professor, they shook it off, saying that he was always eccentric. Then I gave them a wake-up call.

"So that's what you're going to tell the press? It's only a matter of time before they come, with cameras in hand. And you are going to tell them that you knew that a professor was sleeping on the gymnasium floor, surrounded with pictures of naked men and empty bottles of vodka—and that he was attempting to seduce male students—and you concluded that he was just a little eccentric?" When they asked, "What should we do?" I said, "Get him into Saint Francis Hospital and call your lawyers." They did. He got some initial help, left the college, and moved away. He later died of AIDS.

These two examples are not unlike the scenarios that play out all the time, in every institution. It is so easy to suggest reforms, yet the necessary correctives are not always amenable to a new set of guidelines. No one gave me any guidelines. Common sense and the courage to act on it are indispensable attributes in the war on sexual misconduct. Unfortunately, they are in short supply.

It is hard to read about some instances where red flags were dismissed by bishops and where an "I do not want to get involved" attitude prevailed. In some cases, it is too easy to say that ineptitude is the cause. Take the case of an Illinois priest who molested at least a hundred high school boys. When investigators searched his room, they found hundreds of examples of homosexual pornography. The housekeeper told the authorities that the priest had a statue of a man and boy embracing in plain sight in the rectory. Are we to believe that no one ever saw it, aside from the housekeeper? Too bad no one did anything to intervene earlier.[38] What about Father Gilbert Gauthe, the infamous serial abuser? Priests knew he was bringing children to sleep with him, yet they never said a word about it.[39] Another serial abuser from the 1980s was ordained even though his superiors knew he was a sick man.[40]

One of the worst molesters was Father Rudolph "Rudy" Kos. He had been married before he entered the priesthood, and Church officials knew from his divorced wife that he "was gay and was attracted to boys"; he secured an annulment so he could become a priest. Church officials in Dallas also knew that he had sexually abused his brother when they were children. Yet they still ordained him. He then proceeded to rape one boy after another.[41] Whether those in authority were also sick men, covering for each other, or were simply uncaring is unclear. But they bear responsibility for his conduct. This was more than ineptitude—this was unconscionable. There is no place in the Catholic clergy for these enablers, any more than there is for the molesters.

Conditions have improved so much that it is hard to fathom what was going on just a few decades ago. When we read that all five tribunal priests in one diocese were either active homosexuals, or had serious homosexual issues, it does not pass the smell test to say that no one knew what was going on.[42] Of course they did.

The Role of Therapists

The buck stops at the top, so even when bishops are given poor advice by "experts", they have to accept the blame. It is not fair,

---

[38] Berry, *Lead Us Not into Temptation*, 139–40.
[39] Ibid., 55.
[40] Ibid., 141.
[41] D'Antonio, *Mortal Sins*, 206.
[42] Berry, *Lead Us Not into Temptation*, 167.

however, to downplay the role that therapists played in turning bishops into enablers of molesting priests. Their role was consequential.

One reason therapists have not been held accountable for their advice—much of which was terrible—is that critics of the scandal never want to divert attention from episcopal responsibility. Another reason is that critics in the behavioral and social sciences don't want to blame their colleagues or admit to the limits of their expertise. The former is an expression of in-group favoritism and is understandable; the latter is born of arrogance and is inexcusable.

When the clergy sexual abuse scandal was at its worst—from the mid-1960s to the mid-1980s—belief in rehabilitation was the zeitgeist in social science and therapeutic circles. There was no one, no matter how incorrigible, who was incapable of being reformed. From the most hardened prisoner to the most brazen delinquent, there was no one who could not be "fixed". So strongly held was this conviction that anyone who expressed doubts about rehabilitation was quickly marginalized. This was the sociological climate that swelled the heads of therapists and viscerally appealed to bishops.

A bishop wouldn't be a bishop if he did not believe that everyone, including offending priests, is capable of redemption. Many sincerely believed that it would be un-Christian not to help their troubled priests recover. For priests, especially bishops, the impulse to forgive and to renew is strong; it certainly played a major role in explaining what happened. Regrettably, when they were dealing with serial offenders, the bishops should have acted more prudently: they should have pivoted and sought more punitive measures.

Not all accused priests were given therapy, but a substantial number, 37 percent, were.[43] The second of the two John Jay studies found that "the majority of diocesan leaders took actions to help 'rehabilitate' the abusive priests." Why didn't they seek to remove them from the priesthood? "The procedures for formal canonical responses such as laicization, or dismissal from the clerical state, were complicated, time-consuming, and often avoided."[44]

It is also true that social scientists did not really understand the dynamics of sexual abuse when it spiked in the Catholic Church.

[43] Terry, JJCCJ, and USCCB, *Nature and Scope*, 6.
[44] Terry, JJCCJ, and USCCB, *Causes and Context*, 4.

"Victimization was little understood", the John Jay researchers concluded.[45] In fact, it wasn't until 1952 that the *Diagnostic and Statistical Manual*, the definitive source book on mental illness, even mentioned pedophilia; it took until 1980 before it was elevated from a subcategory of "sexual deviation" to the level of primary diagnosis.[46]

A statistic that should have been given more attention by the John Jay researchers is the finding that "the majority of priests who were given residential treatment following an allegation of sexual abuse of a minor also reported sexual behavior with adult partners."[47] This is startling. We know that most of the abusers were homosexuals, not pedophiles, so this conclusion means that most homosexual priests not only abused minors *but also had sex with adult men*. When they were not preying on young adolescents, they were sleeping with other men. It would be unfair to blame therapists for these priests—they had no intention of changing. They also had no business being priests.

Therapists who deserve blame include those who floated the "repressed memory" thesis. They argued that being sexually abused is so horrific that the victim often represses it from his memory, at least temporarily. Importantly, they contend, the victim may later recall what happened. This has been used to great effect by alleged victims who sue the Church.

In November 1993, a few months after I took over as president of the Catholic League, Cardinal Joseph Bernardin, archbishop of Chicago, was hit with a "repressed memory" accusation by Steven Cook. I was skeptical from the beginning. Here was a former mental patient and admitted alcohol, sex, and drug addict making serious charges against a sitting cardinal. Worse, Cook, who was dying of AIDS, stated that his charge was based on a "seeing and feeling memory" that he had repressed for seventeen years. With the help of a hypnotist, Cook said he was able to recover his memory. He soon changed his mind, however, saying that he could no longer trust his memory, and he dropped the charges.

On March 24, 1994, Cardinal Bernardin wrote me a kind letter thanking me for writing a news release, "Bernardin Vindicated",

[45] Ibid., 117.
[46] Erlandson and Bunson, *Pope Benedict XVI and the Sexual Abuse Crisis*, 55.
[47] Terry, JJCCJ, and USCCB, *Causes and Context*, 3.

which helped to clear his name.[48] Unfortunately, my defense of the liberal prelate led some of my conservative Catholic friends to shun me: it took a year before one of them would speak to me again. Fairness should not be dictated by ideology.

In 1993, an important article on "repressed memory" appeared in *Society*, the flagship magazine of Transaction Press, the renowned social science publication edited by Irving Louis Horowitz. "Making Monsters", by sociologist Richard Ofshe and journalist Ethan Watters, contended that repressed memory "has never been empirically demonstrated". They noted with regret that "practitioners of the therapy have developed repression into a psychological phenomenon far more powerful than was ever suspected by Freud or anyone else until recently." After examining the evidence, they concluded that this notion "has never been more than unsubstantiated speculation tied to other Freudian concepts and speculative mechanisms".[49]

Ofshe and Watters are not alone in questioning repressed memory. Dr. Paul McHugh, a professor of psychiatry at Johns Hopkins University School of Medicine and adviser to the bishops, has long dismissed it as a dangerous idea that literally manufactures victims.[50] The American Psychological Association studied this issue and concluded that "most people who are sexually abused as children remember all or part of what happened to them."[51] Researchers at Harvard Medical School concluded that "repressed memory" is a "cultural creation having no basis in science".[52] Clinical psychologists from the University of Nevada, Reno, led by William O'Donohue, studied the literature on this subject and concluded that "there is a large amount of scientific evidence that clearly shows that repressed memories simply do not exist. Furthermore, research studies involving traumatic events that have been verified

[48] Bill Donohue, "Bernardin Vindicated", Catholic League, April 11, 1994, www.catholic league.org.

[49] Richard Ofshe and Ethan Watters, "Making Monsters", *Society* (March/April 1993): 5.

[50] Stephanie Salter, "Victims' Enemy Isn't One", *San Francisco Chronicle*, July 31, 2002, A19.

[51] James Colangelo, "Recovered Memory Debate Revisited: Practice Implications for Mental Health Counselors", *Journal of Mental Health Counseling*, 29, no. 2 (2007): 93–120.

[52] "Repressed Memory Is a Cultural Creation", United Press International, February 26, 2007, posted on Medical Xpress, https://medicalxpress.com/news/2007-02-repressed-memory -cultural-creation.html.

indicate that people do not forget their trauma. Indeed, traumatic events are actually quite memorable."[53]

How many priests have had their reputations tarnished, or worse, on the basis of "repressed memory"? It is hard to say. But it is clear that this discredited idea has wreaked havoc in the lives of many innocent persons, thanks to the unfounded beliefs of some therapists.

Such beliefs are also to blame for some of the ineffectual treatment given to abusing priests. Father John Geoghan was so hopeless that no therapist could save him, but initially he was not treated by a psychiatrist: his therapist was his family doctor.[54] Geoghan did receive therapy from a licensed psychiatrist at another time, but that psychiatrist had no experience in treating sexual offenders.[55] Both of these doctors, Robert Mullins, the family physician, and John Brennan, the psychiatrist, reported Geoghan "fully recovered" in 1984.[56]

This false diagnosis misled Cardinal Law, as did the declaration of the archdiocesan review board that serial rapist Paul Shanley was without "evidence of a diagnosable sexual disorder".[57]

It would be a mistake to think that the opinions and advice given to Cardinal Law were anomalies. No, much of the blame goes to the laypeople, and the clergy, who advised the bishops which "experts" they should choose to counsel them on sexual abuse when they met in Dallas in 2002. For example, no one from the respected Catholic Medical Association was chosen, even though its psychiatrists are known for their competence and fidelity to Church teachings on sexuality.[58] Instead, Dr. Fred Berlin of Johns Hopkins University was chosen.

[53] William O'Donohue, Olga Cirlugea, and Lorraine Benuto, "Psychologists Address Sexual Abuse", Catholic League, May 23, 2012, https://www.catholicleague.org/psychologists-address-sexual-abuse/.

[54] Philip F. Lawler, The Faithful Departed: The Collapse of Boston's Catholic Culture (New York: Encounter Books, 2008), 160.

[55] Michael Rezendes and Matt Carroll, "Doctors Who OK'd Geoghan Lacked Expertise, Review Shows", Boston Globe, January 16, 2002, https://archive.boston.com/globe/spotlight/abuse/stories/011602_doctors.htm.

[56] Michael Rezendes, "Church Allowed Abuse by Priest for Years", Boston Globe, January 6, 2002, A1.

[57] Pam Belluck, "Papers Show Officials Knew of Priest's Troubles in 1991", New York Times, May 15, 2002, A20.

[58] Rod Dreher, "Dallas Diary", National Review, June 13, 2002, posted on BishopAccountability.org, http://www.bishop-accountability.org/news/2002_06_13_Dreher_InTown.htm.

Dr. Judith Reisman, a law professor at Liberty University, described Berlin as a "pedophile apologist" because he "protected the predators in his care while ignoring their acknowledged ongoing child victims".[59] It's not just her opinion of him that counts. Berlin's sexual-deviance clinic at Johns Hopkins has had quite a reputation for harboring molesters. In the mid-1980s, the *Baltimore Sun* revealed that a man under Berlin's care would stop by the downtown arcade to meet young boys before his visits to the clinic. Not only that; the man was an ex-con who was convicted of child molestation.[60] Those who advised the bishops to select Berlin must have known all of this. They should also have known that Berlin contended that therapists should not have to report child molesters to the authorities. "Berlin was one of many researchers who argued that with psychological treatment," writes Michael D'Antonio, "many if not most sex offenders could get control over their compulsions."[61] They were wrong. More important, they misled the bishops.

If it were just one "expert" who failed the bishops, that would be one thing; but, in fact, there were many. The number of therapists who treated abusive priests yet did not accept Catholic sexual morality is mind-boggling. Father Jerry Pokorsky read the spiritual and psychological clinical risk assessment of Father Geoghan that was prepared at Saint Luke Institute in Maryland and was appalled. The "most basic questions of Catholic morality" were never considered, he said, it was entirely secular in orientation.[62] Similarly, the Servants of the Paraclete, a religious order dedicated to troubled priests, employed as its chief psychiatrist Jay Feierman, who complained that a priest is "not allowed to be affectionate, he's not allowed to be in love, he's not allowed to be a sexual being".[63] Father John J. McNeill, S.J., who was openly homosexual and an advocate of gay rights, had once been in charge of counseling gay priests in his Jesuit community in New York City before being expelled from the Jesuits

[59] Jordan Michael Smith, "The Professor of Horrible Deeds", *Chronicle of Higher Education*, February 18, 2018, https://www.chronicle.com/article/the-professor-of-horrible-deeds/.

[60] Ibid.

[61] D'Antonio, *Mortal Sins*, 28.

[62] Jerry Pokorsky, "The Crisis: Déjà Vu All Over Again", Catholic Culture, August 31, 2018, https://www.catholicculture.org/commentary/crisis-dj-vu-all-over-again/. This is an abridged version of a letter sent to ecclesiastical authorities in 2002 after the *Boston Globe* revelations.

[63] The Investigative Staff of the *Boston Globe*, *Betrayal*, 173.

in 1987 at the request of the Vatican.[64] He married his long-term partner in 2008.

The most famous gay priest to counsel Catholic homosexuals was Dr. Michael Peterson. He opposed the Church's teachings on sexuality when he ran a clinic for clergy and religious troubled by substance abuse and sexual problems at Saint Luke Institute. He was one of the "nonjudgmental" types who couldn't bring himself to see trouble when it was staring him in the face. "I know of a missionary who was an alcoholic for thirty-five years", he said. "He'd find boys, poverty-stricken, and hug 'em for five minutes. When he had an orgasm, the child would leave. Is that child abuse? I don't know." No wonder he dreamed of "Peterson's Park", a playground where sexual activities of all kind were acceptable. He made headlines when he died of AIDS at the age of forty-four, but not before offering wrongheaded advice to priests with serious sexual problems and their bishops.[65]

What makes this part of the story about clergy sexual abuse so distressing is the realization that the bishops had at their disposal some excellent therapists associated with the Catholic Medical Association. But they were not given the role they deserved. Perhaps their morality was too traditional for the sages who advised the bishops.

In 2002, at the time of the Dallas conference, the *Linacre Quarterly*, the scholarly publication of the Catholic Medical Association, released a task-force report on the kinds of help that abusive priests were being given by therapists.[66] It would have been an eye-opener if more had read it. It was written by eight physicians, four of whom were psychiatrists, several consulting psychologists, and a moral theologian. Here are three of their more important findings.

- "Many former patients of the Church-related treatment programs have stated that the staff at these centers for priests and religious do not support the teachings of the Church on homosexuality and other areas of sexuality, as detailed in the Catechism of the

[64]Berry, *Lead Us Not into Temptation*, 199.

[65]Ibid., 88 and chapter 12, "The New Confession".

[66]"Linacre Institute Symposium—The Clerical Sexual Abuse Crisis: Inpatient Treatment and Outpatient Psychiatric Evaluation Programs for Priests and Religious, Report of the Task Force of the Catholic Medical Association", *Linacre Quarterly* 69, no. 3, art. 5 (August 2002): 208–212, https://epublications.marquette.edu/cgi/viewcontent.cgi?referer=https://www.google.com/&httpsredir=1&article=2270&context=lnq.

Catholic Church and by the Magisterium. In fact they often criticize patients who do adhere to the Church's moral teachings."

- "Professionals at the evaluated facilities reportedly told patients
  that homosexuality is unchangeable and untreatable. Patients
  who state the belief that their homosexual attractions and behaviors are a result of specific trauma, for example, with a distant or
  critical father or with harsh or unaccepting peers, are regularly
  told that they are in denial of their homosexuality or that they
  are homophobes."
- "Patients are never referred to Courage, the only recovery program in the Church supported by the Pontifical Academy for
  the Family."[67]

Failure to Follow Canon Law and Vatican Directives

As we shall see in part 2, this kind of sabotage—and that is what this
is—played a key role in creating the clergy sexual abuse scandal. It is
true that many bishops made poor judgments. It is doubly true that
many who advised them had their own agenda, offering the kind of
treatment that held their patients back from growing in the virtue
of chastity.

If the bishops can be cut some slack for sending accused priests to
therapy—a treatment that typically failed—they cannot be cut any
slack for their refusal to follow the edicts of canon law.

On May 25, 2010, Religious Sister of Mercy Sharon Euart spoke
at a one-day canon-law conference in Washington, D.C. She began
by saying that "the Church's canon law has made provision for sexual
abuse of minors to be a grave offense since the Middle Ages." Canon
law was not the problem, she said. "The problem was the bishops'
reluctance to utilize the then-existing provisions of canon law for
removing priests from ministry. The canonical tools were there."[68]

Pope Benedict XVI said the same thing in the same year when
he issued his pastoral letter to the Catholics of Ireland. "It cannot
be denied that some of you and your predecessors failed, at times
grievously, to apply the long-established norms of canon law to the

[67] Ibid., 210–211, 212.
[68] "Bishops Actually a Step Ahead in Addressing Scandal", Zenit, June 15, 2010, http://
www.zenit.org/articles/bishops-actually-a-step-ahead-in-addressing-scandal.

crime of child abuse." This failure of judgment, he said, "has seriously undermined your credibility and effectiveness".[69]

The 1917 *Code of Canon Law* was not ambiguous in laying down a strict set of penalties for abusive priests as well as for active homosexual priests; nor was the 1961 Vatican document on this subject, *Careful Selection and Training of Candidates for the States of Perfection and Sacred Orders*: it warned about priests who find it impossible to practice chastity. The document on selecting and training for the priesthood told every bishop "that he should confer Sacred Orders on no one unless he is morally certain, by positive arguments, of the candidate's canonical fitness; otherwise, he not only sins most grievously himself but exposes himself to the danger of sharing in the sins of others". The document was also quite clear about homosexuals. "Advancement to religious vows and ordination should be barred to those who are afflicted with evil tendencies to homosexuality or pederasty, since for them the common life and the priestly ministry would constitute serious dangers."[70]

I once asked Father Mitch Pacwa, S.J., why the bishops kept men in the priesthood who should have been shown the door. They were "afraid of losing them", he said. He was right. Too bad they didn't heed what the 1961 Vatican document said. While vocations to the priesthood should be vigorously promoted, "still care must be taken lest an immoderate desire to increase numbers should interfere with quality and selection."[71]

Unfortunately, some of the changes made in canon law in 1983 were not helpful for disciplining abusive priests. Cardinal Gerhard Müller, the former prefect of the Congregation for the Doctrine of the Faith, said the changes were a "disastrous error". The new *Code of Canon Law* lessened the penalties for abusive priests and eliminated all mention of homosexuality. Müller called the LGBT ideology within the Church "atheistic" and warned against lowering standards for behavioral infractions.[72]

[69] Erlandson and Bunson, *Pope Benedict XVI and the Sexual Abuse Crisis*, 56.

[70] See Sacred Congregation for Religious, *Careful Selection and Training of Candidates for the States of Perfection and Sacred Orders* (February 2, 1961), nos. 1–4, 10, 16, 30, https://adoremus.org/1961/02/religiosorum-institutio/.

[71] See ibid., no. 14.

[72] "Interview: Cdl Müller on Abuse Crisis and Its Link to Homosexuality in Priesthood", LifeSiteNews, November 21, 2108, https://www.lifesitenews.com/blogs/interview-cdl.-mueller-on-abuse-crisis-and-its-link-to-homosexuality-in-pri.

Some important directives on this subject were issued by the Vatican in the early 2000s. The Congregation for Catholic Education addressed the question of whether men with homosexual tendencies should be admitted to the priesthood. It reaffirmed the teaching of the *Catechism of the Catholic Church* that while homosexual acts are grave sins, people with same-sex attractions must be accepted with respect. However, "the Church, while profoundly respecting the persons in question, cannot admit to the seminary or to holy orders those who practice homosexuality, present deep-seated homosexual tendencies or support the so-called 'gay culture'."[73]

This document was read by Father James Martin, S.J., and by the media, as saying that Pope Benedict XVI barred homosexuals from the priesthood. As I replied to Father Martin on CNN, this was not true: the prohibition was limited to those with "deep-seated homosexual tendencies".[74] The difference is important. This was reiterated in 2016 when the Vatican's Congregation for Clergy issued a document on the subject.[75] In 2018, Pope Francis was just as explicit when he said that men with "deeply rooted" homosexual tendencies, or who "practice homosexual acts", should not be allowed into the seminary.[76]

Canon law and Vatican directives are important, but only if they are followed. They haven't always been followed, and that is a big part of the problem. It must also be said that all the canonical proclamations and Vatican documents in the world can never be a substitute for plain common sense, and the fortitude to follow it.

---

[73] Congregation for Catholic Education, *Instruction Concerning the Criteria for the Discernment of Vocations with Regard to Persons with Homosexual Tendencies in View of Their Admission to the Seminary and to Holy Orders* (August 2005), no. 2, https://www.vatican.va/roman_curia/congregations/ccatheduc/documents/rc_con_ccatheduc_doc_20051104_istruzione_en.html.

[74] See the CNN transcript of *The Lead with Jake Tapper*, July 29, 2013.

[75] Inés San Martín, "Vatican Reiterates That Homosexuals Shouldn't Be Priests", *Crux*, December 7, 2016, https://cruxnow.com/global-church/2016/12/vatican-reiterates-homosexuals-shouldnt-priests/.

[76] *Crux* staff, "Pope Doesn't Want 'Practicing' Gays in Seminaries, Reports Say", *Crux*, May 25, 2018, https://cruxnow.com/vatican/2018/05/pope-doesnt-want-practicing-gays-in-seminaries-reports-say/.

PART II

The Origins of Clergy Sexual Abuse

5

The Role of Evil

The priests who abused minors were sick men, but I wouldn't say that all of them were evil. The word "evil" does describe, however, priests who used sacred objects or sacred words when abusing their victims. Similarly, when a senior member of the hierarchy has sex with seminarians—raping them psychologically as well as physically—it makes no sense to say he is a troubled soul. No, what he did was evil personified. This is the work of the devil.

In 1995, Cardinal John O'Connor, the archbishop of New York, wrote a column about the anti-Catholic movie *Priest*, supporting the Catholic League's criticism of it. He said that while most priests were good men, some were evil.[1] At the time, I was not sure whom he meant. Now I know. Pope Francis knows as well. In 2019, he told reporters that there were some things, such as the abuse crisis and child pornography, that "cannot be understood without the mystery of evil".[2]

The problem today is that many deny the existence of evil. Pope Benedict XVI notes that this is a function of moral relativism. When that flourishes, "there are no standards of good or evil." The sexual abuse of minors, he maintains, could not have happened if God were in our lives; the devaluing of the Eucharist illustrates his point. Pope Benedict XVI gave a real-life example that is horrifying: a woman told him that when a priest was abusing her, he uttered the words, "This is my body which will be given up for you."[3] This is a manifestation of evil, and we should not be afraid to say so.

[1] John Cardinal O'Connor, " 'Priest' and Real Priests", *Catholic New York*, April 6, 1995, 7.
[2] Cindy Wooden, " 'Spiritual Combat' Must Be Part of Fight against Sex Abuse, Pope Says", Catholic News Service, March 31, 2019, https://www.catholicnews.com/spiritual-combat-must-be-part-of-fight-against-sex-abuse-pope-says/.
[3] Pope Benedict XVI, "Full Text of Benedict XVI: The Church and the Scandal of Sexual Abuse", Catholic News Agency, April 10, 2019, https://www.catholicnewsagency.com/news/full-text-of-benedict-xvi-the-church-and-the-scandal-of-sexual-abuse-59639.

The first molesting priest to make a big media splash in the 1980s, Gilbert Gauthe, was not only a serial abuser; he was an evil man, according to Glenn Gastal, the father of a boy whom Gauthe abused. He did not choose that word flippantly: his son had to be treated for rectal bleeding because of what Gauthe did to him.[4]

Gauthe was a diagnosed sociopath who had sex with prepubescent boys and teenage boys.[5] Had he been bounced from the seminary, he may have become a predator anyway, but not as a priest. There were early signs that he was a problem. How many seminarians fail courses in ethics, the Sacrament of Penance, and the human knowledge of Christ and are still admitted to the priesthood? He also failed his master of divinity exams twice before passing. In the end, however, it was not his "shallow theology", as some noted, that explained his behavior: it was his propensity to do evil.[6]

James Porter was another one of the first abusing priests to hit the headline news. He was also evil. What else would we call a priest who sodomized an eleven-year-old girl while invoking the power of God? He also had sex on the altar with two boys.

Here are some other examples. A priest from Syracuse is alleged to have had sex with a boy while wearing his clerical garb, telling him he was "doing God's will". While raping him, he prayed the Our Father. When the boy cried out in pain while being anally pene-trated, the priest told him to shut up because "his suffering was noth-ing compared to the pain of Jesus' crucifixion". A Bridgeport priest performed oral sex on a teenage boy and had the boy reciprocate by telling him "the act was a way to receive Holy Communion".[7]

Marcial Maciel

It would be hard to outdo the evil that these priests did, but it would not be impossible. What is worse is when leading figures in the Cath-olic Church go on a rampage abusing young seminarians and priests.

---

[4] Jason Berry, *Lead Us Not into Temptation: Catholic Priests and the Sexual Abuse of Children* (New York: Doubleday, 1992), 155.

[5] Ibid., 75, 139.

[6] Ibid., 68, 69, 84.

[7] Leon J. Podles, *Sacrilege: Sexual Abuse in the Catholic Church* (Baltimore, Md.: Crossland Press, 2008), 260–63.

The two who are easily identified are Father Marcial Maciel Degollado, founder of the Legionaries of Christ, and former cardinal Theodore McCarrick. George Weigel is not alone in seeing evil at work in both of these men: he said they were "demonically possessed".[8]

Maciel was a drug-addicted predator who fathered several children, raped at least sixty postpubescent boys, and had sex with at least twenty seminarians.[9] Many have rightly speculated that Maciel could not have committed his vile behavior without the complicity and the knowledge of other people.

When a news story published in the Hartford Courant in 1997 alleged that "several [of the accusers] said Maciel told them he had permission from Pope Pius XII to seek them out sexually for relief of physical pain",[10] I responded with a letter to the editor. "To think any priest would tell some other priest that the pope gave him the thumbs up to have sex with another priest—all for the purpose of relieving the poor fellow of some malady—is the kind of balderdash that wouldn't convince the most unscrupulous editor at any of the weekly tabloids. It is a wonder why The Courant found merit enough to print it."[11]

One of the authors of the Hartford Courant article was Jason Berry. In his book on the scandal, he listed me as a supporter of Maciel. But my letter was a criticism of those who believed that Pope Pius XII actually gave Maciel the green light to practice sodomy with other priests, not a defense of Maciel. More honest was Father Richard McBrien. After he quoted what Berry wrote about me, I contacted the Notre Dame priest, and he was good enough to correct the record. "Donohue disputes the listing and I am only too happy to make this correction", McBrien wrote.[12]

[8] Jesse Remedios, "Catholic University Sex Abuse Series Wraps with Starkly Different Viewpoints", National Catholic Reporter, May 2, 2019, https://www.ncronline.org/news/accountability/catholic-university-sex-abuse-series-wraps-starkly-different-viewpoints.

[9] "Mexican Catholic Group Founder 'Abused 60 Minors'", video, 1:40, Reuters, December 23, 2019, https://www.reuters.com/video/watch/mexican-catholic-group-founder-abused-60-id646544955?chan=8gwsyvzx. See also D'Antonio, Mortal Sins, 232.

[10] Gerald Renner and Jason Berry, "Head of Worldwide Catholic Order Accused of History of Abuse", Hartford Courant, February 23, 1997, A1.

[11] My letter is available at "Donohue Never Defended Fr. Maciel", Catholic League, April 5, 2010, https://www.catholicleague.org/donohue-never-defended-fr-maciel/.

[12] Richard McBrien, "Our Lady of the Rosary", National Catholic Reporter, October 3, 2011, www.ncronline.org/print/blogs/essays-theology/our-lady-rosary.

Maciel died in Jacksonville, Florida, in the presence of an exorcist; his remains were sent to his Mexican hometown. He was defiant to the end, refusing Confession: he did not believe in God's forgiveness.[13] This was one more sign of his demonic possession.

Theodore McCarrick

Former cardinal Theodore McCarrick is an American, and for that reason alone, his sordid story caused much more grief among American laity than Maciel's. They wanted to know how someone like him could rise through the ranks of the Catholic hierarchy in the United States.

Expectations were high in November 2018 when the USCCB, under its president, Cardinal Daniel DiNardo, met to announce plans to deal with clergy sexual abuse, paying close attention to McCarrick. But on the eve of the meeting, the Vatican told the bishops to hit the pause button, saying that nothing should be done until the Vatican convened a global meeting on sexual abuse in February 2019.[14] As it turned out, nothing was forthcoming from the Vatican on McCarrick for two years. In November 2020, it released what became known as "The McCarrick Report".[15]

The report excels in providing abundant information about the ascent of McCarrick to the highest ranks of the Catholic Church. No other study comes close to providing such rich material, much of it heretofore unknown to the public. To be sure, there are holes in the report, but it nonetheless answers a lot of questions that needed to be answered.

If there was one outstanding flaw, it was the refusal to interview Archbishop Carlo Maria Viganò. This is especially unconscionable

[13]Idoia Sota and José M. Vidal, "The Legionary Who Died Four Times and Did Not Want to Confess", *El Mundo*, no. 746, January 31, 2010, www.elmundo.es/suplementos /cronica/2010.

[14]David McFadden and David Crary, "Bishops Delay Votes on Combatting Church Sex Abuse Crisis", Fox45, November 12, 2018, http://www.foxbaltimore.com/news/local /bishops-delay-votes-on-combatting-church-sex-abuse-crisis. This was an AP story.

[15]"The McCarrick Report" is formally known as *Report on the Holy See's Institutional Knowledge and Decision-Making Related to Former Cardinal Theodore Edgar McCarrick*. It was published on November 10, 2020.

given that the report mentions him 306 times, mostly to discredit him.[16] Yet persons who were mentioned only a few times were interviewed.

The report blames Archbishop Viganò for not investigating McCarrick, something he vigorously denies.[17] I question blaming him myself, given my own experience of the man. In late 2015, after a notable Catholic contacted me about a bishop who refused to do anything about a rogue priest, I reached out to Archbishop Viganò; he was the apostolic nuncio to the United States at the time. He got right on it and acted responsibly. Indeed, he took very seriously my request to investigate this matter.

When I became president of the Catholic League in 1993, McCarrick was the archbishop of Newark. At the time, our office was in the Catholic Center of the Archdiocese of New York. Cardinal O'Connor was kind enough to move our office to the twentieth floor, next to his office, so I got a chance to know him well. He even knocked down a wall in his office to provide more room for our expanding staff.

I was on the job for only a few years when I received a phone call from McCarrick. I remember two comments he made. He was very kind, praising my work combating anti-Catholicism. But he also said something that rocked me: he said it was his desire to come across the Hudson and succeed Cardinal O'Connor as the next archbishop of New York. Why, I wondered, would he tell me this?

McCarrick's quest to assume this post apparently consumed him. The report notes that while talking to two bishops in 1990, he "pounded the table and blurted out 'I deserve New York.'"[18] His sense of entitlement was appalling.

It now becomes clear from reading the report that one of McCarrick's characterological weaknesses, present from the beginning, was his excessively ambitious nature. It was in 1968 that McCarrick, then a monsignor, was first considered for elevation to the episcopate. Those charged with assessing his credentials were impressed by his multiple skills, but "several informants expressed concern that McCarrick might be overly 'ambitious.'"[19]

---

[16] Archbishop Viganò made this comment on EWTN's *The World Over with Raymond Arroyo*, November 12, 2020.

[17] Ibid.

[18] "The McCarrick Report", 91.

[19] Ibid., 23.

He was made auxiliary bishop in the Archdiocese of New York in 1977. Four years later, he was being considered to head the newly created Diocese of Metuchen in New Jersey. He again impressed everyone. The "sole concern" was his "obvious ambition to be promoted in the ecclesiastical hierarchy".[20] His quest for a red hat (that of a cardinal)—in one of the nation's most prestigious dioceses— proved to be an unhealthy preoccupation.

The first signs of trouble became apparent in the 1980s. That is when his homosexual escapades became known. At least three of the four bishops in New Jersey at the time failed to act responsibly: they allowed him to continue his predatory behavior unchecked.

McCarrick's penchant for seducing seminarians is well documented in the report. His house in Sea Girt, on the Jersey Shore, was a favorite spot for him to lure these young men. He intentionally invited more men than he had beds for, and he did this with regularity. He didn't just share a bed with the "extra" seminarians: He attempted to have sex with them. He often succeeded.[21]

What McCarrick did was not simply wrong—it was evil. "Evil" is a strong word. It should not be used promiscuously. But what other word can be used to describe a bishop who intentionally stains young men preparing for the priesthood?

McCarrick had some help from other priests. For example, Monsignor Anthony Joseph Gambino, after listening to a priest who told him what McCarrick did to him, had the nerve to admonish the priest.[22] Just as disconcerting, after Archbishop Gabriel Montalvo, the apostolic nuncio, learned from Father Boniface Ramsey in 2000 about McCarrick's sexually abusive behavior at his beach house, Montalvo never got back to him.[23]

After McCarrick was appointed archbishop of Newark in 1986, Bishop Edward T. Hughes succeeded him as the bishop of Metuchen. When a priest came to Hughes relaying how McCarrick abused him, he listened carefully but failed to take action.[24] In fact, he never said

[20] Ibid., 27.
[21] Ibid., 70–71.
[22] Ibid., 73.
[23] Ibid., 190.
[24] Ibid., 76.

a word to anyone in the United States or in Rome. Hughes did the same thing to every other priest who confided in him.[25]

McCarrick not only abused seminarians at his beach house, he also preyed on them at the Waldorf Astoria in New York City. One of them told Hughes—to no avail—that McCarrick "tried to convince me that priests engaging in sexual activity with each other was normal and accepted in the United States, and particularly in that diocese".[26] While this may be an exaggeration, it still bears much truth. The homosexual network in the Catholic Church in the 1980s was extensive. What did Hughes do when he heard this? Amazingly, he told the priest "to forget about McCarrick's misconduct and to forgive McCarrick 'for the good of the Church'".[27]

On January 25, 1990, soon after Bishop James McHugh was appointed to head the Diocese of Camden, he had dinner with McCarrick and three other priests: Monsignor Dominic Bottino, Newark auxiliary bishop John Smith, and a young cleric. In front of everyone, McCarrick started rubbing the crotch of the cleric. The young man froze while the others looked away. No one said a word.[28] We know this because in 2018, Bottino finally admitted what happened. Neither bishop found what McCarrick did objectionable. In fact, McHugh even commended Bottino for the way he "handled" the incident.[29]

If the New Jersey bishops were delinquent, the archbishop of New York proved to be meritorious. It was Cardinal O'Connor, a man whom I worked with and greatly admired even before the report tallied his integrity, who courageously blew the whistle on McCarrick. Regrettably, he ran into opposition, both in the United States and in Rome.

In early 1994, Cardinal O'Connor started receiving anonymous complaints about McCarrick.[30] O'Connor knew McCarrick for many years, and he also knew how common it was to field all sorts of false complaints about priests, so he understandably passed the letters

[25] Ibid., 77.
[26] Ibid., 84–85.
[27] Ibid., 87.
[28] Ibid., 92.
[29] Ibid., 93.
[30] Ibid., 95–99.

on to McCarrick. Then more letters of this sort reached O'Connor's desk. Also receiving copies was the nuncio at the time, Agostino Cacciavillan.[31] It appears unlikely that Cacciavillan did not also hear the rumors about McCarrick, especially given that he "traveled repeatedly to the Archdiocese of Newark".[32]

We know for certain that Cacciavillan was dismissive of reports about McCarrick's misconduct. In 1994, Mother Mary Quentin Sheridan, superior general of the Religious Sisters of Mary of Alma (Michigan), called Cacciavillan, relaying to him what a priest told her about McCarrick's "bad moral conduct" with young seminarians. Cacciavillan brushed her off with characteristic arrogance, saying that "she wanted to make herself appear important."[33]

Washington archbishop Cardinal James Hickey also rose to the defense of McCarrick. He wrote to Cacciavillan, "I can truly say that I know of no one more dedicated to the service of the Church than Archbishop McCarrick. He truly goes above and beyond the call of duty in supporting the Holy Father and the Church's teaching." Knowing of the rumors about McCarrick, Hickey said he never saw "any evidence of sexual impropriety". Indeed, McCarrick was so holy that he "never told an off-color joke".[34]

We know from the report that accusations made against McCarrick were ignored by these prelates. For example, there was a priest who not only contacted Hickey and Cacciavillan but also talked to Bishop Hughes "on two or three occasions during the late 1980s or early 1990s". The priest acknowledged that he spoke with Hughes regarding "the escalating talk about McCarrick", including "carrying on at the beach house". McCarrick, he said, preferred "the young and good looking among the clergy". The priest eventually realized that Hughes would do nothing about it.[35]

For these reasons, no investigation was deemed warranted at that time.[36] But that all changed after Cardinal O'Connor came forward. In 1999, he spoke to the new nuncio, Archbishop Montalvo, about

[31] Ibid., 101–110.
[32] Ibid., 100. See the footnote.
[33] Ibid., 112–14.
[34] Ibid., 114–15.
[35] Ibid., 116. See the footnote.
[36] Ibid., 116.

McCarrick's suitability to succeed him as archbishop of New York. O'Connor warned him that there are "some elements of a moral nature that advised against" consideration of McCarrick's candidacy.[37] Influencing O'Connor were psychiatric reports on one of McCarrick's seminarian victims; a graphic account of McCarrick's behavior was provided.[38]

While McCarrick was being considered for the New York archdiocese, he was also being assessed as a candidate to assume the duties in two other dioceses. He received the support of several bishops. Cardinal Hickey named McCarrick his number-one choice for promotion.[39] Cardinal Bernard Law of the Boston Archdiocese also rallied to McCarrick's side, admitting, however, that "from time to time 'a cloud' appeared over McCarrick's head regarding what he termed a 'misplaced affection.' "[40] Others might call it sexual abuse.

O'Connor proved his chops when he wrote a six-page letter to Nuncio Montalvo; the letter was dated October 28, 1999.[41] It was so personal and confidential that the Archdiocese of New York does not have a copy of it.[42] But the Vatican does.

The case against McCarrick was sober and convincing. O'Connor relied on the findings of Dr. Richard Fitzgibbons, a psychiatrist, and Monsignor James Cassidy, a psychologist from the Archdiocese of New York.[43] At the end of his letter, after detailing his concerns, Cardinal O'Connor said he could not "in conscience, recommend His Excellency, Archbishop McCarrick for promotion to higher office".[44]

On August 6, 2000, three months after O'Connor died, McCarrick wrote to then Bishop Stanisław Dziwisz, particular secretary to Pope John Paul II, addressing O'Connor's allegations against him.[45] McCarrick admitted that friends of his in the Curia came across O'Connor's letter and "tipped me off about it".[46] He seemed to have friends everywhere.

[37] Ibid., 129.
[38] Ibid., 117–23.
[39] Ibid., 130.
[40] Ibid.
[41] Ibid., 131.
[42] Ibid., 140.
[43] Ibid., 134, 137.
[44] Ibid., 139.
[45] Ibid., 169.
[46] Ibid., 171.

McCarrick accused O'Connor of "deeply attacking my life as a bishop", saying he knew O'Connor "did not want me as his successor".[47] Was he clueless as to why? Or was he just being deceitful? No matter, he definitely lied when he said, "I have never had sexual relations with any person, male or female, young or old, cleric or lay, nor have I ever abused another person or treated them with disrespect."[48]

Pope John Paul II, after learning of O'Connor's letter, asked Cacciavillan, then president of the Administration of the Patrimony of the Apostolic See, and Bishop Giovanni Battista Re, substitute for general affairs of the Vatican's Secretariat of State, to review allegations against McCarrick. The pope held both of these men in high esteem and relied heavily on their advice.[49] That turned out to be a grave mistake.

Both Cacciavillan and Re took McCarrick's side against O'Connor. Cacciavillan said McCarrick was "the best choice for Washington",[50] and Re agreed.[51] Indeed, Re concluded that if rumors persisted against McCarrick, "now certain that the accusations are false, they can easily be denied."[52]

From the report, we learn why the pope was deceived. Cardinal Dziwisz said it best. While noting that the decision to promote McCarrick was made personally by Pope John Paul II, the Holy Father "took into consideration the words of the people he trusted", namely, Cacciavillan and Re.[53]

It is a source of great disappointment that Pope John Paul II believed McCarrick, not O'Connor.[54] Whether it was his experience in Poland of hearing malicious lies about priests told by the Communists, as some have suggested, or his being surrounded by dupes is not clear. Perhaps both. According to Archbishop Viganò, Cardinal Angelo Sodano, secretary of state, was the one most responsible for persuading the pope to side with McCarrick.[55]

[47] Ibid., 169–70.
[48] Ibid., 170.
[49] Ibid., 142.
[50] Ibid., 179.
[51] Ibid., 182.
[52] Ibid.
[53] Ibid.
[54] Ibid., 173–74.
[55] *The World Over with Raymond Arroyo*, EWTN, November 12, 2000.

On the eve of his seventy-fifth birthday, McCarrick submitted his required resignation to Pope Benedict XVI. Nuncio Montalvo wanted McCarrick to stay on for another two years, and Benedict initially agreed.[56] But then new information about McCarrick's homosexual advances came to the pope's attention, and he quickly reversed his decision. McCarrick was told of the Holy Father's desire that he "immediately resign" as archbishop of Washington.[57] On May 16, 2006, Benedict accepted McCarrick's resignation.[58] His problems, however, were only beginning.

A month later, an attorney representing a priest who said McCarrick abused him met with Vatican officials. The priest described a fishing trip in upstate New York that took place in 1987. McCarrick invited him and two other priests to go with him. They had dinner and then went back to a local hotel to watch television. Shortly after going to bed, the priest "rolled over and noticed the Archbishop and another priest having sex on another double bed. At that point the Archbishop noticed that I was looking and invited me to be 'next.' The other priest laughed and joked at the Archbishop's invitation for me to have sex with him."[59] Shaken, he did not accept the invitation. The priest subsequently offered more testimony about another incident. The Diocese of Metuchen reached a settlement with him in November 2006.[60]

More problems emerged when Richard Sipe, a former Benedictine monk and psychotherapist, sent a letter to Pope Benedict about McCarrick's sexual misconduct, providing a lot of information, including reports by Catholic journalist Matt Abbott.[61] Though Sipe's letter was posted on the Internet, it received little attention by the media. Fortunately, it wasn't ignored in Rome.

In 2006, and again in 2008, Archbishop Viganò sent a memorandum to Pope Benedict about what Sipe had said, and what he himself had learned about McCarrick.[62] The evidence of McCarrick's

---

[56] "The McCarrick Report", 230–31.
[57] Ibid., 232.
[58] Ibid., 246.
[59] Ibid., 251.
[60] Ibid., 260.
[61] Ibid., 279–81.
[62] Ibid., 282–86.

misconduct was mounting, becoming ever more difficult to deny, though some still tried to defend him. Among them was Cardinal Kevin Farrell, who lived with McCarrick for six years in Washington, D.C. He claims he never heard of any wrongdoing, and indeed "never suspected, or ever had reason to suspect, any inappropriate conduct in Washington".[63] That would make him unique.

McCarrick proved to be shameless. He was asked many times not to present himself in public and to retire quietly, but he refused to do so. He even claimed victim status, contending that the proposed restrictions amounted to "persecution".[64]

If there was one big mistake Pope Benedict made, it was not laying down the law in writing.[65] When it comes to manipulative and self-absorbed people like McCarrick, the door must be shut firmly in their faces; otherwise they will exploit any remaining opening.

This explains why McCarrick refused to abide by every request to curtail his public appearances: he saw the lack of teeth in the requests as evidence of their impotence. He traveled all over the world under Benedict XVI and did so with greater ease under Pope Francis.[66]

When Pope Francis was elected in 2013, he said he never heard of any rumors related to McCarrick's past sexual conduct. Similarly, he professed not to know of any restrictions on McCarrick's traveling.[67] He said he assumed that allegations against McCarrick must have been without foundation; otherwise Pope John Paul II would have treated him differently.[68]

On June 23, 2013, Pope Francis agreed to meet with Archbishop Viganò; they met again on October 10. Five years later, on August 22, 2018, Viganò claimed that Pope Francis asked him about McCarrick during the June meeting. Viganò says he told him about "a dossier this thick" on McCarrick and explained that "he corrupted generations of seminarians and priests and Pope Benedict ordered him to withdraw to a life of prayer and penance." Viganò added that McCarrick had committed "crimes" and was a "serial predator".[69] Viganò says he discussed McCarrick's exploits again in the October meeting.

[63] Ibid., 290.
[64] Ibid., 308.
[65] Ibid., 298.
[66] Ibid., 370–72.
[67] Ibid., 394.
[68] Ibid., 401–2.
[69] Ibid., 403–4.

According to the report, Pope Francis "does not recollect what Viganò said about McCarrick during these two meetings". In fact, he says he never knew a thing about McCarrick until the Archdiocese of New York revealed allegations against McCarrick in 2017.[70]

On June 8, 2017, the Archdiocese of New York received a complaint about McCarrick's having abused a teenage male in the 1970s. Archbishop Timothy Cardinal Dolan had established an Independent Reconciliation and Compensation Program to deal with past cases of priestly sexual abuse, and it was this mechanism that proved to be McCarrick's last straw. This was the first time anyone had heard of McCarrick's having abused a minor.[71]

An investigation of this matter concluded that the allegations against McCarrick were "credible and substantiated".[72] Following the archdiocese's policies, Dolan recommended that the case be made public. That was done on June 20, 2018, and on July 28, Pope Francis accepted McCarrick's resignation from the College of Cardinals.[73]

How could this sad chapter in the Catholic Church have happened? When the Catholic League had its office at the headquarters of the New York Archdiocese, I heard rumors about McCarrick's sexual behavior in his house on the Jersey Shore in the 1980s. In Catholic circles, it was hard not to have heard these stories. Of course, it is not uncommon to hear all sorts of rumors about priests, many of which are false. In this case, they proved to be true.

McCarrick was well liked and had extensive contacts with elites in and out of the Catholic Church. He was also a magnificent fundraiser. Such factors cannot be dismissed as having no effect on his ability to proceed without sanctions. But there is another reason why he escaped punishment: the overwhelming presence of a homosexual network of priests, both in the United States and in Rome.

Bishops Who Took Action against Abusers

It is important not to forget those who proved to be heroic. Even though Cardinal O'Connor was in very bad health at the time, that

[70] Ibid., 404–5.
[71] Ibid., 433.
[72] Ibid., 434.
[73] Ibid., 435.

did not stop him from doing what was right. His passionate letter laying out the case against McCarrick was a great service to the Church. So was the bravery of another New York archdiocesan leader, Cardinal Dolan. How many other institutions in our society, secular as well as religious, have ever brought charges against one of their own offenders at the top rungs of their organization? None.

Pope Benedict XVI is also deserving of praise. If there is one person who did more than anyone else to sanction both Maciel and McCarrick, it was he. It didn't take him long to do what Pope John Paul II failed to do: he removed Maciel from ministry in 2006, a year into his pontificate. He also accepted McCarrick's resignation when the cardinal turned seventy-five.[74]

Pope Benedict XVI does not get the credit he deserves for the actions he took. Quite frankly, no pope in the modern era worked to punish predator priests more than Benedict. In 1988, when he was a cardinal, he pressed for a "more rapid and simplified penal process" in dealing with abusive priests.[75] In 2005, just before becoming pope, he gave that historic Good Friday homily in which he unloaded on abusive priests. "How much filth there is in the Church, even among those who, in the priesthood, ought to belong entirely to him! How much pride, how much self-complacency!"[76]

The most unjust representation of Benedict's legacy was written by Laurie Goodstein of the New York Times. She was plainly wrong when she said he never removed predators from the priesthood.[77] Not only did he remove Maciel, but he also defrocked some eight hundred molesting priests between 2005 and 2013.[78] He was also treated unfairly in the 2019 movie The Two Popes, which made it

---

[74] Peter Daly, "With McCarrick Scandal, #MeToo Arrives for the Church", National Catholic Reporter, August 6, 2018, https://www.ncronline.org/news/accountability/parish-diary/mccarrick-scandal-metoo-arrives-church?site_redirect=1.

[75] John Thavis, "While a Cardinal, Pope Asked for Swift Action against Abusive Priests", Catholic News Service, December 2, 2010, posted at BishopAccountability.org, http://www.bishop-accountability.org/news2010/11_12/2010_12_02_Thavis_WhileA.htm.

[76] Gregory Erlandson and Matthew Bunson, Pope Benedict XVI and the Sexual Abuse Crisis (Huntington, Ind.: Our Sunday Visitor, 2010), 153.

[77] Laurie Goodstein, "Rome's Fallible Conclave", New York Times, February 27, 2013, A1.

[78] Nicole Winfield, "Pope Quietly Trims Sanctions for Sex Abusers Seeking Mercy", AP News, February 25, 2017, https://apnews.com/64e1fc2312764a24bf1b2d6ec3bf4caf/pope-quietly-trims-sanctions-sex-abusers-seeking-mercy.

seem as though Benedict covered up for Maciel, when the truth was just the opposite.

The Denial of Sin and Evil

Benedict acted bravely because of his conviction that evil had conquered these very sick priests. But to many, not only is there no such thing as evil, there is no such reality as grievous sins. I once heard a priest tell a crowd of about 150 adults that there was no such thing as a mortal sin. He scoffed at the very idea that anyone sitting in front of him could ever commit a mortal sin. His audience seemed to love what he said.

I told this story to Monsignor Michael Wrenn, who did not know this priest, and asked for his opinion. He said the priest must be struggling with some serious sins of his own, explaining that only such a priest would speak this way; it was the priest's way of alleviating guilt, he said. As it turned out, Wrenn was right. Not long after Wrenn and I had this conversation, the priest was removed from ministry for sexually abusing boys. He died of alcoholism in his late fifties.

Psychiatrist Richard Fitzgibbons said that in treating molesting priests, he has "observed that these men almost without exception suffered from a denial of sin in their lives". They adopted a "utilitarian sexual ethic" that allowed them to "see their own pleasure as the highest end and used others—including adolescents and children—as sexual objects". They cleverly sought "a spiritual director or confessor who openly rebelled against Church teachings on sexuality".[79] Sounds very much like the priest I knew.

Archbishop Fulton Sheen would not have been surprised. He said, "Modern man has lost the understanding of the very name of sin." And we have become very good at blaming anyone but ourselves. Modern man has set a trap for himself, he added, "by ignoring the real guilt, he may become either psychotic or neurotic."[80]

---

[79] Richard Fitzgibbons and Dale O'Leary, "Sexual Abuse of Minors by Catholic Clergy", *Linacre Quarterly* 78, no. 3 (August 2011): 260.

[80] Fulton Sheen, *Your Life Is Worth Living: 50 Lessons to Deepen Your Faith* (New York: Image, 2019), 263.

Cardinal Sarah captures the essence of this tragedy: "Satan has a fierce hatred of priests. He wants to defile them, to make them fall, to pervert them. Because by their whole life they proclaim the truth of the Cross."[81] What the cardinal says cannot be exaggerated. No amount of psychological inquiry into the nature of the worst crop of molesting priests can adequately account for their behavior. In the most extreme instances, the hand of the devil can be felt. Prayer is needed to combat such occurrences, but it also takes courage. Serial offenders and those who give scandal to the Church have no place in the priesthood.

[81] Robert Cardinal Sarah, *The Day Is Now Far Spent* (San Francisco: Ignatius Press, 2019), 71.

6

The Role of Homosexuality:
Denying the Obvious

No one denies that slightly more than eight in ten victims of clergy sexual abuse have been males, and that almost eight in ten of those males have been postpubescent. Although many are reluctant to admit it, the fact remains that when an adult male has sex with an adolescent male, he is engaging in homosexuality. Everyone knows this to be true, but it is unpopular to say it. There is no end to the games that the deniers play, doing everything in their power to move the discussion away from homosexual priests. It is totally dishonest, but the dishonesty is so rampant that it carries the day, including in Church circles.

SNAP, for example, has tried to deflect attention away from homosexual priests by demonstrating that women have also been abused.[1] However, there have been relatively few. The former leader of SNAP, David Clohessy, along with people such as Father Thomas Doyle, are known for their outrage at clergy sexual abuse, but as historian James Hitchcock has observed, "They have never been willing to state the obvious."[2] They are hardly alone.

Father Andrew Greeley tried very hard to convince himself that the scandal was not a homosexual one. "Although 81 percent of abusers were homosexuals, it does not follow that all gay men or all gay priests are abusers."[3] Similarly, he has written that "the argument reasons that because most abusers are gay, then all gays are abusers, a fallacy whose false reasoning escapes the dunderheads who make

---

[1] "News Stories about Female Victims of Clergy Sexual Abuse", www.snapnetwork.org/female_victims/female_victims_index.htm.

[2] James Hitchcock, "Defending the Indefensible", *Catholic World Report*, July 2005, 37.

[3] Andrew Greeley, "Both Sides Are Wrong on Church Abuse", *Sun Times*, March 12, 2004, BishopAccounatbility.org, https://www.bishop-accountability.org/news2004_01_06/2004_03_12_Greeley_BothSides.htm.

it."[4] It's too bad Greeley didn't identify the dunderheads. Maybe that's because there aren't any. No one argues that because most of the abusers are gay, therefore all gay priests are abusers. That's a red herring. The real issue is why most of the abusers have been gay. As I have said for many years, most gay priests are not abusers, but most of the abusers have been gay. That is undeniable.

Another way to deny the obvious is to pretend that homophobia, not the sexual abuse of minors by homosexual priests, is the issue. This gambit was tried in April 2002 by Charles Colbert, a reporter for the *National Catholic Reporter*: "I think blaming and scapegoating gay priests is just utterly outrageous, finding a scapegoat for this, while deflecting the real issue ... deep homophobia."[5] But phobias don't molest minors—predators do. The total absence of homophobia would not discourage one sick homosexual priest from victimizing adolescent males.

The 2019 Vatican Summit

The denial of the role of homosexuals in the scandal extends to the Church's hierarchy. In early 2019, a Vatican summit was held in Rome to deal with the sexual abuse scandal. But before it commenced, some influential lay Catholics assembled to address it.

The Leadership Roundtable's Catholic Partnership Summit was held in Washington, D.C., and a report detailing its work was issued; there were six pages of recommendations and six pages of commentary. The Leadership Roundtable had done some good work in the past, but this report was disappointing. The report spoke about the "Twin Crises of Abuse and Leadership Failures" and addressed the "root causes", but regrettably, absolutely nothing in the report even attempted to examine the root causes of sexual abuse; only leadership failures were noted.[6]

[4] Andrew Greeley, "Failed Logic in Banning Gay Priests", *Times Union*, October 7, 2005, A11.
[5] "Allegations against Another Boston-Area Priest Surface", CNN's *The Point*, transcript of April 8, 2002, http://www.cnn.com/TRANSCRIPTS/0204/08/tpt.00.html.
[6] Christopher White, "Catholic Leadership Group Offers Plan to Fight Abuse and Cover-Up", *Crux*, March 4, 2019, https://cruxnow.com/church-in-the-usa/2019/03/catholic-leadership-group-offers-plan-to-fight-abuse-and-cover-up/.

Page 4 of the report said that "there are twin crises that need twin solutions."[7] True. The scandal involves two parties: the molesting priests and their enabling bishops. Why didn't anyone associated with the report bother to question why only the latter was discussed? Three cardinals, Blaise Cupich of Chicago, Joseph Tobin of Newark, and Seán O'Malley of Boston, participated in this event. Surely one of them should have spoken up about the gaping hole in the report.

The subsequent Vatican summit was a spectacular failure: it addressed only the enabling bishops, saying nothing about the molesting priests. This is like blaming drug lords for drug addiction and never mentioning drug users. To be sure, the drug lords are a guilty party, but were it not for drug users, they would be out of business. Similarly, the origins of clergy sexual abuse must begin with the abusers, not with their superiors.

What was most disappointing was the position of Pope Francis. He knew that homosexual priests were the real problem, which is why he said they did not belong in the priesthood. Yet at the summit, he identified clericalism as the root problem.[8] Meanwhile, Archbishop Charles Scicluna of Malta, one of the key organizers of the event, said it was wrong to talk about the role of homosexuals because "to generalize about categories of persons is never legitimate. We have individual cases, we don't have categories of people."[9]

Scicluna's claim is nonsense. Most street crime is committed by young men from fatherless families. Fatherless families are a category of people; not to discuss their role in accounting for violent crimes would be delinquent. Similarly, since homosexual priests commit most of the sexual abuse of minors, to refuse to discuss their role in a summit on sexual abuse is just as inexcusable.

Reporters and pundits in Catholic media spoke openly about the refusal to discuss the role of homosexuality in the scandal. "On 'Gay Lobby' Debate, Pope Again Offers the Sound of Silence": that

[7] Ibid. See also Bill Donohue, "Vacuous Report on Abuse Issued", Catholic League, March 4, 2019, https://www.catholicleague.org/vacuous-report-on-abuse-issued/.

[8] Jason Horowitz and Elisabetta Povoledo, "Vatican Hopes Meeting on Child Sexual Abuse Will Be a Turning Point", New York Times, February 19, 2019, A8.

[9] "Archbishop at Vatican Summit: Homosexuality Isn't 'Something that Really Disposes to Sin'", LifeSiteNews, February 21, 2019, http://www.lifesitenews.com/news/cdf-archbishop-denies-homosexuality-is-an-inclination-to-sin-at-vatican-sex.

was the way *Crux* editor John L. Allen Jr. put it.[10] Similarly, the piece that Michael J. O'Loughlin did for *America* magazine was titled "Despite External Pressure, Little Talk of Homosexuality at Vatican Summit".[11]

Some observers liked what they heard. An editorial in the *National Catholic Reporter* said the clergy sexual abuse scandal has "its roots deep in a clerical culture that valued secrecy, privilege and power over the welfare of child victims and families".[12] John Gehring, an activist at Faith in Public Life, wrote, "The root cause of this existential crisis for the church is clericalism, an insulated patriarchal culture where priests and bishops are viewed as a privileged class set apart."[13] Father Hans Zollner, a Jesuit who helped to organize the summit, fingered "abuse of power" as the cause of the scandal.[14]

Those who saw a massive denial of reality going on were not happy. Father Raymond J. de Souza said the summit was a "turning point in how sexual abuse itself is understood in the Church—with a shift away from sex itself toward abuse of power". As a result, he said, attention has also shifted away "from sexual morality and the virtue of chastity".[15] He's right. Any conversation about priestly sexual abuse that does not speak about sexual morality and the virtue of chastity is absurd.

When something as important as a Vatican summit on clergy sexual abuse denies the obvious, it gives cover to those who have an agenda of

[10]John Allen Jr., "On 'Gay Lobby' Debate, Pope Again Offers Critics the Sound of Silence", *Crux*, March 3, 2019, https://cruxnow.com/news-analysis/2019/03/on-gay-lobby-debate-pope-again-offers-critics-the-sound-of-silence/.

[11]Michael J. O'Loughlin, "Despite External Pressure, Little Talk of Homosexuality at Vatican Abuse Summit", *America*, February 24, 2019, https://www.americamagazine.org/faith/2019/02/24/despite-external-pressure-little-talk-homosexuality-vatican-abuse-summit.

[12]"Editorial: Systemic Malady Has Deep Roots in Clerical Culture", *National Catholic Reporter*, February 20, 2019, http://www.ncronline.org/print/news/accountability/editorial-systemic-malady-has-deep-roots-clerical-culture.

[13]John Gehring, "The Root Cause of the Catholic Crisis: It's the Culture That Views Priests and Bishops as a Privileged Class", *Daily News*, February 20, 2019, http://www.nydailynews.com/opinion/ny-oped-the-root-cause-of-the-catholic-crisis-20190219-story.html.

[14]Maike Hickson, "Swiss Bishop Endorses LifeSite Petition to Stop Homosexual Networks in the Catholic Church", LifeSiteNews, February 19, 2019, https://www.lifesitenews.com/blogs/swiss-bishop-endorses-lifesite-petition-to-stop-homosexual-networks-in-the.

[15]Raymond J. de Souza, "The Danger of Conflating Sexual Abuse with Abuse of Power", *National Catholic Register*, March 23, 2019, https://www.ncregister.com/commentaries/the-danger-of-conflating-sexual-abuse-with-abuse-of-power.

THE ROLE OF HOMOSEXUALITY: DENYING THE OBVIOUS   131

their own. Indeed, it emboldens people like Robert Hoatson, the ex-priest who advocates for victims. He finds it scurrilous even to mention the role that homosexuals have played in the scandal and implores Catholics to "embrace homosexual and transgender priests".[16]

No forum mirrored the failed Vatican summit more than the 2019 Georgetown University event, National Convening on Lay Leadership for a Wounded Church and Divided Nation, organized by John Carr and Kim Daniels of the Initiative on Catholic Social Thought and Public Life.[17] The issue before them was the scandal. Never once did anyone mention homosexual priests. For the fifty-some persons they invited, the scandal was all the result of clericalism. Progress can be made, they said, by retiring terms such as "Your Eminence" and "Your Excellency", as if that had anything to do with why Gauthe, Geoghan, and Shanley became serial homosexual rapists. Just as inane, they said that the Church has to focus more on diversity. What diversity has to do with crazed molesters they did not say. They recommended such sophomoric reforms as "develop a national collaboration of ministries" and "be both humble and bold." In other words, this was another missed opportunity to deal seriously with the problem.

For all the talk about clericalism, the one expression of it that escaped all of these people was "gay clericalism". Jason Berry, who is no conservative, spotted this blind spot before anyone else. "The Catholic left", he said, "fixed on homosexuality as a human rights issue, seemed unable to grasp that the abuse of power by gay clericalism was as valid an issue as homophobia."[18] Ten years later, in 2002, Church historian James Hitchcock wrote, "By now it is apparent, as has been suspected for some time, that there exists in American Catholicism a network of homosexual clergy and that this network,

[16]Ed Condon, "Abuse Survivor: Some 'Victim Advocacy' Groups 'Have Their Own Agendas'", Catholic News Agency, August 2, 2019, http://www.catholicnewsagency.com/news/abuse-survivor-some-victim-advocacy-groups-have-their-own-agendas.

[17]Lay Leadership for a Wounded Church and Divided Nation: Lessons, Directions, and Paths Forward, National Convening Report, Initiative of Catholic Social Though and Public Life, Georgetown University, June 14–15, 2019, https://catholicsocialthought.georgetown.edu/publications/report-of-the-national-convening-on-lay-leadership-for-a-wounded-church-and-divided-nation.

[18]Jason Berry, Lead Us Not into Temptation: Catholic Priests and the Sexual Abuse of Children (New York: Doubleday, 1992), 307.

which extends into the ranks of the episcopacy, has significant influence in the life of the Church."[19] Gay clericalism, as we shall see, formed the basis of a gay subculture in the Church and had a devastating effect.

Far and away the most trenchant analysis of the Vatican summit was given by Pope Benedict XVI. Although he did not make his case in direct response to the February meeting, his six-thousand-word essay in April 2019 was seen, quite correctly, as his way of responding to it. Some non-Catholics were upset with him for breaking his silence. The first sentence of a front-page news story in the *New York Times* set the tone: "In his retirement, Pope Benedict XVI is apparently tired of hiding." The next sentence noted that he previously "declared he would 'remain hidden to the world'".[20] In other words, he has somehow been duplicitous by speaking up. But even worse is that his essay "amounted to the most significant undercutting yet of the authority of Pope Francis".[21]

This position was echoed in the Catholic media, for instance, by John Thavis at the Catholic News Service.[22] There was great irony in the position carved out by Michael Sean Winters of the *National Catholic Reporter*: he criticized the pope emeritus for addressing only the causes of sexual abuse, saying not a word about the enabling bishops.[23] Was it not the wholesale refusal to deal with anything aside from clericalism at the Vatican summit that motivated Benedict to bring some balance to the discussion?

Historian Christopher Bellitto said Benedict's essay "essentially ignores what we learned there". No, Benedict's letter was meant as a corrective to whatever it was that was learned there.[24] English author

---

[19] James Hitchcock, "Secrecy and Subversion in the Church Has Historical Model", Women for Faith and Family, May 31, 2002, http://archive.wf-f.org/JFH-Spies.html.

[20] Jason Horowitz, "With Letter on Sexual Abuse, Retired Pope Returns to Public Eye", *New York Times*, April 12, 2019, A4.

[21] Ibid.

[22] John Bacon, "Theologians: Benedict Wrong to Blame 1960s", *USA Today*, April 12, 2019, 6A.

[23] Michael Sean Winters, "Benedict's Letter about Sex Abuse Crisis Is a Regrettable Text", *National Catholic Reporter*, April 11, 2019, https://www.ncronline.org/news/opinion/distinctly-catholic/benedicts-letter-about-sex-abuse-crisis-regrettable-text?clickSource=email.

[24] Nicole Winfield, "Retired Pope Benedict Wades into Clergy Sex Abuse Debate", Associated Press, April 11, 2019, https://apnews.com/article/c98a296cd9be4da4aabbbd626403d7a4.

THE ROLE OF HOMOSEXUALITY: DENYING THE OBVIOUS 133

Austen Ivereigh was the most critical: "The release of this letter has been schismatic in effect, if not in intention."[25] Pope Benedict XVI obviously struck a nerve; otherwise the reaction would have been muted.

Pedophilia and Ephebophilia

Another way to deny the obvious is to pretend that the real problem is not homosexuality but pedophilia or ephebophilia. The former contention is simply inaccurate, and the latter is a dodge.

There is hardly a news story published that does not refer to clergy sexual abuse as a pedophilia problem. This is true not only in the United States but all over the world. The term "pedophile priest" is voiced on radio, on television, and on the Internet with such abandon that virtually everyone thinks that the Catholic Church has been harboring pedophiles. It has not. This is false. Indeed, it is a lie. Pedophilia has had little to do with clergy sexual abuse.

Pedophilia refers to adult preference for sex with prepubescent children. According to the American Academy of Pediatrics, puberty for boys begins at ten for whites and Hispanics and nine for African Americans.[26] The John Jay researchers found that 3.8 percent of clergy sexual abuse victims were boys ten or younger and correctly identified their abusers as pedophiles.[27] Those who treat molesting priests, such as psychologist Dr. Leslie Lothstein, also say that only a small minority of abusers are pedophiles.[28]

[25] "Retired Pope Benedict Reemerges to Step into the Roiling Clergy Sex Abuse Debate", *Los Angeles Times*, April 14, 2019, https://www.latimes.com/world/la-fg-vatican-pope-benedict-20190412-story.html.

[26] American Academy of Pediatrics, "American Academy of Pediatrics Study Documents Early Puberty Onset in Boys", EurekAlert!, October 20, 2012, https://www.eurekalert.org/pub_releases/2012-10/aaop-aao_2101312.php. See also, Daniel J. DeNoon, "Earlier Puberty: Age 9 or 10 for Average U.S. Boy", WebMD, October 20, 2012, https://www.webmd.com/children/news/20121020/earlier-puberty-age-9-10-average-us-boy#1.

[27] Karen J. Terry, John Jay College of Criminal Justice (JJCCJ), and United States Conference of Catholic Bishops (USCCB), *The Causes and Context of Sexual Abuse of Minors by Catholic Priests in the United States, 1950–2010: A Report Presented to the United States Conference of Catholic Bishops by the John Jay College Research Team* (Washington, D.C.: United States Conference of Catholic Bishops, 2011), 55.

[28] Mark Oppenheimer, "A Psychologist Steeped in Treatment of Sexually Active Priests", *New York Times*, April 9, 2010, https://www.nytimes.com/2010/04/10/us/10beliefs.html.

The John Jay researchers also found that 78.2 of the priests' victims were postpubescent boys.[29] Other experts have found similar numbers and therefore prefer to blame clergy sexual abuse on ephebophilia, which is adult preference for sex with adolescents. Father Stephen Rossetti, a psychologist who has treated many priests, says that over 90 percent "of priests and religious who sexually molest children are not true pedophiles ... [but] ephebophiles".[30] Psychologist Thomas Plante takes the same position.[31] He says that 80 to 90 percent of sexually abusive priests have "engaged with adolescent boys not pre-pubescent children". Thus, he calls them "ephebophiles".[32]

Branding sex between adult and adolescent males as ephebophilia is a linguistic game, the purpose of which is to move the discussion away from homosexuality. Mary Eberstadt astutely figured out the game that was being played. "When was the last time you heard the phrase 'ephebophile' applied to a heterosexual man?" she asked. "The answer is almost certainly that you haven't. That is because 'ephebophile,' in the technical-sounding nomenclature of the scandal commentary, is a term whose chief attraction is that it spares one from having to employ the words 'homosexual' or 'gay' in attempting to describe exactly which sexual crimes the offending priests have committed."[33]

Historian Philip Jenkins, who has authored a book on clergy sexual abuse, commended Eberstadt for her observation. "I think she is exactly right in suggesting that we move away from the overly technical term 'ephebophilia,' which I have indeed used in the past, though I now believe that the word frankly communicates nothing to most well-informed readers. These days I tend rather to speak of these acts as 'homosexuality.'"[34]

[29] Karen J. Terry, JJCCJ, and USCCB, *The Nature and Scope of Sexual Abuse of Minors by Catholic Priests and Deacons in the United States 1950–2002: A Research Study Conducted by the John Jay College of Criminal Justice* (Washington, D.C.: United States Conference of Catholic Bishops, 2004), 6.

[30] Berry, *Lead Us Not into Temptation*, 281.

[31] Thomas G. Plante, "No, Homosexuality Is Not a Risk Factor for the Sexual Abuse of Children", *America*, October 22, 2018, http://www.americamagazine.org/faith/2018/10/22 /no-homosexuality-not-risk-factor-sexual-abuse-children.

[32] Thomas Plante, "A Perspective on Clergy Sexual Abuse" (2002), Psychology of Religion, https://www.psywww.com/psyrelig/plante.html.

[33] Mary Eberstadt, "Correspondence", *Weekly Standard*, July 22, 2002, 8.

[34] See ibid. for his letter.

THE ROLE OF HOMOSEXUALITY: DENYING THE OBVIOUS 135

And so he should. Given that 81 percent of all victims of clergy sexual abuse, no matter their age, were male, that means that homosexual priests were responsible for roughly eight in every ten cases of abuse.

Homosexuality as a "Gift"

Perhaps the most disingenuous deflection from the role that homosexuality has played in the scandal is to insist that homosexuality is a gift. Almost no one talks about heterosexuality as a gift; it is treated as simply a given. Why then is homosexuality—which can be felt as a burden by those who experience it—put on a pedestal?

No one is better known for his defense of homosexual priests in the United States than Father James Martin, S.J. For more than two decades, he has railed against the Church's teaching that homosexual orientation is an objective disorder (homosexual acts, the Church teaches, are intrinsically disordered). It is difficult for the homosexual priest to carry out the Church's work, he says, "while knowing that the church considers him ordered toward an intrinsic moral evil".[35]

To be fair, Martin makes a good point. Yes, it must be difficult for homosexual priests, including chaste ones, to do their work knowing what the Church teaches about their orientation. But if what the Church teaches is true, finding it challenging is hardly a reason to reject it. Following Church teaching is challenging for everyone, because all of us, the whole fallen lot, have tendencies toward evil we must strive to overcome, with the grace and mercy of God.

Father Martin finds support in some Church circles. Berlin's archbishop Heiner Koch, chairman of the Marriage and Family Commission of the German bishops' conference, says homosexuality is a "normal form" of human sexual identity.[36] But if homosexuality

[35] James Martin, "The Challenges and Gifts of the Homosexual Priest", *America*, November 4, 2000, http://www.americamagazine.org/faith/2000/11/04/challenges-and-gifts -homosexual-priest.

[36] "German Bishops Commit to 'Newly Assessing' Catholic Doctrine on Homosexuality and Sexual Morality", Catholic News Agency, December 12, 2019, https://www.catholic newsagency.com/news/german-bishops-commit-to-newly-assessing-catholic-doctrine-on -homosexuality-and-sexual-morality-82866.

were normal, how would reproduction occur? Lesbian author Camille Paglia disagrees with Archbishop Heiner: "Homosexuality is not 'normal.' On the contrary it is a challenge to the norm.... Nature exists whether academics like it to not. And in nature, procreation is the single relentless rule. That is the norm. Our sexual bodies were designed for reproduction."[37] Yes, nature is a stubborn reality, one that cannot be altered by mere opinion.

Martin says that because most homosexuals are acquainted with suffering, and with isolation, they are better suited to be priests.[38] It's a weak argument. While suffering can indeed make people more empathetic, it doesn't always. Some people allow their suffering to make them selfish, embittered, and spiteful. And homosexuals are not the only ones who suffer in this world.

Martin is not alone in his view. Two years after his statements appeared in print, Bishop Thomas J. Gumbleton opined that homosexuality is a gift because it makes homosexual priests more compassionate.[39] In 2017, a Brazilian bishop declared homosexuality to be a "gift from God". He came to this conclusion by noting that since homosexuals do not choose to be that way, their orientation can therefore be considered a gift.[40] But we don't choose cancer or a broken leg either. Does that make them gifts? Causes of suffering can be seen as redemptive, but that's not what is being talked about here.

Pope Francis, in an effort not to marginalize homosexuals, asked Catholics, "Are our communities capable of providing that, accepting and valuing their sexual orientation, without compromising Catholic doctrine on the family and matrimony?"[41] This is a rather clumsy construction, and it could be a bad translation; but if what the pope meant was that we should accept one another as gifts of God regardless of our sexual orientation, then that is unexceptional: it is what the

[37] Camille Paglia, *Vamps & Tramps: New Essays* (New York: Vintage, 1994), 70–71.
[38] Martin, "Challenges and Gifts".
[39] Thomas J. Gumbleton, "Yes, Gay Men Should Be Ordained", *America*, September 30, 2002, http://www.americamagazine.org/issue/403/article/yes-gay-men-should-be-ordained.
[40] Inés San Martín, "Bishop Calls Homosexuality 'Gift from God,' Seeks to End 'Prejudices That Kill'", *Crux*, August 9, 2017, https://cruxnow.com/global-church/2017/08/bishop-calls-homosexuality-gift-god-seeks-end-prejudices-kill/.
[41] Pope Francis made his remarks at the 2014 Synod on the Family, in the interim midterm report, *Relatio Post Disceptationem*. See part 2, section 50 on "Welcoming Homosexual Persons".

Church teaches. Most important is his closing remark. Unlike those who speak about homosexuality as a gift, Pope Francis made it clear that whenever the treatment of homosexuals is discussed, we must keep in mind that we can never compromise Catholic teachings on marriage and the family.

We can never lose sight of the fact that there are good homosexual priests who struggle with chastity just as good heterosexual priests do. They are entitled to our respect. But we can never allow sentimentalism to override the pursuit of the truth, and the truth is that homosexual priests are responsible for the lion's share of clergy sexual abuse.

We need to be honest about why that is the case.

7

The Role of Homosexuality: Admitting the Obvious

When Bishop Thomas V. Daily was the head of the Diocese of Brooklyn, he got into a discussion with one of his priests who identified himself as a homosexual. Daily asked, "Do you really think there are a number of [homosexuals] in this diocese?" "Yes, I do", came the reply. "I think that probably half the priests are gay." Daily's jaw dropped.[1]

Not only are there many priests who are homosexual; some of these men became priests because they are homosexual. In 1990, a man told a reporter that when he was a student in his twenties at Saint Joseph's College in Philadelphia, he fell in love with a forty-year-old Jesuit priest. The Jesuit did not leave the priesthood to join his lover—the lover joined the Jesuits to be with him.[2] That's how confident he was that he would be able to be a sexually active homosexual after being ordained. Similarly, a German Jesuit, Klaus Mertes, director of an elite Catholic boarding school, said in 2016, "The battle for the rights of homosexuals worldwide is a project that makes it worth staying in the Church."[3] In other words, to help the homosexual cause, it made sense for this priest not to leave.

In the 1980s some people began noticing a lack of manliness in the American clergy as well as more homosexuals. "Back when I was coming up, ninety percent of them [seminarians] were more

[1] Carol Eisenberg, "Catholic and Gay: Once They Were Invisible, Now They Are Scapegoats in the Church Sex-Abuse Scandal", *Newsday*, June 9, 2002, A7.

[2] Paul Shaughnessy, "The Gay Priest Problem", *Catholic World Report* (November 2000), posted on Catholic Culture, https://www.catholicculture.org/culture/library/view .cfm?recnum=12047.

[3] Gerhard Cardinal Müller, foreword to Gabriele Kuby, "Abuse: 'Let Not Your Heart Be Troubled'", LifeSiteNews, February 20, 2019, https://www.lifesitenews.com/images/local /files/PDFs/Abuse_by_Gabriele_Kuby.pdf.

masculine, we played football, hardball", said a priest. "There was a noisy, rowdy spirit, full of pep. For [priests] fifty or older, you find a feeling that there are too many expressions of effeminate action and tastes among younger priests. This is a generalization. But without hesitation, I can say it's a real problem."[4]

Dr. Richard Fitzgibbons notes that a "weak masculine identity" among homosexuals was evident "in more than 70 percent of the males" he treated.[5] He says that "poor eye-hand coordination" explains why some men do not excel in some of the more popular sports for boys, and this, in turn, can lead their fathers and their peers to reject them, leaving them with "powerful feelings of loneliness, sadness, and isolation". The consequences of this can be severe. "The craving for acceptance and love from peers results in strong emotional attractions to those of the same sex, which leads many youngsters to think they may be homosexuals."[6]

What Are the Real Numbers?

How many homosexual priests were there when the clergy sexual abuse scandal was raging? No one knows for sure, but there is no shortage of estimates from credible sources. When a lawyer who knew about conditions in the Louisiana Dioceses of Lafayette and New Orleans asked author Jason Berry how many priests he thought were homosexuals, Berry guessed about 40 percent. The lawyer disagreed, saying he thought the figure was 60 to 70 percent.[7]

Another author who has studied this issue, Leon Podles, says, "Estimates range from 3 percent to 80 percent."[8] Podles cites Father Donald Cozzens, another expert on this subject, saying that the figure back then was about a third.[9] Homosexual activist and author

---

[4]Jason Berry, *Lead Us Not into Temptation* (New York: Doubleday, 1992), 56.

[5]Richard Fitzgibbons, M.D., "The Origins and Healing of Homosexual Attractions and Behaviors", in *The Truth about Homosexuality: The Cry of the Faithful*, ed. John F. Harvey, O.S.F.S. (San Francisco: Ignatius Press), 325–26.

[6]Ibid., 309.

[7]Berry, *Lead Us Not into Temptation*, 81.

[8]Leon Podles, *Sacrilege: Sexual Abuse in the Catholic Church* (Baltimore: Crossland Press, 2008), 326.

[9]Ibid.

Andrew Sullivan is probably right when he estimates that "around 30 to 40 percent" of parish priests these days are homosexuals and "considerably more than that—as many as 60 percent or higher" of the men in religious orders like the Franciscans or the Jesuits are homosexual.[10] In 2021, when Jesuit Father James Martin was asked what percent of priests are homosexuals, he replied, "I'm guessing maybe 40 percent. Who knows? If it was 40 percent, I wouldn't be surprised; if it was 80 percent, I wouldn't be surprised."[11] A badly sourced but influential book by a French homosexual author estimates that homosexuals "represent the great majority" of clergy in the Vatican.[12]

Does it matter? When asked by a homosexual reporter if it did, I said, "I'd take a chaste gay priest any day over a promiscuous straight one."[13] But how many of the gay men who sought cover or respectability for their homosexuality by becoming priests intended to be chaste? Perhaps we have no way of knowing a man's true intentions when becoming a priest, no matter what his sexual orientation is, but we do know that homosexuals are overrepresented among the molesting clergy.

Refusal to Admit the Obvious

Mary Eberstadt, commenting on the unwillingness of the bishops to admit the link between homosexuality and clergy sexual abuse, astutely noted what she called the "elephant in the sacristy".[14] When I was asked about this link I said, "The attempt to skirt the obvious is not only disingenuous; it is bad social science." Author Michael D'Antonio was not pleased with my comment but was guilty of only

[10]Jennifer Roback Morse, "Memo to Andrew Sullivan: There's No 'Anti-Gay Purge'", *National Catholic Register*, February 11, 2019, https://www.ncregister.com/commentaries /memo-to-andrew-sullivan-there-s-no-anti-gay-purge.

[11]Sari Aviv and Anna Matranga, *Sunday Morning*, CBS News, "Gay Priests: Breaking the Silence", March 28, 2021, https://www.cbsnews.com/news/gay-priests-breaking-the-silence.

[12]Frédéric Martel, "Excerpt: In the Closet of the Vatican", *National Catholic Reporter*, February 18, 2019, https://www.ncronline.org/news/accountability/excerpt-closet-vatican.

[13]David France, *Our Fathers: The Secret Life of the Church in an Age of Scandal* (New York: Broadway Books, 2004), 421.

[14]Mary Eberstadt, "The Elephant in the Sacristy", *Weekly Standard*, June 17, 2002, 22.

a slight exaggeration when he concluded that "Donohue stood comfortably alone in his position."[15]

Even some so-called progressive Catholics have admitted that homosexuality is a problem in the priesthood. Dr. Michael Peterson, the gay priest whose clinic treated clergy with sexual problems, was candid about it: "Most of the pedophiliac clerics I have seen and my colleagues have dealt with are homosexual pedophiles and not heterosexual pedophiles; this is surprising since the greater percentage in the population is the opposite."[15] Arthur Jones, the Washington, D.C., bureau chief of the *National Catholic Reporter* in the 1990s, said, "Homosexuality in the priesthood is the biggest problem to face the church in years—much larger than most people suspect."[16]

In 2002, Boston lawyer Roderick MacLeish Jr. said that 90 percent of the nearly four hundred victims he has represented are boys, and 75 percent of these are postpubescent, meaning the victimizing priests were homosexuals (though the reporters, of course, refused to draw that conclusion).[17] A year later, two *Boston Globe* reporters said that, of the clergy sexual abuse cases referred to prosecutors in eastern Massachusetts, "more than 90 percent involve male victims"; lawyers in Boston said "about 95 percent of their clients are male."[18] Still others have reported that, of the adolescent victims of clergy abuse, 93 percent were male.[19]

Current members of the National Review Board do not comment on these statistics, but those who sat on the initial panel were willing to connect the dots. When the first John Jay study was released in 2004, Robert S. Bennett, the lawyer who headed the National Review Board, said, "There are no doubt many outstanding priests of a homosexual orientation who live chaste, celibate lives, but any evaluation of the causes and context of the current crisis must be cognizant

[15] Michael D'Antonio, *Mortal Sins: Sex, Crime and the Era of Catholic Scandal* (New York: St. Martin's Press, 2013), 336.

[16] Berry, *Lead Us Not into Temptation*, 73.

[17] Michael Paulson and Thomas Farragher, "Priests Who Abuse Choose Adolescents", *Gazette* (Montreal, Quebec), March 19, 2002.

[18] Thomas Farragher and Matt Carroll, "Church Board Dismissed Accusations by Females", *Boston Globe*, February 7, 2003, posted on BishopAccountability.org, http://www.bishop-accountability.org/news2003_01_06/2003_02_07_Farragher_ChurchBoard.htm.

[19] Louise Haggett, *The Bingo Report: Mandatory Celibacy and Clergy Sexual Abuse* (Freeport, Me.: Center for the Study of Religious Issues, 2005), 118.

of the fact that more than 80 percent of the abuse at issue was of a homosexual nature."[20] What Bennett said, on all counts, is undeniably true. Dr. Paul McHugh, another early member of the National Review Board, said two years later that the John Jay study revealed a crisis of "homosexual predation on American Catholic youth".[21]

Honest Views from the Church Hierarchy

Some members of the Catholic hierarchy have also been willing to tell the truth about the role homosexuality has played in clergy sexual abuse. Cardinal Gerhard Müller is among the most courageous. "We can say 80 percent or more of the victims had been young people, but not girls. Boys, bigger than 14 years. It's more a homosexual attack than a pedophile attack. The victims, the great big majority, they are not children. They are teenagers and older."[22]

When Müller was asked why so many Church leaders continue to talk about clericalism while refusing to discuss homosexuality, the German cardinal replied, "I think they don't want to confront the true reasons for sexual abuse of minors, of boys and young men, and want to make their own agenda. They're against celibacy, against the sixth commandment, and therefore they instrumentalize abuse and this terrible situation for their own agenda."[23] That is quite an indictment. He received support for his position from his German colleague Cardinal Walter Brandmüller. "It would be unrealistic to forget or conceal that 80 percent of cases of abuse in the church context were perpetrated against male adolescents, not children", Brandmüller noted. "This relationship between abuse and homosexuality

---

[20] Kevin Cullen, "National Review Board Report; More Than 80 Percent of Victims Since 1950 Were Male, Report Says", *Boston Globe*, February 28, 2004, https://archive .boston.com/globe/spotlight/abuse/stories5/022804_victims.htm.

[21] Regis Scanlon, O.F.M.Cap., "Clergy Sexual Abuse: The Unaddressed Question of Same-Sex Attraction", *Crisis*, September 10, 2012, http://www.crisismagazine.com/2012 /clergy-sexual-abuse-the-unaddressed-question-of-same-sex-attraction.

[22] Cardinal Müller made his remarks on EWTN's *The World Over with Raymond Arroyo*, October 4, 2018.

[23] Edward Pentin, "Cardinal Müller: Clergy Sex Abuse Involves Sexual Misconduct, Not Merely Clericalism", *National Catholic Register*, January 23, 2019, https://www.ncregister .com/interview/cardinal-mueller-clergy-sex-abuse-involves-sexual-misconduct-not-merely -clericalism.

has been statistically proven—but it has nothing to do with homophobia, whatever one might mean by that term."[24]

Cardinal Robert Sarah is one of the most influential Catholic authors of our day. In 2019, he issued a clarion call to priests, asking them not to be discouraged during these trying times. "Certainly, because of a few ministers," the African prelate said, "you will all be labeled as homosexuals. They will drag the Catholic Church through the mud."[25] He also had some words to say about those in the Church who are sanitizing the discussion of homosexuality. "As for the churchmen who deliberately entertain ambiguities about the Christian view of homosexual behavior by saying that, morally speaking, all forms of sexuality are strictly equal, I tell them that they are doing the work of the prince of lies and that they lack charity toward the persons involved. Why such statements? Is it to justify their own behavior? Is it because they seek popularity? How can they offer ideological talk to those who ask us for the word of God?"[26]

Pope Emeritus Benedict XVI also posited a link between clergy sexual abuse and the rejection of Church teachings on sexuality: "There were—not only in the United States of America—individual bishops who rejected the Catholic tradition as a whole and sought to bring about a new, modern 'Catholicity' in their dioceses."[27] The brutal honesty of Benedict stands in stark relief to his critics, most of whom simply lash out at him for daring to speak the truth.

Pope Francis has also weighed in on the role of homosexuality in the scandal, but when he does, the media typically underreport or ignore what he has said. This is in keeping with the media's overall strategy, and that is to keep out of the news anything that might tarnish the pope's reputation as a progressive reformer. They are quite protective of him, in a dishonest way, and this is especially noticeable when we consider the media's often brutal treatment of his more conservative predecessors.

[24] Anian Christoph Wimmer, "The Church and Sexuality: An Interview with Cardinal Brandmüller", Catholic News Agency, January 9, 2019, https://www.catholicnewsagency.com/news/the-church-and-sexuality-an-interview-with-cardinal-brandmller-92738.

[25] Robert Cardinal Sarah, The Day Is Now Far Spent (San Francisco: Ignatius Press, 2019), 13.

[26] Ibid., 167.

[27] Benedict XVI, "Full Text of Benedict XVI: The Church and the Scandal of Sexual Abuse", Catholic World Report, April 10, 2019, http://www.catholicworldreport.com/2019/04/10/full-text-of-benedict-xvi-the-church-and-the-scandal-of-sexual-abuse.

If there is one line that Pope Francis uttered that endeared him to the media early on in his pontificate, it was "Who am I to judge?" It has been widely quoted inaccurately. The pope was not justifying homosexual acts but refusing to condemn publicly a man being accused of sexual impropriety.

In 2013, on the papal plane, Pope Francis was asked about Monsignor Battista Ricca. The pope had appointed him to head the Vatican Bank. Ricca was alleged to have had homosexual encounters, including being caught in an elevator with a boy prostitute,[28] but a preliminary investigation found that there were no accusations made against him.[29] It was Ricca whom the pope was asked to comment on; he proceeded to make a generic statement about homosexuality. Inexcusably, words were put in his mouth by reporters.

No one was more inaccurate in his reporting this incident than *Washington Post* journalist Anthony Faiola. Here is what he said: "On a flight back from his visit to Brazil in July 2013, Francis struck a different note on homosexuality than his predecessor, Pope Benedict XVI, who had described it as an 'intrinsic moral evil.' In contrast, Francis had this to say about homosexuals: 'If someone is gay and he searches for the Lord and has good will, who am I to judge?'"[30]

Faiola was twice wrong. Pope Francis' famous quip was not about homosexuality; it was about homosexual persons. This is not a small difference. Both Francis and Benedict uphold the teaching of the Church that homosexual acts cannot be morally justified, nor can any sexual act outside a marriage between a man and a woman. But the Church also teaches that someone with same-sex attraction is not deserving of condemnation on that account. To conflate sodomy and sexual orientation, which is what the reporter did, is inexcusable.

Like other reporters, Faiola excised the last word from the pope's comment: he left out the pronoun "him". What the pope actually said was "Who am I to judge him?"[31] Again, that is not a small

[28] Robert Royal, "The Abuse Summit: It's Only the Beginning", The Catholic Thing, February 20, 2019, http://www.thecatholicthing.org/2019/02/20/the-abuse-summit-its-only-the-beginning.

[29] John L. Allen Jr., "Pope on Homosexuals: 'Who Am I to Judge?'", *National Catholic Reporter*, July 19, 2013, http://www.ncronline.org/print/blogs/ncr-today/pope-homosexuals-who-am-i-judge.

[30] Anthony Faiola, "8 Things Pope Francis Has Done That Have Rankled Church Conservatives", *Orange County Register*, September 8, 2015, http://www.ocregister.com/2015/09/08/8-things-pope-francis-has-done-that-have-rankled-church-conservatives.

difference. The full sentence makes clear that the pope was talking about not judging a particular person.

The media gave considerably less coverage to what Pope Francis had to say about the "gay mentality". When a bishop told the Holy Father that it was no big deal that several priests in his diocese were homosexuals—it was just an "expression of affection"—the pope strongly disagreed. "In the consecrated life and in the priestly life, there is no place for that kind of affection." He also warned priests against aligning themselves with the "gay movement".[32]

There is no question that Pope Francis sees homosexual behavior in the priesthood to be a scourge. Why else would he issue this warning about homosexuals in the seminaries? "Homosexuality is a very serious issue that must be adequately discerned from the beginning with the candidates. The Church recommends that people with this ingrained tendency not be accepted into the ministry or the consecrated life. The ministry or the consecrated life is not his place." He also expressed his concerns about the trendiness of homosexuality. He noted that "in our societies it even seems that homosexuality is fashionable, and that mentality, in some way, also influences the Church."[33]

The Gay Subculture

Almost no one denies that there has been a gay subculture in the seminaries and in the priesthood. This would include those who attempt to shield homosexual priests from unfair criticism. Spanish Father Jordi Bertomeu is one of the Vatican's experts on clergy sexual abuse, and while he says, quite rightly, that being a homosexual does not cause one to be a molester, he does not deny that "a certain homosexual subculture typical of some clerical groups and present

[31] "Pope's First Trip Abroad Changes View of Church", Voice of America, July 30, 2013. See also transcript of *60 Minutes Presents: Inside the Vatican*, December 28, 2014, https://www.cbsnews.com/news/60-minutes-presents-inside-the-vatican/. Catholic News Agency used the word "person" instead of "him". See "Pope Francis Explains 'Who Am I to Judge' in His New Book", Catholic News Agency, January 12, 2016, https://www.catholicnewsagency.com/news/pope-francis-explains-who-am-i-to-judge-in-his-new-book-21443.

[32] Roger J. Landry, "Pope Francis and the 'Gay Mentality' That Has 'Influenced the Church'", *National Catholic Register*, December 12, 2018, https://www.ncregister.com/commentaries/pope-francis-on-the-gay-mentality-that-has-influenced-the-church.

[33] Ibid.

in certain seminaries or novitiates, with the consequent tolerance towards active homosexual behaviors, can lead to pedophilia."[34] That this can be asserted by a Vatican expert on the subject who bears no animus toward homosexuals is impressive.

Heterosexual priests who break their vows to have sex tend to become involved with adult women; no one argues that their sexual activity *can lead to pedophilia*. And they do not create a subculture or a network to encourage, protect, or promote each other. According to Father Roger Landry, "When priests cheat on their vocations with women, in general they do so alone, without forming cliques or collared mafias."[35] Now it may be that homosexual priests more naturally bond together because of their social status, but that would not account for what Father Bertomeu says about the potential for this to *lead to pedophilia*.

There must therefore be something peculiar about the sexually active homosexual, and this peculiarity lends support to the position taken by Pope Benedict XVI and Pope Francis against admitting active homosexuals into the priesthood. Benedict has warned of "homosexual cliques" in the seminaries,[36] and both popes have spoken about problems caused by a "gay lobby".[37]

Even priests who have never been labeled "orthodox" have discussed the causes and the effects of the gay subculture in the priesthood. At the turn of this century, Father Donald Cozzens, an author and professor, noted that "the need gay priests have for friendship with other gay men, and their shaping of a social life largely comprised of other homosexually oriented men, has created a gay subculture in most of the larger United States dioceses. A similar subculture exits in many of our seminaries."[38] Cozzens concluded that there has been a "heterosexual exodus from the priesthood" and an equally

---

[34] Inés San Martín, "Top Vatican Official Says Celibacy, Homosexuality Not Cause of Abuse Crisis", *Crux*, December 14, 2019, http://www.cruxnow.com/vatican/2019/12/top -vatican-official-says-celibacy-homosexuality-not-cause-of-abuse-crisis.

[35] Roger Landry, "After the Vatican Summit on the Protection of Minors in the Church", *National Catholic Register*, March 11, 2019, http://www.ncregister.com/blog/fatherlandry /after-the-vatican-summit-on-the-protection-of-minors-in-the-church.

[36] Benedict XVI, "The Church and the Scandal".

[37] Inés San Martín, "Benedict XVI Says He Dismantled Vatican's 'Gay Lobby'", *Crux*, July 1, 2016, https://cruxnow.com/vatican/2016/07/benedict-xvi-says-dismantled-vaticans -gay-lobby/.

[38] Eberstadt, "The Elephant in the Sacristy".

important diversion of heterosexual candidates away from the priesthood, all caused by the gay subculture.[39]

This same phenomenon was recognized by the head of the bishops' conference when the scandal hit the front page in 2002. Bishop Wilton Gregory said, "One of the difficulties we do face in seminary life or recruitment is when there does exist a homosexual atmosphere or dynamic that makes heterosexual men think twice" about joining the priesthood. He said that this was "an ongoing struggle" and that the Church must be careful not to be "dominated by homosexual men".[40] Heterosexual priests have not driven out the homosexual ones; it's the other way around.

Father Andrew Greeley, who was always quick to defend homosexual priests from conservative critics of the scandal, did not shy away from stating the truth about the gay subculture. In 1989, he made known his concerns. "Blatantly active homosexual priests are appointed, transferred and promoted. Lavender rectories and seminaries are tolerated. National networks of active homosexual priests (many of them administrators) are tolerated."[41] In 2000, he testified that seminary professors "tell their students that they're gay and take some of them to gay bars, and gay students sleep with each other."[42]

Greeley did not just note the prevalence of a gay subculture: he said the Church was rife with sexually active homosexual priests. Let's be clear about this. It is one thing for a priest to break his vows in order to have sexual relations; it is quite another for a network of philanderers to be tolerated, if not embraced, by Church officials. When promiscuity is accepted, no matter how it is expressed, it is highly unlikely that it will not spill over into other areas. Reckless people have a way of destroying everything in their path.

Bishop Robert Morlino, of the Diocese of Madison, Wisconsin, was a gregarious man and a loyal son of the Church. "He was ordained in 1974 and experienced as a young priest the upheaval in the Society of Jesus, as theological confusion, disciplinary breakdown, widespread

[39]Michael S. Rose, *Goodbye, Good Men: How Liberals Brought Corruption into the Catholic Church* (Washington, D.C.: Regnery, 2002), 86–87.

[40]The Investigative Staff of *The Boston Globe*, *Betrayal: The Crisis in the Catholic Church* (Boston: Little, Brown and Company, 2002), 170.

[41]Eberstadt, "The Elephant in the Sacristy".

[42]Rose, *Goodbye, Good Men*, 57.

homosexuality and a culture of dissent sent Jesuits heading for the exits in droves."[43] That is how Father Raymond J. de Souza put it after Morlino died in 2018. Morlino was one of the many priests I have met who started as a Jesuit (or a Franciscan) and left to become a diocesan priest because putting up with the homosexual subculture was too much to bear. In some cases, conditions were so bad that the homosexual culture was *dominant*.

In the 1960s the modern manifestation of the gay subculture became evident in the Church, particularly after Vatican II.[44] How much of it was caused by external events—the explosion of the sexual revolution—and how much was caused by the aftereffects of the Second Vatican Council is debatable. Surely both factors contributed to the problem. The first National Review Board referenced the 1970s and the 1980s as the heyday of the gay subculture, but as Philip Lawler said, the bishops failed to discuss this at the Dallas conference.[45] Some places were worse than others. Detroit's Sacred Heart Seminary and St. John's Provincial Seminary in Plymouth, Michigan, were reportedly "veritable hotbeds" for homosexuals during the 1970s and the 1980s.[46]

Alcohol is central to the gay subculture, including that among priests. At an LGBT conference, a Jewish woman learned about "a practice of certain Catholic priests who described going into gay bars in full clerical garb: They would sit in the bar, and when queer Catholics approached them, the priests would affirm God's love and their belonging in the church."[47] That's how out in the open some homosexual priests are. Indeed, I was told by a woman who tended bar in the 1990s at a pub near the Diocese of Rockville Centre's headquarters that homosexual priests used to frequent there and had no qualms about "making out" in front of patrons.

Drugs and frequent casual sex with strangers are also commonplace among gays. Some homosexual leaders blame the addiction problems

---

[43] Raymond J. de Souza, "Bishop Morlino Was Truly a Churchman of His Time", *National Catholic Register*, November 27, 2018, https://www.ncregister.com/commentaries /bishop-morlino-was-truly-a-churchman-of-his-time.

[44] Podles, *Sacrilege*, 322.

[45] Philip F. Lawler, *The Faithful Departed: The Collapse of Boston's Catholic Culture* (New York: Encounter Books, 2008), 172.

[46] Rose, *Goodbye, Good Men*, 58.

[47] Rabbi Avram Mlotek, "I'm an Orthodox Rabbi Who Will Start Officiating LGBTQ Weddings. Here's Why", *Jewish Standard*, April 8, 2019, https://jewishstandard.timesofisrael .com/im-an-orthodox-rabbi-who-is-going-to-officiate-at-lgbtq-weddings-heres-why/.

on "homophobia", but they nonetheless concede that "frequent impersonal sexual encounters [and] an inability to establish long-lasting relationships" are features of the gay subculture.[48]

As this culture spread in Catholic seminaries, some professors and seminarians did try to resist it, and they suffered repercussions. Threats of violence against seminary professors—those who were seen as being too orthodox—were not common but they did occur. The threats came not only from seminarians but from faculty members. As for the orthodox seminarians, where they were not driven out they were "pressured by [their] superiors to espouse, defend, and take part in homosexual acts".[49] It is important not to mince words: this is demonic.

Why didn't good men speak up? In 2018, Father Robert Altier, a Minnesota priest, answered this question when he candidly told his parishioners about the homosexual network. "Number one, if I would have stood here even a couple of years ago, would you have believed what I am telling you? Number two, who were we supposed to go to? It was at every single level all the way to the top. You wanted to be ordained a priest, you couldn't say a word. And even as a priest you can't."[50] Unfortunately, such silence is what allowed the molestation of minors to go unchecked. Here is how one homosexual author put it: "The problem is that some abusers that commit crimes within the church were protected by this culture of secrecy that was mainly to protect homosexuality."[51]

Reform in Seminaries

Whether it is the Dallas reforms, numerous Vatican directives, or other factors, it is clear the word has gone out to those who sought to join the priesthood for the wrong reasons: the party is over.

---

[48] Enrique Rueda, *The Homosexual Network: Private Lives and Public Policy* (Old Greenwich, Conn.: Devin Adair, 1982), 24.

[49] Rose, *Goodbye, Good Men*, 78–79.

[50] Robert Altier made his remarks in a homily given at the Church of St. Raphael in Crystal, Minnesota. See his article "The Enemy Within", *Catalyst* (October 2018), https://www.catholicleague.org/the-enemy-within/.

[51] Associated Press, "The Latest: Son of Priest Meets with Vatican Investigator", Yahoo! News, February 20, 2019, https://www.yahoo.com/news/latest-author-links-abuse-church-culture-silence-102550487.html.

Father Carter Griffin is a priest in the Archdiocese of Washington and the rector of Saint John Paul II Seminary in Washington, D.C. Monsignor Andrew Baker is rector of Mount St. Mary's Seminary in Emmitsburg, Maryland. Both testify that it is much harder for men with sexual disorders to join the priesthood these days. "The screening and the formation are far more rigorous than before, and unlike [in] the past where probing a candidate's moral character was not done, they are today; psychological examinations are now routine. Are there still men with same-sex attractions entering the seminaries? Yes, but they tend to be celibate. The seminary rectors are not naïve." They add that "it is equally clear that the *great majority* of priest abuse cases have involved the homosexual abuse of boys and young men" (their emphasis).[52]

What brought about the changes? Griffin and Baker credit Pope John Paul II for his 1992 document *Pastores Dabo Vobis*, which raised the bar by "demanding a set of spiritual, human, intellectual and pastoral expectations for seminary admissions and formation". They readily admit that this document was not welcome in every seminary, and its implementation has been uneven. Still, it set a new tone, inspiring American seminaries to issue a handbook, *Program for Priestly Formation*, that offers practical advice and standards. They also credit a new generation of seminarians and instructors: dissent from Church teachings is no longer tolerated the way it was in the past.[53]

The second John Jay study also credits the handbook, which was published in 2005: "From about 2006–2010, immense changes were recorded demonstrating greater awareness of the need for human formation, including education about the role of sexuality and celibacy in the life of a priest."[54] Monsignor Stephen Rossetti agrees, saying today's seminarians "are determined not to make the mistakes that

---

[52] Andrew Baker and Carter Griffin, "What Has Changed at Catholic Seminaries?", *National Catholic Register*, July 19, 2019, https://www.ncregister.com/commentaries/what-has-changed-at-catholic-seminaries.

[53] Ibid.

[54] Karen J. Terry, John Jay College of Criminal Justice (JJCCJ), and United States Conference of Catholic Bishops (USCCB), *The Causes and Context of Sexual Abuse of Minors by Catholic Priests in the United States, 1950–2010: A Report Presented to the United States Conference of Catholic Bishops by the John Jay College Research Team* (Washington, D.C.: United States Conference of Catholic Bishops, 2011), 44.

we made, and that is a good thing".[55] This is certainly true for most seminarians, though a 2012 investigation of Holy Apostles Seminary in Connecticut revealed that a homosexual subculture still existed.[56] More recently, matters were so impossible at Christ the King Seminary in Buffalo—faculty were accused by seminarians of "raunchy gatherings"—that it was shut down in 2020.[57]

Perhaps the most encouraging news came in 2019, when researchers at the University of Notre Dame's McGrath Institute for Church Life and the Center for Applied Research in the Apostolate at Georgetown University released a study of American seminaries. They found that 6 percent of seminarians have experienced some form of sexual harassment, and that 84 percent said that their administration and faculty took reports of sexual misconduct seriously. Seventy-five percent reported that sexual harassment was "not at all a problem" at their seminaries, and nearly nine in ten said they hear little or no talk of sexual promiscuity.[58] This is a significant change from the 1970s, when sexual misconduct in the seminaries was a serious problem. That was when Father Andrew Greeley spoke of the "Lavender Mafia" of homosexual subcultures in the seminaries. Reports of sexual misconduct in seminaries are rare nowadays, and they are vastly outnumbered by stories of misconduct on American college campuses.[59]

Regrettably, there is reason to believe that if there is any place in the Catholic Church that still tolerates a homosexual subculture, it is the Vatican. That is the conclusion of Frédéric Martel, a homosexual observer of the gay scene in Rome. While much of his book on the subject, *In the Closet of the Vatican: Power, Homosexuality, Hypocrisy,*

[55] Stephen J. Rossetti, "The Sexual Abuse Crisis: Didn't We Fix This?", *Priest* (December 2018), https://d2y1pz2y630308.cloudfront.net/11878/documents/2019/2/Priest%20magazine%20article-%20The%20Sexual%20Abuse%20Crisis.pdf.

[56] Thomas Wehner, "Unholy Activity Uncovered at Holy Apostles Seminary", *National Catholic Register*, November 29, 2018.

[57] Raymond J. de Souza, "Buffalo Seminary Closure Speaks Volumes to Other Dioceses", *National Catholic Register*, February 6, 2020, http://www.ncregister.com/daily-news/buffalo-seminary-closure-speaks-volumes-to-other-dioceses.

[58] "Study: 6% of US Seminarians Have Experienced Sexual Harassment, Abuse or Misconduct", Catholic News Agency, September 23, 2019, https://www.catholicnewsagency.com/news/study-6-of-us-seminarians-have-experienced-sexual-harassment-abuse-or-misconduct-71971.

[59] Bill Donohue, "Sexual Misconduct in Seminaries Is Rare", Catholic League, September 24, 2019, https://www.catholicleague.org/sexual-misconduct-in-seminaries-is-rare/.

is heavy on innuendo and cannot therefore be regarded as a scholarly account, there appears to be some truth to what he says. Father Paul Mankowski was not persuaded by many of Martel's findings, but he acknowledged that "the bulk of their testimony [priests who have worked in the Vatican] has the ring of truth, especially with respect to the blind-eye toleration permitted by their superiors to discreet homosexual recreation, and the willingness of the same superiors to cover up indiscretions that become known, provided silence is maintained by all parties."[60]

No doubt there are pockets of resistance to reforms in the United States also, but we can be thankful for the progress that has been made to restore the identity of the priest as a man who strives to imitate the example of Christ.

---

[60] Paul V. Mankowski, "Comfort to Predators," *First Things*, May 2019, https://www .firstthings.com/article/2019/05/comfort-to-predators.

8

The Role of Homosexuality:
An Analysis of the John Jay Thesis

It is not just in the United States that most of the victims of clergy sexual abuse have been postpubescent males: this is the situation all over the world.[1] Wherever the problem exists, it is homosexual priests who are largely responsible. Even in the comparatively small proportion of cases involving pedophilia, as gay priest Dr. Michael Peterson admitted, "We don't see heterosexual pedophiles at all."[2] Dr. Richard Fitzgibbons, who treated molesting priests for many decades, made an even more startling observation. He said that every molesting priest he had treated had "previously been involved in adult homosexual relationships".[3] He didn't say *most*—he said *every* priest who sexually abused minors was actively involved in homosexual relationships with other men at one time.

Are there studies to back up these observations? The *New York Times* insists there aren't,[4] but that is simply not true. To be sure, given the politically correct nature of academia, there aren't many such studies. Dr. Gerard J.M. van den Aardweg captured what has been going on in these circles. "The general trend is to interpret and present the findings one-sidedly as supportive of the wished-for biological causation; psychologists and social psychologists try to

[1] Gabriele Kuby, "Abuse: 'Let Not Your Heart Be Troubled'", LifeSiteNews, February 20, 2019, https://www.lifesitenews.com/images/local/files/PDFs/Abuse_by_Gabriele_Kuby.pdf.

[2] Mary Eberstadt, "The Elephant in the Sacristy", *Weekly Standard*, June 17, 2002, 22.

[3] Richard Fitzgibbons and Dale O'Leary, "Sexual Abuse of Minors by Catholic Clergy", *Linacre Quarterly* 78, no. 3 (August 2011): 259.

[4] Elizabeth Dias, "'It Is Not a Closet. It is a Cage.' Gay Catholic Priests Speak Out", *New York Times*, February 17, 2019, https://www.nytimes.com/2019/02/17/us/it-is-not-a-closet-it-is-a-cage-gay-catholic-priests-speak-out.html.

demonstrate the normalcy of homosexual relations and gay parenting. By contrast, research and publications at variance with the normality view are virtually taboo at universities and research institutes and unwelcome with most professional journals and publishing houses."[5]

This is not an exaggeration. From my sixteen years in the professoriate and my twenty years serving on the board of directors of the National Association of Scholars (which monitors academic freedom), I can testify that in almost every college and university in the nation, it would be virtually impossible for a social scientist to receive tenure if it were known that he had done work showing even a modest link between homosexuality and the sexual abuse of minors. There is no freedom of speech on campuses these days for anyone who dares challenge the LGBT agenda.

The issue is so thoroughly politicized that government agencies are also biased. To cite one example, the Centers for Disease Control and Prevention (CDC) published a study in 2020 of HIV infection among men who claim to be women (transgender women), and it concluded that the high rate of infection was attributable to "multiple factors, including stigma related to gender identity, unstable housing, limited employment options, and high-risk behaviors, such as sex work, unprotected receptive anal intercourse, and injection drug use."[6] Now, one does not need a Ph.D. to know that stigma, housing problems, and employment opportunities have practically nothing to do with HIV infections. But male prostitution, promiscuity, unhealthful sex acts, and dirty needles do. The need to shade the truth about LGBT problems is compelling among elites in many quarters.

Nonetheless, some studies have made it to print, and they are quite revealing.

Dr. Timothy J. Dailey reviewed the literature on the link between homosexuality and the sexual abuse of minors and found that homosexuals are overrepresented in such cases.[7] A study in the *Journal of Sex*

[5] Gerard J. M. van den Aardweg, "On the Psychogenesis of Homosexuality", *Linacre Quarterly* 78, no. 3 (August 2011): 330–54.

[6] Wei Song et al., "HIV Partner Service Delivery among Transgender Women—United States, 2013–2017", *Morbidity and Mortality Weekly Report* 69, no. 2, January 16, 2020, https://www.cdc.gov/mmwr/volumes/69/wr/mm6902a3.htm.

[7] Timothy J. Dailey, "Homosexuality and Child Sexual Abuse", 2002, posted on Lantern Project, http://lanternproject.org.uk/library/general/articles-and-information-about-sexual-abuse-and-its-impact/homosexuality-and-child-sexual-abuse/. Dailey provides the citations for the journals mentioned.

Research, for instance, found that although homosexuals are a small percent of the population, they account for one-third of all child sex offenses.[8] An article in the *Archives of Sexual Behavior* put the figure at 25 percent.[9] A study published in the same journal by another author found something even more startling: "One of the most salient findings of this study is that 46 percent of homosexual men and 22 percent of homosexual women reported having been molested by a person of the same gender. This contrasts to only 7 percent of heterosexual men and 1 percent of heterosexual women reporting having been molested by a person of the same gender."[10] Even homosexual authors agree that homosexuals are disproportionately represented in sex crimes against minors. They found that 73 percent of homosexuals surveyed had sex with boys sixteen to nineteen years of age or younger.[11]

Brian W. Clowes and David L. Sonnier studied the research on this subject and came to the same conclusion: homosexuals are more likely to abuse minors than heterosexuals are.[12] In a nationwide survey of school principals, it was found that they received thirteen times as many complaints about homosexuals molesting students than they did about heterosexuals abusing students.[13] Other studies report that homosexual teachers are ninety to a hundred times more likely to molest students than their heterosexual colleagues are.[14]

The John Jay Studies

An important dissenting voice on this subject was raised by the John Jay researchers. Regarding the prevalence of homosexuals in the

[8] Kurt Freund, Robin Watson, and Douglas Rienzo, "Heterosexuality, Homosexuality, and Erotic Age Preference", *Journal of Sex Research* 26 (February 1989): 107.

[9] Ray Blanchard et al., "Fraternal Birth Order and Sexual Orientation in Pedophiles", *Archives of Sexual Behavior* 29 (2000): 471.

[10] Marie E. Tomeo et al., "Comparative Data of Childhood and Adolescence Molestation in Heterosexual and Homosexual Persons", *Archives of Sexual Behavior* 30 (2001): 539.

[11] Karla Jay and Allen Young, *The Gay Report: Lesbians and Gay Men Speak Out about Sexual Experiences and Lifestyles* (New York: Summit Books, 1979), 275.

[12] Brian W. Clowes and David L. Sonnier, "Child Molestation by Homosexuals and Heterosexuals", *Homiletic & Pastoral Review* (May 2005): 44–54.

[13] J. Dressler, "Gay Teachers: A Disesteemed Minority in an Overly Esteemed Profession", *Rutgers/Camden Law Journal* (1978): 399–445.

[14] Ibid.

priesthood and the sexual abuse of minors, they concluded that "if it were the case that there were more homosexual men in the seminaries in the 1980s, this increase does not correspond to an increase in the number of boys who were abused."[15] If this is true, they reason, it provides evidence that there is no relationship between homosexuals and the sexual abuse of minors.

What this line of reasoning fails to grasp is that it is not so much the influx of homosexuals into seminaries that matters most; it is the composition and culture of the priesthood that counts. Heterosexual priests were driven to leave in the 1970s after a surge in the number of homosexuals entering the priesthood, the net result being a higher concentration of homosexuals in the priesthood than ever before. In addition, a welcoming culture greeted homosexuals in the 1960s and the 1970s, making life more appealing to them while having a reverse effect on heterosexual priests.

Father Krzysztof Olaf Charamsa, an author on this subject and an admitted homosexual, came to the same conclusion:

> Throughout the 1970s, several hundred men left the priesthood each year, many of them for marriage. As straight priests left the church for domestic bliss, the proportion of remaining priests who were gay grew. In the United States the *Los Angeles Times* found that 28 percent of priests between the ages of 46 and 55 reported that they were gay. This statistic is higher than the percentage found in other age brackets and reflected the outflow of straight priests throughout the 1970s and 1980s.[16]

Even Father James Martin, a champion of LGBT rights, agrees. He says that "in some venues, groups of homosexual priests may develop a network of close friendships among themselves that consciously or unconsciously exclude heterosexual priests." This, he concedes, "makes heterosexual priests feel marginalized"; some then choose to

---

[15] Karen J. Terry, John Jay College of Criminal Justice (JJCCJ), and United States Conference of Catholic Bishops (USCCB), *The Causes and Context of Sexual Abuse of Minors by Catholic Priests in the United States, 1950–2010: A Report Presented to the United States Conference of Catholic Bishops by the John Jay College Research Team* (Washington, D.C.: United States Conference of Catholic Bishops, 2011), 100.

[16] Ross Benes, "How the Catholic Priesthood Became an Unlikely Haven for Many Gay Men", *Slate*, April 20, 2017, https://slate.com/human-interest/2017/04/how-the-catholic-priesthood-became-a-haven-for-many-gay-men.html.

move to another residence. "Such insularity can also effectively discourage heterosexual vocations from feeling welcome in rectories, seminaries and religious communities."[17]

Father Paul Sullins holds a doctorate in sociology and has published a study of clergy sexual abuse that directly challenges the John Jay conclusion. "The [John Jay] authors reported that they came to this conclusion without collecting or examining any direct data on 'the sexual identity of priests and how it changed over the years'", Sullins noted. Instead, they relied on "subjective clinical estimates and second-hand narrative reports of apparent homosexual activity in seminaries." He faults them for this, saying, "such reports could not establish 'whether the open expression of sexual identity in seminaries in [the 1980s meant] that more men were entering the seminary understanding themselves as homosexual [or were] more likely to *reveal* themselves as homosexual ... than in prior decades'" (his emphasis).[18] He raises an important point. More important, he did his own study of this issue.

Sullins examined the data on homosexuals in the priesthood and the prevalence of sexual abuse. "The share of homosexual men in the priesthood rose from twice that of the general population in the 1950s to eight times the general population in the 1980s. This trend was strongly correlated with increasing child sex abuse." He does not exaggerate. His findings showed that "the increase or decrease in the percent of male victims correlated almost perfectly (.98) with the increase or decrease of homosexual men in the priesthood." He also delved into the homosexual subculture. "A quarter of priests ordained in the late 1960s report the existence of a homosexual subculture in the seminary, rising to over half of priests ordained in the 1980s. This trend was strongly correlated with increasing child sex abuse."[19]

In an interview, Sullins explained his findings with even greater clarity. "In the 1950s, about 3% of priests were of a homosexual orientation, by their own reports. By the 1980s, that had risen to over

[17]James Martin, "The Challenges and Gifts of the Homosexual Priest", *America*, November 4, 2000, http://www.americamagazine.org/faith/2000/11/04/challenges-and-gifts-homo sexual-priest.

[18]D. Paul Sullins, "Is Catholic Clergy Sex Abuse Related to Homosexual Priests?", The Ruth Institute, 2018, 2–3.

[19]Ibid.

16%. So we have a fivefold increase in the percentage of priests who were homosexual, in a pretty straight line from the 1950s through the 1980s. And we have a very similar increase in abuse incidents over that same period, and we don't know the sexual orientation of any particular abuser. So we're inferring from the association of those two correlations that there's some influence of one on the other. So my conclusion has to be the opposite of that of the John Jay report."[20]

Identity versus Behavior

My training as a sociologist also led me to examine critically some portions of the John Jay studies. Importantly, I find the methodology used by these researchers to be competent. My criticisms are limited to their interpretation of some of the data, not the collection of it, which was done professionally.

It has been widely noted by those who deny any association between homosexuality and the sexual abuse of minors that the John Jay authors came to this same conclusion. They did. But how could they when they admit that most of the abuse involved male-on-male sex acts? Their answer: many of the priests who had sex with adolescent males did not consider themselves to be homosexuals. "It is therefore possible that, although the victims of priests were most often male, thus defining the *acts* as homosexual, the priest did not at any time recognize his *identity* as homosexual" (their italics).[21] They also found that while over 75 percent of priests had a clear sense of their sexual identity prior to entering the seminary, the figure for accused priests was only 63 percent (it was 83 percent for nonaccused priests).[22]

Sexual identity is an interesting psychological variable, but it can never be a substitute for reality. We know that in the clergy sexual abuse scandal, men had sex with men. That is called homosexuality.

[20] Matthew Bunson, "Is Catholic Clergy Sex Abuse Related to Homosexual Priests?", *National Catholic Register*, November 2, 2018, https://www.ncregister.com/news/is-catholic-clergy-sex-abuse-related-to-homosexual-priests.

[21] Terry, JJCCJ, USCCB, *Causes and Context*, 36.

[22] Ibid., 65.

It matters not if the victimizer does not consider his behavior to be homosexual in nature. Nor does it matter if he is unsure of his sexual identity. What matters is what he did—he is defined by his behavior, not his perception of it.

To be sure, perception may *function* as reality, but that is not the same as saying that reality is determined by perception. It is not. Rachel Anne Dolezal's parents are both white, yet the former NAACP chapter president and college instructor said she was black. She was not. Her parents, who were of European ancestry, said she tried to pass as black. When this hit the media, she resigned from her NAACP post and was dismissed from her position as an instructor at Eastern Washington University. In 2015, she finally admitted that she was "born white to white parents". Yet she still considered herself to be black.[23] She is delusional, as are homosexual priests who think they are not homosexuals. Self-identity is not a dispositive criterion upon which the truth turns.

Here's another way to look at this issue. If the priests who had sex with adolescent males considered themselves to be heterosexual, would it make any sense to call this a heterosexual scandal? Would the John Jay researchers list them as heterosexual? This is a dodge. Indeed, it is a sleight of hand, one grounded in politics, not in science. Men who choose to have sex with women are heterosexual; men who choose to have sex with men are homosexual.

Margaret Smith is a criminologist who worked on the John Jay studies. Here is what she said in reply to a comment I made about the "homosexual crisis" in the Church. "The participation in homosexual acts is not the same as sexual identity as a gay man."[24] She is technically right, but it is of no consequence. Yes, behavior and identity are not the same. So what? The fact remains that if most of the abuse is homosexual in nature, then we have a "homosexual crisis"; it is quite independent of the molester's sexual identity.

It should not come as a surprise that the person most responsible for pushing the notion of sexual identity in Catholic circles was a homosexual priest, Father Donald Goergen, O.P. He was

---

[23] "Rachel Dolezal Admits She's White on 'The Real'", *Hollywood Reporter*, November 2, 2015, https://www.hollywoodreporter.com/news/rachel-dolezal-white-the-real-836121.

[24] Fitzgibbons and O'Leary, "Sexual Abuse of Minors", 255.

a member of the Catholic Coalition for Gay Civil Rights. In his 1974 book, *The Sexual Celibate*, he insisted that sexual identity "in its most mature phase" was a *"feeling"*, not an empirically verifiable condition.[25] It is this kind of subjectivism, which is central to the gay agenda, that allows for wrongheaded conclusions. Today it has evolved into the idea that a man who thinks he is a woman is therefore a woman. This is madness. No one can change his or her chromosomal makeup.

Ironically, the John Jay researchers' denial of the role of homosexuals in clergy sexual abuse is undercut by their own data. For instance, they found that priests accused of sexually abusing a minor were "more likely to have had same-sex and/or bisexual experiences than nonaccused priests".[26] Given what we have learned from the data, this is exactly what we would expect: it confirms the proposition that homosexual priests are mostly responsible for the scandal.

The John Jay researchers found that those priests who identified as being homosexual were more likely to be sexually active after they entered the priesthood than those who identified as being heterosexual. Priests who had more positive views toward homosexuality were also more likely to have had sex after ordination.[27] This makes sense: if a man with homosexual tendencies thought homosexual acts were not wrong, why would he not engage in them?

The researchers also found that the majority of those priests who had sex with men before they entered the seminary often had sex in the seminary.[28] Again, this is hardly surprising. Had they been carefully screened, this might not have happened. Moreover, priests who had sex with other men before they entered the seminary and who abused minors after ordination were more likely to victimize males than females.[29] It would be incomprehensible if the researchers had found otherwise.

It is significant that nothing was said in either of the two John Jay reports about heterosexual men who had sex with women before

[25] Enrique Rueda, *The Homosexual Network: Private Lives and Public Policy* (Old Greenwich, Conn.: Devin Adair, 1982), 334–35.
[26] Terry, JJCCJ, and USCCB, *Causes and Context*, 65.
[27] Ibid., 63.
[28] Ibid., 62.
[29] Ibid.

entering the seminary. Were they sexually active during or after their seminary years? Perhaps owing to the fact that they account for only a small portion of the abuse, the researchers did not probe this issue.

It is interesting to note that only those who had sex while in the seminary, but not before, were significantly more likely to abuse a male.[30] This suggests that the collapse of accountability that took place in many of the seminaries gave a green light to homosexual seminarians, some of whom became promiscuous. This abandonment of restraint, in turn, led them to become sexually active with innocent adolescent males. That is quite an indictment of these seminaries.

What about those priests who were given residential treatment following an allegation of sexually abusing a minor? Did they change their behavior? No. The majority continued to be sexually active.[31] It seems nothing was going to stop them. Had they been bounced from the priesthood, they would no doubt have continued their ways, but at least they would no longer have caused harm as ministers of Christ and his Church.

Rejection of Celibacy

How many homosexual priests are sexually active? Jason Berry explored this question with several priests. One who had recently left the priesthood told Berry, "Every gay priest I know is sexually active, without exception."[32] Of the eighteen homosexual priests Berry interviewed for a reporting assignment, only two were not sexually active.[33] In a study of fifty gay priests, forty-eight of them were sexually active, and 60 percent admitted to having group sex. Ninety percent said they rejected mandatory celibacy.[34]

Regarding the last figure, it is easy to understand why these promiscuous homosexual priests reject the Church's teaching on celibacy: they say it doesn't apply to them. "I am still chaste", said a sexually active homosexual priest (he was interviewed by the *Baltimore Sun*).

[30] Ibid.
[31] Ibid., 3.
[32] Jason Berry, *Lead Us Not into Temptation* (New York: Doubleday, 1992), 213.
[33] Ibid., 211.
[34] Ibid., 185.

Pointing to his head and heart, he said, "I define chastity up here, not at the genitals."[35]

Priests who have sexual relations, whether heterosexual or homosexual, sometimes claim that their vow of celibacy forbids them only from marriage, not from sexual relations. A case in point is a homosexual priest who had sex with adolescent males and was sent to Saint Luke for treatment. He rationalized his behavior by saying celibacy "meant being single and not having a wife".[36] Even some bishops agree with this assessment. Bishop Thomas J. Gumbleton said, "Active homosexuality would not violate the vow of celibacy or the promise of celibacy." He added that active homosexuality "violated the Sixth Commandment",[37] but since the sexual revolution, who cares about that or even knows what it means? Is it any wonder that gay priests have been morally malformed?

Father James Martin explains that many homosexuals, including gay priests, have not "received" the Church's teaching on leading a celibate life, defined as abstaining from sexual relations. He says that for a Church teaching to be considered authoritative, it must be accepted by Catholics. "From what I can tell, in the LGBT community, the teaching that LGBT people must be celibate their entire lives—not just before marriage as it is for most people, but for their entire lives—has not been received."[38] When asked why he did not discuss chastity in a book he wrote about LGBT Catholics, he said that because they have not received this Church teaching, he decided to focus on "places of common ground".[39] He did not explain why, as part of his outreach to these people, he did not make it his goal to help them "receive" this teaching.

David Carlin notes that, for many bishops, to get rid of the abuse is all that counts. "But clerical homosexuality is more fundamental than abuse of minors", he says. "The way some bishops talk," he

---

[35] Ibid., 212.

[36] Ibid., 139.

[37] Ibid., 216.

[38] Father James Martin's remarks were offered in a YouTube interview on September 20, 2017, quoted in Dan Hitchens, "Fr. Martin Does Not Actually Say", *First Things* (October 2, 2017), https://www.firstthings.com/web-exclusives/2017/10/fr-martin-does-not-actually-say.

[39] Judy Roberts, "Father James Martin Explaining His Vision Regarding 'LGBT' Catholics", *National Catholic Register*, July 10, 2017, http://www.ncregister.com/daily-news/father-james-martin-explains-his-vision-regarding-lgbt-catholics.

adds, "it's as if, when they speak of cleaning up the Church, they mean that they'll put an end to priestly sex with minors; when priests limit themselves to consensual sex with adults, either adult men or women, then we'll have solved our problem." He properly sees this position as "absurd". If a priest can't keep his vows, as they are properly understood, Carlin opines, "he should resign from the priesthood".[40]

The John Jay researchers should have allowed their own data to drive their conclusions. Instead, they employed the subjective notion of sexual identity. The objective evidence they culled so authoritatively indicates that there is a clear link between homosexuality—at least as evidenced in the priesthood—and the sexual abuse of minors.

[40]David Carlin, "'Gay' Priests and Indulgence of Homosexuality", The Catholic Thing, November 30, 2018, https://www.thecatholicthing.org/2018/11/30/gay-priests-and-indulgence-of-homosexuality/.

9

The Role of Homosexuality:
Does Homosexuality Cause
the Sexual Abuse of Minors?

Does homosexuality cause the sexual abuse of minors? No. Is there a link between homosexuality and the sexual abuse of minors? Yes. What is that link? Immaturity.

Father Hans Zollner is a German Jesuit and a member of Pope Francis' Commission for the Protection of Minors. When asked about whether homosexuality causes the sexual abuse of minors, he lost his temper. He said, "There's a small, but very fierce part of people who think that homosexuality causes abusive behavior, which if you think a little bit is pretty much nonsense, but people stick to that."[1] While he is technically correct, his answer was misleading.

Almost all human behavior is caused by multiple factors. That is why social scientists speak about multivariate analysis. Unicausality, behavior resulting from only one cause, is extremely rare. One such example would be a person who pulls his hand away when he inadvertently touches a hot stove. The heat is the cause, or the independent variable, and the pulling away of the hand is the effect, or the dependent variable. Sometimes there are intervening variables: when the independent variable does not adequately explain the existence of the dependent variable, there may be some variable between the two that better explains the relationship. For instance, there is a relationship between education level (the independent variable) and

[1] Shannon Levitt and Inés San Martín, "Sex Abuse Prevention Expert Says 'No Simple Answers to Complex Problems'", *Crux*, November 13, 2019, https://cruxnow.com/church-in-the-americas/2019/11/sex-abuse-prevention-expert-says-no-simple-answers-to-complex-problems/.

income (the dependent variable). But does education level determine how much money one earns? No, but if we add occupation as the intervening variable, we see that education level is related to higher-status jobs, and that, in turn, explains the income level.[2]

We have already seen that homosexuals, in and out of the priest-hood, are overrepresented among those who sexually abuse minors. But this is not the same as saying that homosexuality causes abuse: it is simply not true that most homosexuals abuse minors. We still need to explain, however, why homosexuals are disproportionately repre-sented in abuse cases.

Let us consider two other examples to make the same point. The Irish are overrepresented among alcoholics. Chinese Americans are overrepresented among gamblers. Obviously, being Irish does not cause one to become an alcoholic, any more than being Chinese causes one to be a gambler. But something must explain the relationship. That something is history.

Dr. Garrett O'Connor has studied Irish history—alcoholism is nothing new to the Irish—and offers a cogent observation: "The net effect of religious persecution, land rape, extreme poverty and inter-mittent abuse of military power by English colonists in Ireland during 700 years of continuous occupation was to produce a national inferi-ority complex in Irish Catholics which I identify as cultural malignant shame, characterized by chronic fear, suppressed rage, self-loathing, procrastination, low self-esteem, false pride and a vulnerability to use alcohol for suffering—past and present."[3]

There are many causes and effects in this account. Suffice it to say that once a culture has been shaped by such powerful forces, certain characteristics are baked into it. Alcohol use is one of those cultural characteristics. So it may be that the intervening variable between being Irish (the independent variable) and alcoholism (the dependent variable) is the adversity that marks Irish history.

From 1882 to 1943, the Chinese Exclusion Act barred migration from China to the United States. At that time, there were many

---

[2] Ashley Crossman, "How Intervening Variables Work in Sociology", ThoughtCo, May 15, 2019, https://www.thoughtco.com/intervening-variable-3026367.

[3] Garrett O'Connor, "Breaking the Silence: The Irish and Drink", *Irish America*, January 26, 2012, http://www.irishamerica.com/2012/01/breaking-the-code-of-silence-the-irish-and-drink.

more Chinese men than Chinese women in America. Chinese men had come to California in droves after gold was discovered in 1849. Then the 1882 law made matters worse by barring Chinese women from coming to the States. How does this explain the overrepresentation of the Chinese among gamblers? Whenever there is a high concentration of men, such as in the armed services, certain male characteristics (e.g., risky behaviors) tend to dominate. One of them is gambling. It is the high concentration of Chinese men, shaped by their history in America, that explains their relatively high rates of gambling. In other words, it is their demographic profile, shaped by historical factors, that explains their propensity to gamble.

Regarding homosexuals, their higher rates of sexual abuse is not caused by their sexual orientation. However, their sexual orientation is related to their immature status, and that explains their greater likelihood to abuse minors. Immaturity is the intervening variable. In other words, their immaturity is a function of their sexual orientation—homosexuals are more likely to be immature than heterosexuals—and immaturity is linked to the molestation of minors.

Factors That Contribute to Abusive Behavior

Before examining the evidence of immaturity and the role it plays in the psychological profile of homosexuals, it is helpful to discuss other factors that account for the higher rates of molestation among homosexuals.

Men with same-sex attractions are much more likely to have been sexually abused than other men. Some studies have found that the prevalence is significantly higher. There is a consensus that men who have been sexually abused as children are more likely as adults to abuse children.[4] Saint Luke Institute's records on priests who are sex offenders found that more than 50 percent of them were abused as children; the estimate in the general male abuser population is about 30 percent.[5]

---

[4] Richard Fitzgibbons and Dale O'Leary, "Sexual Abuse of Minors by Catholic Clergy", *Linacre Quarterly* 78, no. 3 (August 2011): 255.

[5] Curtis Bryant, "Psychological Treatment of Priest Sex Offenders", *America*, April 1, 2002, 15.

Similarly, the John Jay authors found that "priests who were sexually abused as minors themselves were more likely to abuse minors than those without a history of abuse."[6] This is a tragic fact of life that must enter into the screening process of candidates for the priesthood. There are other problems, of a more organic nature, that also bear scrutiny.

After reviewing the scientific research on the psychological profile of homosexuals, Dr. Richard Fitzgibbons and Dale O'Leary found that men with same-sex attractions "are more likely than the general public to have psychiatric disorders, substance abuse problems, suicidal ideation, STDs, and a lack of fidelity and permanency in loving relationships."[7] They cite studies from New Zealand, the Netherlands, and England that come to similar conclusions. Even gay-rights advocates admit that homosexuals are plagued with psychiatric problems, though they tend to blame their condition on a hostile society. But as Fitzgibbons and O'Leary point out, the Netherlands is quite tolerant of homosexuals, yet the same problems are evident there.

They conclude that "the evidence is overwhelming that self-identified 'gay' men are more likely to have psychological issues, substance abuse problems, and problems with authority figures."[8] For these reasons, they recommend implementing the policy of prohibiting homosexuals from entering the priesthood if they exhibit "deep-seated homosexual tendencies". This would cut down on "future homosexual abuse of adolescents and children".[9]

The lack of fidelity and permanency of loving relationships that Fitzgibbons and O'Leary mention as a characteristic of homosexuals is expressed most visibly in the promiscuous lifestyle of many homosexuals. According to practicing psychotherapist Zev Ballen, commenting on promiscuity in general, "the correlation between sexual

[6] Karen J. Terry, John Jay College of Criminal Justice (JJCCJ), and United States Conference of Catholic Bishops (USCCB), *The Causes and Context of Sexual Abuse of Minors by Catholic Priests in the United States, 1950–2010: A Report Presented to the United States Conference of Catholic Bishops by the John Jay College Research Team* (Washington, D.C.: United States Conference of Catholic Bishops, 2011), 4.

[7] Fitzgibbons and O'Leary, "Sexual Abuse of Minors", 264–65.

[8] Ibid., 269.

[9] Ibid.

promiscuity, depression, and suicide is very clear. Multitudes of people are attempting to fill up with sex—this breeds guilt, self-hatred, emptiness and shame."[10] Promiscuous homosexuals have these problems as well as others.

In 2017, *Huffington Post* published a brutally frank account by journalist Michael Hobbes of promiscuity in the gay community. "Gay people are now," he said, "depending on the study, between 2 and 10 times more likely than straight people to take their own lives. We're twice as likely to have a major depressive episode." Much of this is traced to the failure of homosexuals to form strong bonds. "Despite all the talk of our 'chosen families,' gay men have fewer close friends than straight people or gay women."[11]

How can it be that, in a time of growing acceptance of gay rights, so many homosexuals are unhappy? The conventional wisdom, one widely shared by those working in the media, the schools, and the government, was that the legalization of gay marriage and its acceptance by the public would lead to an overall increase in the well-being of gays. It sounds plausible, but there is no evidence to support it.

Indeed, as Hobbes shows, "in the Netherlands, where gay marriage has been legal since 2001, gay men remain three times more likely to suffer from a mood disorder than straight men, and 10 times more likely to engage in 'suicidal self-harm.'" It is no different in Sweden, the sexual Shangri-la of elites. The Swedes have had civil unions since 1965 and gay marriage since 2009, but "men married to men have triple the suicide rate of men married to women."[12]

Were gays better off in the closet than out? According to Hobbes, "A study published in 2015 found that rates of anxiety and depression were higher in men who had recently come out than in men who were still closeted."[13] This is not a brief to force homosexuals back into the closet, but it is a wake-up call to those who think that social acceptance redounds to better psychological health for homosexuals.

---

[10] Zev Ballen, "Sexual Promiscuity and Suicide", Breslev, updated December 29, 2020, https://www.breslev.co.il/articles/family_daily_life/physical_and_emotional_health/sexual_promiscuity_and_suicide.aspx?id=18424&language=english.

[11] Michael Hobbes, "Together Alone: The Epidemic of Gay Loneliness", *Huffington Post*, March 2, 2017, https://highline.huffingtonpost.com/articles/en/gay-loneliness/.

[12] Hobbes, "Together Alone".

[13] Ibid.

Immaturity in Homosexuals

It seems that immaturity is the variable that best explains the link between homosexuality and the sexual abuse of minors. It is worth recalling that the John Jay researchers reported that accused priests often cited their own immaturity as a way of rationalizing their behavior: "A common excuse for offending was sexual immaturity." The report also noted that "in addition to the sexual immaturity, they also expressed emotional immaturity."[14] While this cannot be accepted as exculpatory, these molesting priests have an accurate understanding of their own condition. Indeed, they made the correct diagnosis: their homosexual condition is related to their immaturity, both sexually and emotionally, which explains their propensity to abuse minors. They are immature males who relate, developmentally, to other immature males.

Sigmund Freud studied homosexuals and was inconclusive as to the origins of same-sex attraction. He did not see homosexuals as being abnormal, but he described people who are attracted to those of the same sex as having "contrary sexual feelings" or as being "inverts", thus calling homosexuality "inversion".[15] Freud did not quarrel with the conventional understanding of heterosexuality, saying that "the normal sexual aim is regarded as being the union of the genitals in the act known as copulation",[16] and he certainly understood what drives heterosexuals: "No doubt the strongest force working against a permanent inversion of the sexual object is the attraction which the opposing sexual characters exercise upon one another."[17]

Freud attributed homosexuality to "a certain arrest of sexual development".[18] He came to this conclusion because he saw normal psychosexual development as leading to heterosexuality.[19] What blocks this development? According to Freud, a man's psychosexual

---

[14] Terry, JJCCJ, and USCCB, *Causes and Context*, 105.

[15] James Strachey, *Sigmund Freud: Three Essays on the Theory of Sexuality* (New York: Basic Books, 2000), xxxix, 2.

[16] Ibid., 15.

[17] Ibid., 95.

[18] Sigmund Freud, "Letter to an American Mother", *American Psychiatric Journal* 107, no. 10 (1951): 787, Internet History Sourcebooks Project, Fordham University, https://source books.fordham.edu/pwh/freud1.asp.

[19] Joseph Nicolosi, "What Freud Really Said about Homosexuality—and Why", *Journal of Human Sexuality* 7 (2016): 24–42.

development can be hindered by an inordinate attachment to his mother: "In all our male homosexual cases the subjects had had a very intense erotic attachment to a female person, as a rule their mother.... This attachment was evoked or encouraged by too much tenderness on the part of the mother herself, and further reinforced by the small part played by the father during their childhood."[20]

Freud was quite blunt about the immaturity of homosexuals. He said that "any established aberration from normal sexuality" was "an instance of developmental inhibition and infantilism". He further noted that "sexual aberration in adults—perversion, fetishism, inversion (homosexuality) ... will reveal an event such as I have suggested, leading to a fixation in childhood."[21]

Carl Jung also linked homosexuality to a problem with the mother-son relationship. In his masterful book on Jung, Robert H. Hopcke wrote that "Jung viewed homosexuality as a form of immaturity caused, in part, by a disturbance of the relationship with the parents, particularly the mother."[22] Like Freud, he posited that the most natural human expression of sexuality was heterosexual. As Hopcke put it, "Jung's attitude toward homosexuality as psychologically immature or infantile is based on a teleology that sees human sexuality resulting invariably in genital heterosexual practice."[23] This should not be controversial, but given the reluctance of scholars to say anything that could be seen as critical of homosexuals, it is. Even Hopcke is dismayed by Jung's position.[24]

Attempts have been made to discredit the Freudian link between immaturity and homosexuality. For example, a study by California State University professor Mark Biernbaum, which claimed to show that there was no difference between heterosexuals and homosexuals in their level of maturity, came to this conclusion by measuring how college students employed certain defense mechanisms.[25] The

---

[20]James Strachey, *The Standard Edition of the Complete Psychological Works of Sigmund Freud*, vol. 11 (London: Hogarth Press, 1932), 99. The original work was published in 1910.

[21]Nicolosi, "What Freud Really Said".

[22]Robert H. Hopcke, *Jung, Jungians, and Homosexuality* (Boston: Shambhala Publications, 1991), 23.

[23]Ibid., 58.

[24]Ibid.

[25]Mark A. Biernbaum and Michele Ruscio, "Differences between Matched Heterosexual and Non-Heterosexual College Students on Defense Mechanisms and Psychopathological Symptoms", *Journal of Homosexuality* 48, no. 1 (2004): 125–41.

measure he decided upon, however, is only tangentially related to what Freud was discussing. Defense mechanisms have little to do with mature sexual development.

If homosexuals are suffering from a lack of psychosexual maturity, how does this relate to the sexual abuse of minors? It might be easier for homosexual adults to relate to those who, like themselves, have not matured. Some could be stuck in their own adolescence. Monsignor Stephen Rossetti, a psychologist, has observed that

> a significant number of priests who sexually molest minors are involved with post-pubescent adolescent males, about 14 to 17 years of age. It appears to be true that many in this sub-population of priest child-molesters are homosexually oriented. But theirs is a particular kind of homosexuality, which one might call "regressed" or "stunted." These homosexual men are emotionally stuck in adolescence themselves, and so are at risk for being sexually active with teenage males. The issue is not so much homosexuality but rather their stunted emotional development.[26]

Yes, homosexuality is not the cause of sexual abuse, but the inability of some homosexuals to free themselves of their adolescence puts them "at risk for being sexually active with teenage males".

A priest at the University of Chicago who studied the homosexual clergy estimated that, in the 1980s, about half of American priests were homosexual and "a large number of them psychosexually arrested".[27] While others may be reluctant to speculate why this is so, it seems that their homosexual orientation is a result of their psychosexual immaturity. Sister Marie-Paul Ross, a Canadian sister who holds a Ph.D. in clinical sexology, noted the sexual immaturity of molesting priests and the need to "treat deep anxieties", such as childhood traumas, as experienced by these priests.[28]

Sister Fran Ferder, a therapist who treated abusing priests in Seattle, witnessed the same phenomenon. She argues that "there is a tendency among many homosexual men, particularly in their twenties,

[26] Stephen J. Rossetti, "The Catholic Church and Child Sexual Abuse", *America*, April 22, 2002, 11.

[27] Jason Berry, *Lead Us Not into Temptation* (New York: Doubleday, 1992), 186.

[28] Philippe Vaillancourt, "Sexual Immaturity, Poor Formation to Blame for Abuse Crisis, Says Nun", *CatholicPhilly.com*, April 1, 2019, https://catholicphilly.com/2019/04/news/world-news/canadian-nun-sexologist-catholics-must-increase-their-sexual-maturity/.

to experience a delayed adolescence." How does this affect men studying for the priesthood? "I think some Catholic gay men delay it altogether and choose seminary as an acceptable way of not having to deal with sexuality. And then it comes out when they're in their twenties or thirties, emotionally at an age fifteen or sixteen—a regressive homosexuality."[29]

In the late 1960s, at the start of the sexual revolution, four psychologists studied the psychosexual development of men entering the priesthood. They found that 70 percent were "psychosexually immature, exhibiting traits of heterosexual retardation, confusion concerning sexual role, fear of sexuality, effeminacy and potentially homosexual dispositions."[30] Much of the abuse could have been avoided if bishops and seminary rectors had seen these traits as warning signs and refused to ordain men whose severe immaturity rendered them unfit for the priesthood.

David Finkelhor is often cited as an authority on this subject in the John Jay reports. He identified three factors associated with the sexual abuse of minors. First, he said, the molesting priest has "immature emotional needs", which allow him to "relate better to children than adults". Second, "many who abuse children have some level of sexual arousal to children, either innate or learned." Third, abusers "may experience some type of blockage, or an inability to have sexual and/or emotional needs met in adult relationships".[31] While this is the profile of abusers, it also resembles the profile of many homosexuals.

Father John Geoghan, the infamous Boston molester, exhibited the very characteristics we would expect. After graduating from high school in 1952, he entered Cardinal O'Connell seminary. In 1954, his rector wrote, "Geoghan has given the faculty of this seminary cause for concern in the past two years.... He has a pronounced immaturity ... a little feminine in his manner of speech and approach."[32] They did not know then that "pronounced immaturity" was a red flag. Today, there are many who still don't know it.

[29]Berry, *Lead Us Not into Temptation*, 267.

[30]Leon Podles, *Sacrilege: Sexual Abuse in the Catholic Church* (Baltimore: Crossland Press, 2008), 93.

[31]Terry, JJCCJ, and USCCB, *Causes and Context*, 68.

[32]Podles, *Sacrilege*, 144.

One priest who understands what immaturity signals is Father Paul Shaughnessy. He writes of the "psychological disorder of the man locked into a compulsive homosexual libido which is marked by an adolescent selfishness and hunger for gratification and an adolescent irresponsibility and lack of control". He contends that these men evince in their sexuality an "immaturity, hostility, and irresponsibility" that leads them to put their own gratification above the common good.[33]

USA Today issued a revealing study of accused priests in 2019. A former Roman Catholic brother, John Dagwell, pleaded guilty to molesting a student in 1988. When released from prison, he said, "I've stayed away from adolescents." The reporter took note of his apartment. "As he spoke, three teddy bears sat on his television and a half-dozen stuffed Disney dolls—Mickey Mouse, Goofy, Jiminy Cricket—were carefully arranged on a China cabinet."[34] Another abuser, a former Franciscan monk, said, "There is something about me that is happier when accompanied by a small boy.... Perhaps besides the sexual element, the child in me wants a playmate."[35]

Narcissism

If there is one factor other than immaturity that is common among abusers, it is narcissism. Indeed, narcissism is a close cousin of immaturity, and when the two are combined in the same person, they create a potent force for doing harm to others.

Freud defined narcissism as the adoration one gives oneself in light of being an object of sexual desire. Freud noted a narcissistic element in the homosexuals he studied: "A strong libidinal fixation to the

[33] Paul Shaughnessy, "The Gay Priest Problem", *Catholic World Report* (November 2000), posted on Catholic Culture, https://www.catholicculture.org/culture/library/view .cfm?recnum=12047.

[34] Lindsay Schnell and Sam Ruland, "Thousands of Catholic Priests Were Accused of Sexual Abuse, Then What Happened? An Investigation Reveals Most Have Become the Priest Next Door", *USA Today*, updated November 13, 2019, https://www.usatoday.com /in-depth/news/nation/2019/11/11/catholic-sexual-abuse-accused-priests-arent-sex -offender-registry/4012206002/.

[35] Ibid.

narcissistic type of object-choice is to be included in the predisposition to manifest homosexuality."[36]

A priest I know who was in a supervisory role governing young priests once told me how difficult it was for him to deal with homosexual clerics. He had to confront them on several occasions, and eventually they decided to resign rather than live under his strictures. I asked if they were sexually active. He said he did not know. Then what was the problem? Their spending habits: they spent money on food and booze far exceeding their budget. It was not greed that he observed so much as narcissism. Jason Berry tells the story of "Father X", a homosexual abuser who "spent lavishly decorating his previous rectory; boys spent the night there."[37]

The efforts to make oneself sexually attractive to oneself can cost a lot of money. Father Paul Shanley confessed to one of his victims, Kevin English, who was seventeen, that he stayed in the priesthood for the money. The $1,500 monthly stipend wasn't enough, he said, even though $1,500 was not a meager amount in 1990. English told *Vanity Fair* that Shanley drove flashy cars, exercised regularly, and carried $500 cash in his pocket.[38]

This same kind of behavior has been noted among high-ranking clerics. A close adviser to Pope Francis, Cardinal Rodríguez of Honduras, had an auxiliary bishop resign "over homosexual and financial impropriety", leading forty seminarians in his diocese to "publish a letter asking him to please root out the homosexual network in the seminary".[39]

The link between alleged sexual and financial misconduct is what did in West Virginia's leading Catholic, Bishop Michael J. Bransfield, in 2019:

---

[36] Sigmund Freud, *Introductory Lectures on Psychoanalysis*, trans. James Strachey (New York: W. W. Norton, 1977), 530.

[37] Berry, *Lead Us Not into Temptation*, 141.

[38] Maureen Orth, "Unholy Communion", *Vanity Fair*, April 18, 2008, https://www.vanityfair.com/news/2002/08/orth200208.

[39] Ralph Martin, "Dear Troubled Catholics—A Letter from Ralph Martin on the Crisis", *National Catholic Register*, August 2, 2018, posted on Renewal Ministries, July 31, 2018, https://www.renewalministries.net/dear-troubled-catholics-a-letter-from-ralph-martin-about-the-current-crisis/.

During his 13 years as bishop in West Virginia, one of the poorest states, Bransfield spent $2.4 million in church money on travel, much of it personal, which included flying in chartered jets and staying in luxury hotels, according to the report. Bransfield and several subordinates spent an average of nearly $1,000 a month on alcohol, it says. The West Virginia diocese paid $4.6 million to renovate Bransfield's church residence after a fire damaged a single bathroom. When Bransfield was in the chancery, an administrative building, fresh flowers were delivered daily, at a cost of about $100 a day—almost $182,000 in all.[40]

Narcissism goes beyond sexuality and expresses itself in other forms of self-absorption. Ray Mouton, Father Gilbert Gauthe's attorney, expressed the exasperation caused by dealing with his serial-abuser client: "Gilbert is complaining about the *food* now. I tell him it's worse in prison. You notice how pedophiles are so *narcissistic*? The self-obsession staggers me" (his italics).[41] Dr. Gerard J.M. van den Aardweg writes that "the best-established facts in relation to homosexuality point to developmental-psychological, not genetic or physiological, causation." He focuses on the effects of self-dramatization, or "inherent self-centeredness, self-importance, and perception that they are the center of the world". When this occurs, "emotional maturity is more or less severely hampered, for psychic maturity depends on the process of the young person's de-egocentrization. Connected to this, the core of homosexual love is immature self-love; the friend/partner must love *me* before anything else. This is part of the explanation of the instability and utopian character of homosexual affairs."[42]

Some homosexual writers and scholars have been very honest about the immature and narcissistic characteristics of some homosexuals. An Italian writer told an association of psychologists that homosexuality is the result of an "acute lack of love in childhood [and] an affective

---

[40] Michelle Boorstein, Shawn Boburg, and Robert O'Harrow Jr., "W. Va. Bishop Gave Powerful Cardinals and Other Priests $350,000 in Cash Gifts before His Ouster, Church Records Show", *Washington Post*, June 5, 2019, A1.

[41] Ibid., 72.

[42] Gerard J.M. van den Aardweg, "On the Psychogenesis of Homosexuality", *Linacre Quarterly* 78, no. 3 (August 2011): 340.

immaturity". He confessed, "Many men like me are not easy to love. We are self-centered and capricious as children." He dreamed of the day when he would "stop passing whole days looking for an occasional sexual relationship on the internet" and when he would no longer "watch a muscular guy that goes into the metro [subway] and imagine the anatomical parts of his body".[43]

Self-Destructive Behaviors

Marshall Kirk, a researcher in neuropsychiatry, and Hunter Madsen, who earned a Ph.D. in politics from Harvard University, coauthored an influential book on homosexuality that won great praise from activists; it is still heralded for its launch of the LGBT agenda. Both men are homosexuals, and though most of their book, *After the Ball*, is a pro-homosexual manifesto of sorts, in one chapter they list ten "misbehaviors" that bedevil homosexuals.[44]

At base, Kirk and Madsen attribute most homosexual problems to a rejection of morality, a condition they say is widespread. Indeed, they consider the homosexual lifestyle "the pits".[45] Why do so many homosexuals reject morality? Because "amorality is damned convenient. And the moral enemy of that convenience is the value judgment." The logical consequence of this perception, Kirk and Madsen point out, is that "anything goes", leading ineluctably to a host of physical and emotional problems.[46]

According to Kirk and Madsen, the most common effects of the homosexual rejection of morality are narcissism and self-indulgent and self-destructive behavioral problems. Pathologically self-absorbed, many homosexuals find it almost impossible to form lasting relationships, considering it more attractive to ventilate their sexual drives among a number of partners. The idea that self-restraint equals

---

[43] Hilary White, "Homosexuality Due to 'Acute Lack of Love in Childhood'; Gay Blogger to Chief Italian Psychologist", LifeSiteNews, August 27, 2013, https://www.lifesitenews.com/news/homosexuality-due-to-acute-lack-of-love-in-childhood-gay-blogger-to-chief-i.

[44] Marshall Kirk and Hunter Madsen, *After the Ball: How America Will Conquer Its Fear and Hatred of Gays in the '90s* (New York: Doubleday, 1989).

[45] Ibid., 276.

[46] Ibid., 292.

self-hatred is also prevalent, leading inevitably to "drugs and kinky sex". Some resort to raunch and aggression, meaning coprophilia (the use of feces for sexual excitement) and "mere wallowing in filth", as well as other dangerous practices.[47]

Those who have studied sexual abusers have found among them such characteristics as the need for uncritical and continuous admiration; exhibitionist tendencies; affectations of mannerism, dress, and speech; impaired capacity for love; and self-destructive patterns of behavior.[48] This is a psychological profile that begets serious maladies, not only for the afflicted but for those with whom he interacts.

The self-destructive behaviors that are known to bedevil homosexuals begin in the teen years. Dating violence, forced sexual contact, suicide, and drug abuse are much more common among homosexual teens. Astonishingly, homosexual teens are more likely to report being pregnant or getting someone else pregnant.[49] That such patterns of behavior are going on well after Western societies have become increasingly tolerant of homosexuality is disturbing. This aspect was given much prominence in a documentary that aired in England, *The Trouble with Gay Men*.

The film is the work of Simon Fanshawe. A homosexual himself, he says, "I set out to expose the fact that we gay men are living the lives of teenagers, still obsessed with sex, bodies, drugs, youth, and being 'gay.'" He admits that homosexuals refuse to pass judgment on their behaviors or the lack of a moral code. The back of gay magazines, he says, "is full of rent-boy ads", so much so that "we've normalised prostitution." This has happened at a time when "we have all-but total equality. Yet we continue to behave as if we are a disconnected minority, shut out from the world of responsibility."[50]

Another homosexual writer, Jim Mangia, wrote a piece in 2020 in the *New York Times* that echoed what Fanshawe said. "It's an unfortunate reality that certain insidious practices and beliefs are upheld

[47] Ibid., 297–305.

[48] Podles, *Sacrilege*, 298–99.

[49] Maggie Gallagher, "Don't Blame Me for Gay Teen Suicides", *New York Post*, October 20, 2010, https://nypost.com/2010/10/20/dont-blame-me-for-gay-teen-suicides/.

[50] Simon Fanshawe, "Society Now Accepts Gay Men as Equals. So Why on Earth Do So Many Continue to Behave Like Teenagers?", *Guardian*, April 20, 2006, https://www.theguardian.com/commentisfree/2006/apr/21/gayrights.comment.

within gay male culture that put all of us in danger of adopting risky behaviors. We put intense pressure on one another to be thin, hot and have a lot of sex." It must be said, too, that the kind of sex these men practice—anal sex—is extremely dangerous. It is not only a transmitter of STDs; it causes several other physical problems as well. It was not for nothing that gay activist Larry Kramer branded the gay lifestyle a "death style".[51]

Alcohol and drug abuse have long been noted by those who have studied homosexuals who molest minors. As far back as 1985, Father Thomas Doyle and Ray Mouton picked up on this trait. "Statistically, at least in regard to adolescent sexual abuse by priests, drugs and alcohol are the primary complicating or 'mitigating' factor that the treatment of professionals must deal with."[52] It is also true that many of those priests treated at Saint Luke were adult children of alcoholics.[53] The most recent risky behavior that is now consuming homosexuals, he says, is crystal methamphetamine; it is at a crisis level.[54]

Promiscuity

Sexual promiscuity is another self-destructive behavior, and it deserves to be studied separately. "The dirty little secret: Most gay couples are not monogamous." That is how reporter Hanna Rosin puts it.[55] This has been known for some time by scholars.

By the late 1970s, social scientists Alan P. Bell and Martin S. Weinberg were able to conclude that promiscuity was the norm for a sizable segment of the homosexual population. Their study showed that almost half the white homosexuals and about one-third of blacks each had had at least five hundred sexual partners; almost one in ten white

[51] Charles W. Socarides, "How America Went Gay", *America*, November 18, 1995, 20.

[52] Thomas P. Doyle and F. Ray Mouton, *The Problem of Sexual Molestation by Roman Catholic Clergy: Meeting the Problem in a Comprehensive and Responsible Manner* (1985), http://www.bishop-accountability.org/reports/1985_06_09_Doyle_Manual/.

[53] Berry, *Lead Us Not into Temptation*, 195.

[54] Jim Mangia, "Gay Men Are Dying from a Crisis We're Not Talking About," *New York Times*, January 23, 2020, A.27.

[55] Hanna Rosin, "The Dirty Little Secret: Most Gay Couples Aren't Monogamous", *Slate*, June 26, 2013, https://slate.com/human-interest/2013/06/most-gay-couples-aren-t-monogamous-will-straight-couples-go-monogamish.html.

males had over a thousand partners, while the figure for blacks was two in ten.[56]

Sociologists Philip Blumstein and Pepper Schwartz found that 82 percent of homosexuals cheated on their partners, and that 88 percent of them were aware that their partners cheated on them, leading them to conclude that "nearly all gay men have other sexual partners". This, they said, was due to the "trick mentality"—that is, the impersonal nature of homosexual encounters. For example, 90 percent of homosexual men admit that they have had sex with another man on the same day they met him. This is not as prevalent among heterosexuals and lesbians.[57]

The Need to Screen Candidates for the Priesthood

Could it be that the sexual urges experienced by homosexuals, especially those who have adopted a gay lifestyle, are so strong as to preclude a vow of celibacy and the chastity needed to fulfill it? And if so, shouldn't Church leaders follow the pastoral guidance of the last three popes and screen for such men seeking to enter the priesthood?

Yes, they should, says Daniel Mattson, who has turned away from the gay lifestyle. "I am convinced that most homosexual priests are good and holy men", he writes. He nonetheless believes that men like himself, who harbor deep-seated homosexual tendencies, should not be ordained. Why? "The first reason is that men with homosexual tendencies find it particularly difficult to live out the demands of chastity."[58] He finds persuasive the work of Father James Lloyd, a psychologist who has worked with homosexuals, including priests. "It is clear enough from clinical evidence that the psychic energy needed to contain homosexual drives is far greater than that needed by the straying heterosexual."

---

[56] Alan P. Bell and Martin S. Weinberg, *Homosexualities: A Study of Diversity among Men and Women* (New York: Simon and Schuster, 1978), 69.

[57] Philip Blumstein and Pepper Schwartz, *American Couples* (New York: Morrow, 1983), 195, 269–75, 570, 585–86.

[58] Daniel Mattson, "Why Men Like Me Should Not Be Priests", *First Things*, August 17, 2018, https://www.firstthings.com/web-exclusives/2018/08/why-men-like-me-should-not-be-priests.

The lesson for the Church is clear, says Father Lloyd. "If the Church wants to avoid sex scandals, it must stop ordaining the sorts of men who have the hardest time remaining chaste." It is hard to argue with that. Indeed, the burden is on those who disagree to show why this is not a logical conclusion.

10

The Role of the Sexual Revolution

When the John Jay study on "the causes and context" of the clergy sexual abuse scandal was released in 2011, it was greeted with howls of protest by liberal critics of the Catholic Church—the most astonishing outpouring of sociological illiteracy I have ever seen. One pundit after another argued that the study was flawed because it cited the role of the sexual revolution as a causative agent in the scandal. Had the social scientists *not* done so, they would have looked positively foolish. Not surprisingly, the critics were mostly journalists and those who make up the chattering class: they had no training in the social sciences, and it showed.

First out of the gate was Laurie Goodstein, a religious reporter for the *New York Times*. She criticized the John Jay study for promoting the "blame Woodstock" explanation, one that she said played right into the hands of the Church hierarchy.[1] Of course, no Church figure, or the John Jay researchers, used this term; Goodstein made it up and falsely attributed it to them. In an editorial, the newspaper said the study cited "the sexual and social turmoil of the 1960s as a possible factor in priests' crimes". Then it got angry by claiming that "this is a rather bizarre stab at sociological rationalization."[2]

Goodstein and the editorial board of the *New York Times* read the John Jay study as an exculpatory document, one that sought to move the burden of responsibility for the scandal from the Church hierarchy to the effects of the sexual revolution. It was nothing of the sort. It was a professional response. Sociologists always look at the social

---

[1] Laurie Goodstein, "1960s Culture Cited as Cause of Priest Abuse", *New York Times*, May 18, 2011, A1.

[2] "The Vatican Comes Up Short", *New York Times*, May 18, 2011, https://www.nytimes.com/2011/05/19/opinion/19thu4.html.

and cultural environment—the macro forces—that help to explain deviant or criminal behavior committed by groups or institutions. Unless the explanation becomes excessive and deliberately works to exonerate or minimize individual responsibility, it should be understood for what it is: an attempt to appreciate the particular milieu in which group or institutional misconduct takes place.

The *New York Times* was playing politics. When it comes to understanding the race riots of the 1960s, the newspaper is quick to mention the "root causes" of the violence. It cites such things as poverty, poor educational opportunities, racial discrimination, and the like. It does not treat the riots in a social vacuum. Nor should it. But when it comes to clergy sexual abuse, any reference to its social context—the sexual revolution—is seen as a ploy or a "sociological rationalization".

No sooner had the *Times* played its "blame Woodstock" card when one critic after another parroted the same line. Tony Auth captioned his cartoon on this subject in the *Philadelphia Inquirer* "It Was the Sixties, Man".[3] A *Boston Globe* guest columnist titled her piece "Blame it on the '60s, Man".[4] Jon Carroll branded his piece in the *San Francisco Chronicle*, "The '60s Made Them Do It".[5] A Canadian writer wrote, "Church Study Blames Swinging Sixties".[6] Others who chimed in, all echoing the established talking point, included Marci Hamilton, Rabbi Shmuley Boteach, and Mark Silk. Some were more creative: a Minnesota writer said the Church blamed the band Jefferson Airplane, and a Florida writer argued that the Church put the blame on Janis Joplin.[7]

In 2019, Pope Emeritus Benedict XVI set off the alarms again when he referenced the role of the sexual revolution while discussing clergy sexual abuse. He mentioned the need to discuss "the

---

[3] Tony Auth's cartoon ran in the May 20, 2011, edition of the *Philadelphia Inquirer*.

[4] Joan Vennochi, "Blame It on the '60s, Man", *Boston Globe*, May 29, 2011, http://archive.boston.com/bostonglobe/editorial_opinion/oped/articles/2011/05/29/blame_it_on_the_60s_man/.

[5] Jon Carroll, "The '60s Made Them Do It", *San Francisco Chronicle*, May 19, 2011, posted on BishopAccountability.com, http://www.bishop-accountability.org/news2011/05_06/2011_05_19_Carroll_The60s.htm.

[6] Kelly McParland, "Church Study Blames Swinging Sixties for Deviant Priests", *National Post*, May 20, 2011, https://nationalpost.com/full-comment/church-study-blames-swinging-sixties-for-deviant-priests.

[7] Bill Donohue, "Left Critics of John Jay Study", Catholic League, June 3, 2011, https://www.catholicleague.org/left-critics-of-john-jay-study/.

wider social context" of the scandal, "without which the problem cannot be understood". He was not exaggerating when he wrote, "It could be said that in the 20 years from 1960 to 1980, the previously normative standards regarding sexuality collapsed entirely, and a new normalcy arose that has by now been the subject of laborious attempts at disruption." He tied what was happening outside the Church—an "all-out sexual freedom"—to what was happening inside the Church—"Catholic moral theology suffered a collapse."[8] This is exactly what happened.

Liberal thinkers and writers unsurprisingly disagreed. Julie Hanlon Rubio, who teaches at the Jesuit School of Theology at Santa Clara University, was angered at Pope Benedict's "willingness to blame a permissive culture and a progressive theology for a problem that is internal and structural".[9] Rachel Donadio of the *Atlantic* found it "strange" for Pope Benedict to talk about the "destabilizing" forces of the sexual revolution.[10] Brian Flanagan at Loyola Marymount University said that to blame the 1960s and a "supposed collapse of moral theology" is "embarrassingly wrong".[11] Others who took a similar position include Marquette University professor James Bretzke, *Washington Post* columnist David Von Drehle, Virginia Commonwealth University professor R. Andrew Chesnut, and historian Christopher Bellitto.[12]

Father Richard John Neuhaus, one of the most influential voices in the Catholic Church in the late twentieth and early twenty-first centuries, noted the role of the sexual revolution, in particular the "gay activism" that drove the scandal. He said that the Church had

---

[8] Benedict XVI, "Full Text of Benedict XVI: The Church and the Scandal of Sexual Abuse", *Catholic World Report*, April 10, 2019, http://www.catholicworldreport.com/2019/04/10/full-text-of-benedict-xvi-the-church-and-the-scandal-of-sexual-abuse.

[9] Jason Horowitz, "With Letter on Sexual Abuse Pope Benedict Returns to Public Eye", *New York Times*, April 11, 2019, https://www.nytimes.com/2019/04/11/world/europe/pope-benedict-letter-sex-abuse.html.

[10] Rachel Donadio, "Pope Benedict Says Blame the '60s for Priests' Abuse", *Atlantic*, April 12, 2019, https://www.theatlantic.com/international/archive/2019/04/priest-abuse-catholic-church-1960s-pope-benedict/587044/.

[11] Delia Gallagher, "Ex-Pope Benedict XVI Breaks Silence on Church's Sex Abuse Crisis and Blames the Sexual Revolution and Liberals", CNN News, April 12, 2019, https://www.cnn.com/2019/04/11/world/benedict-sex-abuse/index.html.

[12] Bill Donohue, "Benedict XVI Incurs Wrath of Critics", Catholic League, April 17, 2019, https://www.catholicleague.org/benedict-xvi-incurs-wrath-of-critics/.

taken on "a distinct lavender hue". Adolescents, not small children, he emphasized, were the victims, thus making this a homosexual crisis.[13]

Archbishop Rembert Weakland said that, for many priests, Vatican II, which occurred at the onset of the sexual revolution, made sex "into something positive".[14] Father Andrew Greeley said it was debatable whether a sexual revolution took place in American society in the 1960s and the 1970s, but he added that "there is in the Roman Catholic clergy a definite change in sexual values away from the traditional Catholic teaching."[15]

To appreciate how convulsive the sexual revolution was, consider how different the 1950s were from the decades that followed. It was a time of social and economic stability. The rates of inflation, divorce, and crime were low. People married young, and few remained single. It was also a time when the Catholic Church blossomed. Its population doubled between 1940 and 1960, and as Charles Morris recounts, Archbishop Fulton J. Sheen became "the public face of American Catholicism in the 1950s". Morris astutely observed that "he may have been the finest popular lecturer ever to appear on television", helping to make the Catholic Church the "preeminent" institution in society.[16]

Not only was there no sexual revolution in the 1950s; there was no birth control pill, there was little sex education in the schools, and the rates of out-of-wedlock births, STDs, and abortion were low. Clergy sexual abuse existed, but it was on a very small scale, and it never made headlines. Attitudes about sex, interestingly, were in some respects much more relaxed than they are today. Take the case of men swimming naked with boys.

When the first indoor pool opened in the Brooklyn YMCA in 1885, men and boys were required to swim naked. The YMCA took this position because the wool swimsuits that were common at that time carried disease and bacteria, and the fibers clogged the pool's filtration system. But there was more to this than hygiene and

---

[13] Michael D'Antonio, *Mortal Sins: Sex, Crime, and the Era of Catholic Scandal* (New York: St. Martin's Press, 2013), 179.

[14] Ibid., 88.

[15] Andrew Greeley, "The Sexual Revolution among Catholic Clergy", *Review of Religious Research* 14, no. 2 (Winter 1973): 98.

[16] Charles Morris, *American Catholic: The Saints and Sinners Who Built America's Most Powerful Church* (New York: Times Books, 1997), 221, 223, 225.

plumbing. At the time, naked swimming was said to prepare boys for manhood. In 1926, the American Public Health Association declared that "at indoor pools used exclusively by men nude bathing should be required" (at indoor pools for women, they were expected to wear bathing suits "of the simplest types"). During that time, it was common to see pictures of boys swimming naked in *Life* magazine. Even as late as 1959, the YMCA in Bridgeport, Connecticut, ruled that "at no time will suits be worn in the pool and boys will not need them any time during the entire program." It was also common for older boys to swim clothed with naked younger boys, and they regularly engaged in "horse play".[17]

The ironies are striking. Today we hear how contraceptives, sex education, and abortion need to be made more widely available so we can cut down on out-of-wedlock births and STDs. Yet when there was no pill, sex ed, or legalized abortion, rates of illegitimacy and STDs were almost nonexistent. Moreover, when boys swam naked with older men, there was little chatter about the boys being sexually abused. That's because sexual restraint was the accepted norm. Then came the sexual revolution of the 1960s, throwing restraint to the wind.

"Social and cultural changes in the 1960s and 1970s manifested in increased levels of deviant behavior in the general society and also among priests of the Catholic Church in the United States." That was the conclusion of the John Jay social scientists. In fact, they found that the sexual abuse of minors by priests "increased steadily from the mid-1960s through the late 1970s, then declined in the 1980s and continues to remain low". This, of course, is when the sexual revolution flourished, making unpersuasive the idea that it did not affect the Church. "The rise in abuse cases in the 1960s and 1970s was influenced by social factors in American society generally."[18] The John Jay researchers got it just right.

[17] Hannah Dellinger, "Greenwich Lawsuit from a Time When Boys Swam Naked", *Greenwich Time*, April 27, 2019, updated August 20, 2019, https://www.ctinsider.com/news/green wichtime/article/Greenwich-lawsuit-from-a-time-when-boys-swam-naked-13800918.php.

[18] Karen J. Terry, John Jay College of Criminal Justice (JJCCJ), and United States Conference of Catholic Bishops (USCCB), *The Causes and Context of Sexual Abuse of Minors by Catholic Priests in the United States, 1950–2010: A Report Presented to the United States Conference of Catholic Bishops by the John Jay College Research Team* (Washington, D.C.: United States Conference of Catholic Bishops, 2011), 2–3.

As previously noted, it was not so much the surge of homosexuals into the priesthood that proved determinative; it was the changing attitudes about sexuality that mattered most. Michael Rose studied this issue and concluded that "the big revolution in the seminaries happened in the late 1960s, when a lot of the disciplinary codes were thrown out the window in favor of a new, very much liberalized, more university-like atmosphere with a lot of freedom and so forth."[19] Father Eugene Kennedy, a psychologist, said, "There were plenty of homosexuals among the old [pre–Vatican II] priests, but it was dealt with differently. The culture was intact; there was not the acting out you find today."[20] He is exactly right. When homosexuals in the priesthood were expected to behave, most did. But when the strictures were relaxed in the late 1960s—at the time of the sexual revolution in society—priests were given the green light to act out. They did.

The John Jay authors found that priests who lacked social bonds, and those who were reared in families that either spoke negatively about sex or not at all, were more likely than others to abuse minors. Priests with this profile were commonplace among those ordained in the 1940s and the 1950s.[21] But it is also true that they kept their id in check at that time. When the Church dropped its guard, beginning in the latter part of the 1960s, some became predators. "Men ordained in the 1930s, 1940s, and 1950s", the John Jay writers said, "did not generally abuse before the 1960s or 1970s. Men ordained in the 1960s and early 1970s engaged in abusive behavior much more quickly after their entrance into ministry."[22]

The inescapable fact is that the sexual revolution in the greater society hit the Catholic Church like a whirlwind. The libertine ideas that generated the sexual revolution took root in the 1960s, but it was in the 1970s when it flourished behaviorally, in and out of the Church. It makes perfect sense to learn that "more abuse occurred in the 1970s than [in] any other decade, peaking in 1980."[23]

---

[19] Bill Steigerwald, "Origins of a Scandal: 10 Minutes with ... Michael Rose", *Jewish World Review*, June 25, 2002, jewishworldreview.com/0702/steigerwald062502.asp

[20] Jason Berry, *Lead Us Not into Temptation* (New York: Doubleday, 1992), 189.

[21] Terry, JJCCJ, and USCCB, *The Causes and Context*, 4.

[22] Ibid., 3.

[23] Karen J. Terry, JJCCJ, and USCCB, *The Nature and Scope of Sexual Abuse of Minors by Catholic Priests and Deacons in the United States 1950–2002: A Research Study Conducted by the John Jay College of Criminal Justice* (Washington, D.C.: United States Conference of Catholic Bishops, 2004), 5.

In 1978, when Alexsandr Solzhenitsyn, the great Russian dissident, spoke at Harvard University, he told the graduating class how disappointed he was with the state of freedom in the West. There is much talk about rights, he said, but little in the way of human obligations. "Voluntary self-restraint is almost unheard of", he noted.[24] Indeed, self-restraint was treated as taboo. Irving Kristol, a brilliant Jewish intellectual, credited Pope Paul VI with understanding the social and cultural currents of the day. He said the pope was "absolutely right" to contend that "once you cut the link between sex and reproduction and permit sexual activity to become a pleasurable end in itself, all sorts of ghastly things will happen to your society."[25] He was referring to the commercial debut of the birth control pill in 1960 and its predictable results.

The sexual revolution coincided with the gay rights movement. "Flaunting one's sexuality was considered a revolutionary act", notes David Horowitz. "The gay liberation activists were not merely trying to get attention or offend heterosexual society, or, more importantly, to persuade society to accept them as individuals on their own terms. They were trying to change the world by forcing *society* to accept aggressive public sexuality and, more importantly, promiscuous sexual behavior."[26] Homosexual leaders agreed. Larry Kramer, founder of the Gay Men's Health Crisis in New York and AIDS Coalition to Unleash Power (ACT UP), said, "The movement of the 60's and the 70's legitimized promiscuity."[27]

Unfortunately, for many homosexuals this meant frequenting gay bathhouses. Homosexual writer Randy Shilts knew where this led. "Bathhouses guaranteed the rapid spread of AIDS among gay men."[28] It is sad to note that gay activists demanded that the bathhouses stay open, even after the spread of AIDS was at a crisis level.[29] Kramer, furious with homosexuals for their anonymous sex in the bathhouses,

---

[24] Aleksandr I. Solzhenitsyn, *East and West* (New York: Harper and Row, 1980), 48, 64–66.

[25] Patrick G.D. Riley, "Contraception: A Worldwide Calamity?", *Catholic Social Science Review* (2005): 320.

[26] David Horowitz, *Dark Agenda: The War to Destroy Christian America* (West Palm Beach, Fla.: Humanix Books, 2018), 114–15.

[27] William A. Donohue, *The New Freedom: Individualism and Collectivism in the Social Lives of Americans* (New Brunswick, N.J.: Transaction Publishers, 1990), 134.

[28] Ibid., 133.

[29] Ibid., 133–34.

exploded, "How many of us have to die before *you* get scared off your ass and into action?"[30]

Boston Epitomizes the Problem

Those who continue to deny that the sexual revolution created the fertile cultural soil that gave rise to clergy sexual abuse must explain why Boston was the epicenter of the scandal. It celebrated the sexual revolution as much as any city in the nation, and what happened is now a matter of historical record. Los Angeles, another hub for the sexual revolution, also witnessed an explosion in clergy sexual abuse: the Archdiocese of Los Angeles paid out hundreds of millions in settlements in the 2000s.

In the 1940s and 1950s, Boston was a vibrant Catholic city, with swelling church attendance and an increasingly vocal role in politics. Today Boston is one of the most "unchurched" big cities in the nation.[31] Changes began in the 1960s, when the Boston Archdiocese witnessed a sharp decline in admissions to the seminary.[32] The sexual revolution had dropped anchor, and nowhere was this more evident than in the gay community. In the 1970s, Boston was home to the international office of Dignity, the Catholic group of gay priests who reject Church teachings on sexuality.[33] Boston was also home to the North American Man/Boy Love Association, or NAMBLA, an organization of homosexuals who justify sex between adult men and children.[34] Guess who attended NAMBLA's first conference in 1978? Father Paul Shanley.[35]

[30] Michael Specter, "Larry Kramer, the Man Who Warned America about AIDS, Can't Stop Fighting Hard—and Loudly", *New Yorker*, May 13, 2002, 56.

[31] Leah Jessen, "The Top Five Big Cities for Church Attendance in America; New Research Has Identified the Most 'Churched' and 'Unchurched' Areas of the Country", LifeZette, June 10, 2017, http://www.lifezette.com/faithzette/the-top-five-big-cities-church-attendance.

[32] David France, *Our Fathers: The Secret Life of the Catholic Church in an Age of Scandal* (New York: Broadway Books, 2004), 87.

[33] Enrique Rueda, *The Homosexual Network: Private Lives and Public Policy* (Old Greenwich, Conn.: Devin Adair, 1982), 311.

[34] Nicole M. King, "Legalization of Pedophilia: The Wave of the Future?", *Family in America* (Winter 2014): 68.

[35] Rueda, *The Homosexual Network*, 295–96.

It is fair to say, then, that Boston was the epicenter not only of the scandal but of gay activism in and out of the Church. When the scandal broke in the pages of the *Boston Globe* in 2002, Senator Rick Santorum explained why Boston was hit so hard. "When a culture is sick, every element in it becomes infected. While it is no excuse for this scandal, it is no surprise that Boston—a seat of academic, political, and cultural liberalism in America—lies at the center of the storm."[36]

Boston is known for its philandering politicians, all of whom keep getting elected despite the tawdry stories. The Kennedys are a prime example. John, Bobby, and Teddy made the rounds with celebrities and many others and never paid a price for it at the ballot box; they learned their ways from their father, Joe, who was another philanderer. The voters were just as kind to homosexuals who bounced around with their lovers. Representative Gerry Studds was censured by the House in 1983 for his sexual romp with a teenage boy, but he continued to be reelected. (Apparently, those Boston Catholics who are enraged over molesting priests are more accepting if the offender is a politician.) Representative Barney Frank hooked up with a male prostitute in 1989, but that didn't bother his constituents, most of whom voted for him time and again with wide margins.

The Boston electorate also likes pro-homosexual legislation. In 2003, the state legislature held hearings on a bill that would have defined marriage as a union between a man and a woman. No one from the Archdiocese of Boston or the Dioceses of Worcester, Fall River, and Springfield spoke on behalf of the bill. But four priests testified against the measure. As Phil Lawler noted, this meant "in effect that same-sex couples should be allowed the legal privilege of marriage".[37] The following year, Massachusetts became the first state to recognize gay "marriage". Lawler aptly observed that this represented the "collapse of Catholic influence" in the state.[38]

It was in the Boston Archdiocese where Father James Porter, Father John Geoghan, and Father Paul Shanley, three of the most notorious abusers in the history of the Catholic Church, held court. Porter

---

[36] Philip F. Lawler, *The Faithful Departed: The Collapse of Boston's Catholic Culture* (New York: Encounter Books, 2008), 15.

[37] Lawler, *The Faithful Departed*, 204.

[38] Ibid., 4.

molested boys and girls in their homes, on the beach, and on church property, including on the altar.[39] Geoghan was a true pedophile, usually choosing elementary school boys to molest, though one of his victims was just four years old.[40] While Porter and Geoghan were sick men, it was Shanley who was emblematic of Boston's culture.

When Shanley was ordained in 1960, he was a clean-shaven young man. Within a few years, he grew his hair long, looked disheveled, and stopped wearing his collar, choosing instead plain shirts and blue jeans. This was the beginning of his "hippie priest" years. He not only changed his appearance; he changed his thinking. He quickly became known for challenging Church teachings on sexuality, especially homosexuality, and clashed frequently with Cardinal Medeiros. He didn't just espouse a libertine sexual ethos; he lived it. Young boys whom he counseled were his prey. As the *Boston Globe Spotlight* reporters said, "Therapy sessions became settings for molestation and rape."[41] One reason Shanley was able to get away with his serial offenses was the total lack of oversight on the part of his superiors. During the 1970s, when the Church lost its nerve, Shanley lived on his own in an apartment in Boston's Back Bay. That is where he had sex with teenage boys who came for therapy.[42]

Shanley was active in the gay community as early as 1970, seeking out adolescent boys for oral and anal sex.[43] Incredibly promiscuous, he contracted venereal disease and showed the teenage boys how to inject drugs. All of this was known to his superiors: it was in his priest personnel file.[44]

The "street priest" not only enjoyed a very liberal lifestyle; he entertained a very liberal political ideology. He pushed for the legalization of marijuana and blamed the federal government for

[39] Leon Podles, *Sacrilege: Sexual Abuse in the Catholic Church* (Baltimore: Crossland Press, 2008), 115.

[40] Michael Rezendes, "Church Allowed Abuse by Priest for Years", *Boston Globe*, January 6, 2002, https://www.bostonglobe.com/news/special-reports/2002/01/06/church-allowed -abuse-priest-for-years/cSHfGkTIrAT25qKGvBuDNM/story.html.

[41] The Investigative Staff of *The Boston Globe*, *Betrayal: The Crisis in the Catholic Church* (Boston: Little, Brown and Company, 2002), 65–66.

[42] Ibid., 70.

[43] Podles, *Sacrilege*, 159,

[44] The Investigative Staff of *The Boston Globe*, *Betrayal*, 69.

heroin use because it did not make pot more widely available. The predator priest was also a champion of the poor, a big-time social-justice activist. He was known for lashing out at white people, calling them racists, and assigning blame to the parents of runaway kids. He also hated the police, accusing them of planting drugs on young men and beating those who resisted.[45] Shanley was a man at war with himself, the Catholic Church, and society. For all of this, the liberal Boston establishment embraced Shanley as if he were some sort of hero.

Leon Podles, who authored an important book on clergy sexual abuse, called Shanley "the darling of liberal Boston".[46] The "hippie priest" won the Mayor's Citizenship Award in Boston and was adored by young people for running a disco with all the familiar psychedelic lighting.[47] Representative Barney Frank, the liberal homosexual icon, worked with him when he was a state lawmaker, and the son of former mayor John B. Hynes sought him out for therapy. Nuns, both current and former, heralded his work with troubled youth, never noting how he helped to create trouble for them. Victims' lawyer Carmen Durso represented several of Shanley's victims, yet he said, "If he weren't a damned pervert, [he] would be my hero."[48]

Left-wing secular elites in Boston gravitated to Shanley, as did priests who were in open rebellion against the Church. In the 1970s, wayward priests, especially in Boston, could do pretty much anything they wanted, and this was doubly true of dissidents. When Shanley tangled with Cardinal Medeiros, the archbishop never confronted him the way he should have. It is important to note that this child rapist was embraced by the Association of Boston Urban Priests, a dissident group. Some wrote letters of support for Shanley, and so did municipal leaders.

In the late 1970s, Medeiros tried to rein Shanley in, but it was too late. Shanley went on the offensive and had his buddies from the Association of Boston Urban Priests go to bat for him. He contacted

[45] France, *Our Fathers*, 86.
[46] Podles, *Sacrilege*, 155.
[47] Ibid., 158.
[48] Sally Jacobs, "'If They Knew the Madness in Me': A Search for the Real Rev. Paul Shanley Suggests He Was Part Hero, Part Horror", *Boston Globe*, July 10, 2002.

the media, telling them that the archbishop was no longer reaching out to homosexuals. He went directly to the *New York Times* and the Associated Press with tales of victimhood, and Medeiros was accused of cracking the whip. Shanley did not stop there. He recruited support from his liberal admirers in colleges and universities. Gay activists also wrote positively about him. Finally, Medeiros told Shanley in 1979 that he was being relieved of his appointment to the ministry to alienated youth. Shanley went ballistic, but this time the archbishop, knowing that Rome was watching these developments play out, stuck to his guns.[49] The drama was something right out of a play, though it happened in real time. Liberals in Boston had chosen sides, casting their vote for the serial homosexual rapist.

It wasn't just Medeiros who didn't handle the clergy sexual abuse scandal the way he should have; Cardinal Bernard Law bears much of the responsibility as well. Knowing all he did about Geoghan, he still praised him at the end of 1996, when the serial pedophile retired. "Yours has been an effective life of ministry, sadly impaired by illness. On behalf of those who you served well, and in my own name, I would like to thank you."[50] When the scandal exploded in the media in January 2002, Law wasted no time saying he was "profoundly sorry" for having sent Geoghan to a new assignment in 1984.[51]

In 1996, when Shanley retired, Law said, "Without doubt over all of these years of generous and zealous care, the lives and hearts of many people have been touched by your sharing of the Lord's Spirit. You are truly appreciated for all that you have done."[52]

Was Law clueless or malicious? He wasn't clueless: he knew what Geoghan and Shanley had done. Was he malicious? No. His admirers, including Phil Lawler, say such a conclusion is unfair. Lawler stresses the many good things that Cardinal Law had done, often without seeking the limelight. He emphasized that Law was not the "callous tyrant" that many made him out to be.[53]

---

[49] France, *Our Fathers*, 126–28.

[50] Podles, *Sacrilege*, 152.

[51] Walter V. Robinson and Michael Paulson, "A 'Grieving' Law Apologizes for Assignment of Geoghan", *Boston Globe*, January 10, 2002, A1.

[52] The Investigative Staff of *The Boston Globe*, *Betrayal*, 69.

[53] Lawler, *The Faithful Departed*, 7.

So if Law wasn't clueless or malicious, what explains his failure to rein in molesting priests? He may have been a theological conservative, but he did not know how to govern wayward priests. That was his seminal failure. This weakness marked the legacy of many bishops: they allowed some very sick men to act out, never holding up a stop sign or taking command of their dioceses. It is too bad Cardinal Law did not rule as sternly as his critics alleged he had.

Some prelates were, in fact, clueless. Philadelphia archbishop Cardinal John Krol, a staunch theological conservative, was laughed at by homosexual priests who worked under him. In the pages of *Communication*, a newsletter for homosexual clerics, they bragged about their efforts to promote the radical gay agenda. "Little does Cardinal Krol know what great ministries bubble under his umbrella", a reference to their subversive goals.[54] But for the most part, conservative bishops allowed theological dissent to set the tone and were afraid to challenge it. That is the conclusion reached by historian James Hitchcock.

Hitchcock singles out the reforms of Vatican II that were implemented in education. The older generation of bishops failed to gain control of the postconciliar process of education, thus ushering in disastrous results. This meant that "Church officials—from bishops themselves to kindergarten teachers—were systematically inducted into a view of 'renewal' that was increasingly at odds with official teaching and with the actual words of the Council." Middle management in the Church, he says, became a hotbed of dissent. Moreover, during the 1970s, a whole slew of liberal bishops were appointed. But even in those dioceses where a conservative bishop was appointed, liberalism won out. "Whatever his intentions", Hitchcock writes, "a new bishop quickly discovers how tightly the liberals control the diocesan machinery—the school office, the priests' senate, the office of social justice, and other bureaus—and he realizes that dislodging such people will be no easy task and will be unpleasant."[55]

[54] Rueda, *The Homosexual Network*, 349.

[55] James Hitchcock, "Conservative Bishops, Liberal Results", *Catholic World Report* (May 1995), posted on Ignatius Insight, http://www.ignatiusinsight.com/features2005/print2005/hitchcock_bishops_may05.html.

In Washington, they have a saying, "If you want to get along, go along." This is also true of the Catholic Church.

Justifying Man-Boy Sex

The outrage that greeted the news about the clergy sexual abuse scandal was shared by everyone, though some were totally insincere. A sincere person would not justify man-boy sex and then complain when the victimizer is a priest. Who would do such a thing? Mostly well-educated white persons who call themselves liberals, many of whom hate the Church's teachings on sexuality yet shamelessly make the case *for* pedophilia. It's an example of Scandal II in its most extreme form. This bizarre condition is inseparable from the sexual revolution and helps explain why the sickest of priests were able to take comfort in their condition.

On October 31, 2013, the American Psychological Association (APA) issued a statement saying that "pedophilia is a mental disorder" and that "sex between adults and children is always wrong."[56] Why would a group of respected professionals have to make such a pedestrian statement? Because it was thrust upon it.

The APA was still reeling from the public-relations fallout of an article that was published in 1998 in its *Psychological Bulletin*. The authors contended that it is erroneous to conclude that all sexual relations between adults and minors have a negative effect; many victims reported they had neutral or even positive effects. The researchers recommended that pedophilia be referred to as "adult-child sex" so it would be "value neutral".[57] Thus did they set off the alarms in some quarters. Others liked what they heard. For example, it was greeted as "good news" by NAMBLA, the

---

[56]"Statement of the American Psychological Association Regarding Pedophilia and the Diagnostic and Statistical Manual of Mental Disorders (DSM-5)", American Psychological Association, October 31, 2013, https://www.apa.org/news/press/releases/2013/10/pedophilia-mental.

[57]Bruce Rind, Phillip Tromovitch, and Robert Bauserman, "The Meta-Analytic Examination of Assumed Properties of Child Sexual Abuse Using College Samples", *Psychological Bulletin* 124, no. 1 (July 1998), posted on PubMed, https://pubmed.ncbi.nlm.nih.gov/9670820/.

organized proponents of man-boy sex, as sociologist Anne Hendershott noted.[58]

Two prominent homosexual intellectuals, Andrew Sullivan and Jonathan Rauch, sounded off as well, but they directed their anger at those who criticized the study. Sullivan said "there was reason for relief" in learning from the study that "lasting psychological trauma among adult survivors of abuse, particularly for men, was much less than feared". Rauch recommended that we drop references to "abuse" when speaking about what he preferred to call "adult-child sex" or "adult-adolescent sex".[59]

The American Psychological Association may believe that sex between adults and minors is wrong, but by publishing this article, it gave the appearance of giving cover to it. The sad fact is that man-boy sex has its followers, enablers, and practitioners, and no group is more notorious than NAMBLA.

"NAMBLA takes the view that sex is good, that homosexuality is good not only for adults, but for young people as well." This is how David Thorstad, a spokesman for NAMBLA, put it in the association's formative years.[60] Its motto, "Eight is too late", succinctly explains NAMBLA's mission. It is important to note that while there are heterosexuals who molest children, there is no analogue to NAMBLA in their ranks. This is unique to homosexuals.

Is NAMBLA accepted in the gay community? Yes and no. On the twenty-fifth anniversary of the Stonewall riots—when homosexuals clashed with the police in Greenwich Village—there were two gay-pride parades in New York City. I attended both events and hired a photographer to take pictures. The International March on the United Nations to Affirm the Human Rights of Lesbian and Gay People refused to allow NAMBLA to parade with it up First Avenue. Their march was well behaved. But NAMBLA was allowed to march up Fifth Avenue in an alternative event comprising more-radical homosexual groups. Thousands participated, many marched totally

---

[58] Anne Hendershott, "Empowering Pedophiles", *New York Post*, January 16, 2013, https://nypost.com/2013/01/16/empowering-pedophiles/.

[59] Mary Eberstadt, "'Pedophilia Chic' Reconsidered; The Taboo against Sex with Children Continues to Erode", *Weekly Standard*, January 1, 2001, 18.

[60] Rueda, *The Homosexual Network*, 80.

naked in an illegal parade (they were denied a permit—yet were escorted by police on scooters), and some masturbated in the street in front of St. Patrick's Cathedral while others did satanic dances. I showed the pictures to New York City officials, and they intervened the following year to restore order.

Holland has a NAMBLA-like organization called Vereniging Martijn. It also advocates for the legalization of pedophilia; both NAMBLA and Vereniging Martijn are populated by priests. These groups take the position that man-boy sex can be fun for both parties.[61] Paul Shanley even went so far as to say that "the kid is the seducer" and that this "kid" is not at all traumatized by man-boy sex.[62] Geoghan took a slightly different tack. According to *Boston Globe* reporters, his standard answer to child rape was, "It was the children's fault."[63]

It would be one thing if such sentiments were limited to radical homosexuals and disturbed priests, but that is not the case at all. Respected therapists have rallied to normalize man-boy sex, and its supporters include activists, celebrities, and scholars. All of these proponents rode the waves of the sexual revolution, and some of them crested in the Catholic Church.

If the American Psychological Association feels squeamish about adopting the "value neutral" lexicon of its published authors on sex between adults and minors, there is another organization of professional therapists who prefer to speak in a softer language. B4U-ACT is an association of psychiatrists and others in the therapeutic field who reject such terminology as "man-boy sex" and "pedophile". They like to speak about minor-attracted persons, or MAPs. These are adults who are sexually attracted to children or adolescents (they are almost all men). Some MAPs have had sex with kids, and others have just fantasized about it. We are told that the rest of the population is the problem: MAPs suffer from stigma, shame, and fear.[64]

In a B4U-ACT conference held in 2011, psychiatrists from such distinguished places as Harvard, Johns Hopkins, and the London

[61] D'Antonio, *Mortal Sins*, 27.
[62] Podles, *Sacrilege*, 161.
[63] The Investigative Staff of *The Boston Globe*, *Betrayal*, 24.
[64] "Psychotherapy for the Minor-Attracted Person", B4U-ACT, February 2020, https://www.b4uact.org/wp-content/uploads/2020/02/Psychotherapy-for-MAPs-2020.pdf.

School of Economics assembled to criticize the American Psychiatric Association for declaring pedophilia to be a mental illness. At the event, speakers made plain their position: "We are not required to interfere with or inhibit a child's sexuality"; "Children are not inherently unable to consent" to sex with an adult; "An adult's desire to have sex with children is 'normative' "; and "The majority of pedophiles are gentle and rational."[65]

Dr. Fred Berlin, the psychiatrist who argues that it is wrong to report child molesters (recall that he was an adviser to the bishops at the Dallas conference), gave the keynote address. He was proud to be there. "I want to completely support the goal of B4U-ACT", he said.[66] Berlin made the case that we should treat child molesters the same way we do drunk drivers: give them help and don't depend on legal solutions. Conservative critics accused Berlin of trying to normalize child rape (no liberals criticized him), forcing officials at Johns Hopkins to issue a statement saying that he speaks for himself, not for the university.[67]

B4U-ACT may be relatively new, but the idea that sex between adults and children is okay is not. Alfred Kinsey found it to be a perfectly acceptable research methodology to garner data from adult men who sexually stimulated infants and young children. He documented babies and young boys who had "experienced" orgasms, taking tabs on the number and length of their orgasms. One of his sexually abused subjects was two months old; twenty-eight were under the age of one.[68]

Gay activists have long justified man-boy sex. Harry Hay is regarded by some as the founder of the gay rights movement. He not only endorsed sexual relations between adults and minors; he also said the young men would love it. "If the parents and friends of gays are truly friends of gays," he said, "they would know from their gay kids that the relationship with an older man is precisely what thirteen,

---

[65] Matt Barber, " 'Time to Normalize Pedophilia': Firsthand Report on B4U-ACT Conference", Illinois Family Institute, August 22, 2011, https://illinoisfamily.org/marriage/time-to-normalize-pedophilia-firsthand-report-on-b4u-act-conference/.

[66] Ibid.

[67] Jordan Michael Smith, "The Professor of Horrible Deeds", *Chronicle of Higher Education*, February 18, 2018, https://www.chronicle.com/article/the-professor-of-horrible-deeds/.

[68] King, "Legalization of Pedophilia", 66.

fourteen, and fifteen-year-old kids need more than anything else in the world."[69] Naturally, Hay was also a fan of NAMBLA.[70]

Larry Kramer, another champion of gay rights, argued that kids like to have sex with adults. "In those cases where children do have sex with homosexual elders ... I submit that often, very often, the child desires the activity, and perhaps even solicits it, either because of a natural curiosity ... or because he or she is homosexual and innately knows it."[71] This is the position taken by Paul Shanley.

There is no shortage of celebrities who have endorsed pedophilia, including child rapists. Roman Polanski is a convicted child molester—he drugged and raped a thirteen-year-old—yet he is still adored by movie industry people such as Cate Blanchett (she named one of her sons after him), Martin Scorsese, Meryl Streep, Harrison Ford, Penelope Cruz, Whoopi Goldberg, Harvey Weinstein, and Woody Allen.[72] Had Polanksi been a priest, they would have condemned him. This tells us that for some people it is not the victim that matters: it is the identity of the victimizer.

When Michael Jackson was accused of sexually exploiting children in the documentary *Leaving Neverland*, Barbra Streisand rushed to his defense: "His sexual needs were his sexual needs, coming from whatever childhood he has or whatever DNA he has." She put quotation marks around "molested", as if to say the kids were not really molested. "You can say 'molested,' but those children, as you heard say, they were thrilled to be there."[73] She later apologized, although Jackson was found not guilty of the charges made against him.

In 1999, Elton John stunned a crowd in London when he honored a homosexual rights group by including in his performance six

---

[69] Michael Brown, "Childhood Sexual Abuse Often Contributes to Homosexuality", *Christian Post*, February 24, 2017, https://www.christianpost.com/news/childhood-sexual-abuse-often-contributes-to-homosexuality.html.

[70] John Weir, "Mad about the Boys", *Advocate*, August 23, 1994, 37.

[71] Brown, "Childhood Sexual Abuse".

[72] Maureen Callahan, "Why Does Hollywood Keep Defending Roman Polanski?", *New York Post*, October 5, 2017, https://nypost.com/2017/10/05/why-does-hollywood-keep-defending-roman-polanski/.

[73] Brent Bozell and Tim Graham, "Streisand's Bizarre Michael Jackson Defense", CNS News, March 29, 2019, https://www.cnsnews.com/commentary/l-brent-bozell-iii/streisands-bizarre-michael-jackson-defense.

teenage strippers dressed as Cub Scouts.[74] Four year later, he came to the defense of Pete Townshend after the musician admitted accessing child porn: "I love Pete and my thoughts are with him."[75] Another fan of child porn, Pee-wee Herman, was roundly defended by *Friends* star Courteney Cox Arquette and her husband, David Arquette.[76]

Many intellectuals have also defended the indefensible. The *New Republic* is an important source of liberal thought, so when Hanna Rosin wrote sympathetically about NAMBLA, saying there was "some bravery" to its decision to list its phone number in the New York directory, she spoke for more than herself. Why was this so brave? Because, she said, "it is still heresy even to consider the legitimacy of their feelings."[77] The *New York Times* pretty much took the same position. When Peter Melzer, a NAMBLA leader, was removed from his New York City public school teaching post and then reinstated, the *Times*, which is ever so condemnatory of the bishops, applauded his return. Hilton Kramer saw this as a classic example of what Daniel Patrick Moynihan described as "defining deviancy down".[78] NAMBLA has also garnered the support of noted homosexual intellectuals such as Gore Vidal and Allen Ginsberg.[79] Camille Paglia said she admired Ginsberg's "pro-NAMBLA stand".[80]

Intellectuals tend not to like sexual taboos. For example, feminist Andrea Dworkin says we need to get rid of the "incest taboo".[81] Author Judith Levine wrote a book about sexual taboos in general, claiming we need to evolve in our thinking. "In America today", she wrote, "it is nearly impossible to publish a book that says children and teenagers can have sexual pleasure and be safe too." She admits that she had sex with an adult when she was a minor and has some advice for us all. "Teens often seek out sex with older people, and they do so for understandable reasons: an older person makes them feel sexy and

[74] King, "Legalization of Pedophilia", 70.

[75] Robert Kahn, "Rockers Back Up Townshend", *Newsday* (Queens edition), January 17, 2003.

[76] Todd Peterson, "Courteney Defends Pee-Wee" *People*, November 25, 2002, https: people.com/celebrity/passages-courteney-defends-pee-wee.

[77] Hanna Rosin, "Chickenhawk", *New Republic*, May 8, 1995, 42.

[78] Hilton Kramer, "Advancing the Cause of Deviancy", *New York Post*, October 12, 1993, 19.

[79] France, *Our Fathers*, 397.

[80] Podles, *Sacrilege*, 339.

[81] Ibid.

grown-up, protected and special." She also said that when a priest has sex with a young person, the sexual relationship could "conceivably" be positive, though she later backed away from that position after a furor erupted over her remark.[82]

Some European intellectuals have said similar things. Colm Tóibín, a homosexual author who spent time in an Irish seminary, said that at ages fifteen and sixteen he "found some of the priests sexually attractive", and if one of them tried to seduce him, "it would have been absolutely no problem for me aged 15. It didn't happen, but it wouldn't have been a problem."[83] English atheist Richard Dawkins admits that when he was in a boarding school, one of his male teachers "pulled me on his knee and put his hand inside my shorts." The same teacher molested other students. "I don't think he did any of us lasting harm", Dawkins said, preferring to categorize such incidents as "mild pedophilia".[84]

No country is more known for vigorously defending adult-child sex than France. In 2020, a controversy erupted when one of the many victims of Gabriel Matzneff, then eighty-three, published a book about his experiences. He never tried to deny that he had sex with boys and girls in their early teens or even younger. He also admitted to having sex with eight-year-old boys in the Philippines.[85] Indeed, he wrote many books about his sexual exploits and willingly gave interviews on television, bragging about them. Not only did he never go to jail; he won the acclaim of the literati for decades. And he never showed remorse, even when some in France started to turn against him.[86] When one of his victims, Francesca Gee, sought a publisher for her account detailing how he abused her when she was a teenager, no one was interested. The editor of one publishing house said that the subject was "too sensitive"

[82] David Crary, "Children's Sexuality Book Turns Up Heat on Publisher", *Los Angeles Times*, April 7, 2002, A24.

[83] Susanna Rustin, "Review: A LIFE IN WRITING: Colm Toibin", *Guardian*, October 23, 2010, 12.

[84] Abby Ohlheiser, "Richard Dawkins Defends 'Mild' Pedophilia, Again and Again", *Atlantic*, September 10, 2013, https://www.theatlantic.com/international/archive/2013/09/richard-dawkins-defends-mild-pedophilia-again-and-again/311230/.

[85] Norimitsu Onishi, "A Pedophile Writer Is on Trial. So is the French Elite", *New York Times*, February 12, 2020, A1.

[86] Ibid.

and that two members of his editorial committee were "close to Matzneff".[87]

Matzneff benefited greatly from the social revolution of 1968. The slogan that was popular at the time, "It's forbidden to forbid", was used by him to great effect. He advocated the legalization of sex with children, saying, "To sleep with a child, it's a holy experience, a baptismal event, a sacred adventure." He garnered the applause of such intellectual giants as Michel Foucault, Roland Barthes, Jean-Paul Sartre, and Simone de Beauvoir, all of whom were sexually promiscuous.[88] Foucault was a homosexual predator who justified rape, and Barthes, Sartre, and de Beauvoir advocated eliminating all the laws barring sex between adults and children.[89]

The clergy sexual abuse scandal happened because of predatory homosexual priests and their enabling bishops. But they did not live in a social vacuum. The sexual revolution that occurred in Western societies blew through the Church with a fury. Instead of challenging it, too many in the Church succumbed to it. Though much progress has been made by the Church hierarchy to prevent the sexual abuse of minors by Catholic clergy, it is still fashionable in some circles outside the Church to celebrate sexual libertinism. That many of these activists, celebrities, and intellectuals continue to hammer the Church while defending the sexual exploitation of children and adolescents makes them worse than hypocrites: they are facilitators of evil.

[87]Norimitsu Onishi, "Long-Silenced Victim of a Pedophile Writer Gets to Tell Her Story", *New York Times*, March 31, 2020, https://www.nytimes.com/2020/03/31/world /europe/gabriel-matzneff-victim-france.html.

[88]Norimitsu Onishi, "A Victim's Account Fuels Reckoning over Abuse of Children in France", *New York Times*, January 7, 2020, https://www.nytimes.com/2020/01/07/world /europe/france-pedophilia-gabriel-matzneff.html.

[89]Bill Donohue, *Why Catholicism Matters: How Catholic Virtues Can Reshape Society in the 21st Century* (New York: Image, 2012), 251–52.

11

The Role of Dissent in the Church

Monsignor Kevin Wallin was known in the Diocese of Bridgeport as a superb homilist and a "towering figure" in southwestern Connecticut. At one time, he was secretary to Bishop Edward Egan (who would later become the archbishop of New York). Wallin was involved in many charities and was active in several endeavors, serving as a board member of Sacred Heart University. But then, sometime around 2010 or 2011, he began to crack up. He lost a lot of weight, walked stooped over, and did not show up for scheduled events. Some spotted him entertaining "suspicious" men who would come and go from his rectory. "Neighbors said men streamed into Monsignor Wallin's apartment, many of them arriving in cars like BMWs and Corvettes. Sounds of sex could be heard." In 2013 he was locked up for being a drug dealer.[1]

There were many red flags that were noticed by legions of priests, nuns, and laypeople, yet everyone ignored them. Here was a distinguished priest who trafficked in crystal meth and was open about his homosexuality, and no one opened his mouth. But the biggest red flag of them all was his rejection of Catholicism. Years before his arrest, he was in a setting with other priests where the discussion turned to God's mercy. Wallin said, "You don't really believe that, do you?"[2] Wallin was obviously in free fall. Absent faith, how could he function as a priest?

Loss of faith is the number-one reason that priests go rogue. Father Richard John Neuhaus said that the problem of clergy sexual abuse is traceable to "dissent and departure from the teaching of the Church".

---

[1] N.R. Kleinfield, "A Dazzling Priest's Lurid Fall, to Drug Suspect", *New York Times*, February 20, 2013, A1.

[2] Ibid.

Indeed, he claimed, avoiding sexual trouble comes down to "three things: fidelity, fidelity and fidelity".[3] Of course, fidelity includes not only intellectual assent to the teachings of the Church but also a life of prayer in order to live by them. When a priest stops praying, trouble usually follows.

Yes, the clergy sexual abuse scandal is unintelligible without understanding the crucial role played by dissent. Pope Benedict XVI hit a chord with his detractors when he cited the role of dissent, and that is because he hit them square between the eyes.

To be sure, most dissident priests are not inclined to abuse minors sexually, but they may be more inclined than their loyal colleagues to violate Church teachings. Why? For one, the absence of guilt. When guilt is taken to extremes, it is unhealthy. But it is also unhealthy when it is barely present or not present at all. For example, if someone does not believe that stealing from the rich is wrong, he is more likely to do so, if given the opportunity, than those who consider it wrong. What about a priest who rejects the Church's teachings on celibacy and chastity? Would he not be more likely to have a sexual encounter than a priest who accepts these teachings? What about a priest who suffers from a disorder—he is sexually attracted to minors—and who learns from dissident theologians that his sexual feelings are his business and that there is no such thing as "deviant" feelings? Would he not be more inclined to indulge his feelings?

Catholics who consider themselves to be progressives—by rejecting Church teachings on sexuality and marriage—have helped to bring about the conditions that contributed to clergy sexual abuse. Those progressives in positions of influence, such as activists, theologians, writers, instructors, and Church workers, encouraged dissidence among seminarians and priests. To be sure, normal men who are taught to sneer at the Church's sexual morality are not about to seduce a minor, but an already disturbed young man is more likely to do so *after being given tacit permission.*

Catholic progressives often complain about crackdowns on dissent. What crackdowns? Here is the truth about the way the Catholic Church has operated for the past several decades: there is no institution in society that has more rules and enforces them less than the

---

[3] Neuhaus made his remarks on the April 28, 2002, edition of NBC's *Meet the Press.*

Catholic Church. The Catholic Church tolerates more in the way of free speech than most colleges and universities do. The Church is even more tolerant of dissent than the mainstream media, who are insisting more and more on uniformity of thought, especially when it comes to questions of sexuality. How long would someone last on the editorial board of the *New York Times* if he said publicly that he didn't think a true marriage between two men was possible?

Yet progressives portray the pontificates of John Paul II and Benedict XVI as times when dissidents were punished. Father Richard McBrien was particularly harsh, saying the administration of Pope John Paul II was responsible for silencing dissidents, insisting on loyalty oaths, and the like. He compared his rule to that of the Kremlin under the Soviet dictators. Phil Lawler noted, however, that in the pope's early years, there was some movement to address dissent, but it never amounted to anything, aside from a few warnings. In fact, "the crackdown that liberals feared (and conservatives longed for) never occurred. Theological dissent remained commonplace, particularly at the most prestigious Catholic colleges and universities."[4]

Cardinal Joseph Ratzinger, who would become Pope Benedict XVI, was scorned by progressives for his alleged disciplinary efforts while serving under Pope John Paul II. After assuming papal duties, he was similarly criticized for cracking the whip too harshly and too frequently. Though Benedict was known as "God's Rottweiler" by his detractors, Benedict's papacy was actually quite reserved. "Measured over the full seven years of Benedict's papacy," observed Catholic journalist John Allen, "the total number of occasions when Rome has called someone on the carpet remains relatively limited." Allen listed one theologian who was publicly admonished, and "when discipline was imposed, even by recent historical standards, it's often been fairly light." He further noted that no one's license to teach theology was pulled and no one was fired from teaching at a Catholic college or university because of Rome's intervention.[5] So if anything, dissidents got off easy.

---

[4]Philip Lawler, *The Faithful Departed: The Collapse of Boston's Catholic Culture* (New York: Encounter Books, 2008), 92.

[5]John L. Allen Jr., "Has the 'Real Ratzinger' Come Out to Play?", *National Catholic Reporter*, April 29, 2012, https://www.ncronline.org/blogs/ncr-today/has-real-ratzinger-come-out-play.

Theologian Father Matthew Lamb sees the nexus between dissent and clergy sexual abuse. "How many of the priests and bishops who have brought such suffering to minors and scandal to the public were encouraged by teachers and theologians to cut corners and dissent from the truth of Catholic faith and moral teaching? Many priests and future bishops read articles dissenting from Catholic sexual ethics in the 1960s and 1970s. A climate of dissent was promoted by wholesale dissent from Catholic sexual ethics."[6]

Lamb is not engaging in hyperbole. When seminarians are assigned readings from Alfred Kinsey and his disciples, all of whom promote a sexual free-for-all ideology, what are we to expect?[7] What are we to expect when psychologists weed out men from the priesthood because they *don't* reject the Church's teachings on sexuality?[8] Worse, some of them who are sent for therapy—because they *believe* what the Church teaches—begin to question themselves. One seminarian who went through this ordeal, wondered, "Am I nuts?"[9] Another candidate for the priesthood who accepted the Church's teachings on women was declared inadequate by a feminist nun; she labeled him "insensitive to the needs of women". An appeal to the bishop yielded nothing: he said he would not "interfere".[10]

Father Robert Altier minces no words about "an intentional and malicious infiltration of the Church for the purpose of destroying her from within". He says that when he was in the seminary in 1985, "if you were not a homosexual or a radical feminist you were in big trouble." One of his professors called for his students to engage in mutiny by saying, "Martin Luther had the right idea, but he did it the wrong way—he left the Church. You can't change

[6]Leon Podles, *Sacrilege: Sexual Abuse in the Catholic Church* (Baltimore: Crossland Press, 2008), 454.

[7]Judith A. Reisman, "Reliance of the U.S. Catholic Church on the Discredited Field of 'Human Sexuality' and on Sexology Advisors Whose 'Scientific' and Moral Foundation Deviates Radically from That of the Church", Judith A. Reisman, 2002, http://www.drjudithreisman.com/archives/US-CathChurch_Reliance_DiscScience.pdf.

[8]Michael Rose, *Goodbye, Good Men* (Washington, D.C.: Regnery, 2002), 9–10, 31–32, 40–41, 129–31.

[9]Ibid., 131.

[10]James Hitchcock, "Conservative Bishops, Liberal Results", *Catholic World Report* (May 1995), posted at Ignatius Insight, http://www.ignatiusinsight.com/features2005/print2005/hitchcock_bishops_may05.html.

the Church from the outside, you can change it from the inside, so we're not leaving."[11]

Father Patrick Klekas is a young priest who noted that in his seminary years, there was a clear line between men like him and sexually active homosexual classmates who dissented from Church teachings. "The majority of seminarians who act out on their same-sex attractions tend to support heterodox moral teaching", he said. They will dissent at the dinner table, he added, but will appear loyal in class. "The process of ordaining discontented seminarians contributes to the popular notion that a rise in clerical dissent will increase the likelihood of change in the Church."[12]

Given this state of affairs, no wonder many of the laity are confused. If those in the hierarchy are publicly dissenting from Church teachings on homosexuality, why should the laity pay any attention to them on other matters? Cardinal Sarah is not happy with this development. "The sign of Satan is division. Today there are serious conflicts within the clergy. And the devil is partying. The devil loves to divide the Church." From all indicators, he is doing a pretty good job. "He seeks to instill lukewarmness and doubt in priests."[13] What makes this so problematic is that the Church teaching in question has clear behavioral consequences, making the damage that much more severe. When the issue is homosexuality, the fallout can be horrific.

Vatican II and *Humanae Vitae*

Catholic observers of all persuasions agree that the decision by Pope Paul VI to maintain the Church's teaching on artificial birth control, as outlined in *Humanae Vitae*, threw the clergy and the laity into tumult. When his predecessor, Pope John XXIII, established a commission to

---

[11] Father Robert Altier, "The Enemy Within," *Catalyst* (October 2018), https://www .catholicleague.org/the-enemy-within/.

[12] Father Patrick Klekas, " 'Don't Ask, Don't Tell' Is Still the Rule in Seminary", *Crisis Magazine*, July 31, 2019, http://www.crisismagazine.com/2019/dont-ask-dont-tell-is-still -the-rule-in-seminary.

[13] Robert Cardinal Sarah, *The Day Is Now Far Spent* (San Francisco: Ignatius Press, 2019), 134–35.

study this issue, expectations were that a change was imminent. But it never happened, thus setting in motion widespread dissent.

Leading the dissent was Father Charles Curran, professor of moral theology at the Catholic University of America. He argued that the pope's encyclical was not infallible and could therefore be in error. This would legitimize dissent, he said. He commanded a big, influential audience of priests, nuns, and laypeople, some of whom took out a full-page ad in the *New York Times* to justify their rejection of *Humanae Vitae*. The bishops, faced with a growing public relations problem, issued a pastoral letter in November 1968, *Human Life in Our Day*, wherein they accepted what they called "licit dissent". According to Kenneth Whitehead, what they meant by this term was "mere academic-style disagreement". The effect, he said, was that "huge numbers of Catholics not unreasonably concluded that dissent was indeed licit." It was not until 1979 that the Vatican began an investigation of Father Curran. In 1986, he was informed that he was no longer "suitable nor eligible to exercise the function of a professor of Catholic theology".[14] But the damage had already been done. His eighteen years of dissent at a pontifical university legitimized for many Catholics their rejection of Catholic sexual morality.

The 1968 encyclical that reaffirmed the Church's opposition to contraception may have been ignored by the laity, but they did not engage in open rebellion. That was left to nuns and priests. Cardinal Patrick O'Boyle of the Archdiocese of Washington disciplined nineteen Washington priests for what any other organization would call insubordination. But the rebels appealed to Rome, and they won: the Vatican ordered O'Boyle to lift his sanctions. What drove the decision was fear of schism. The pope believed it was better to risk dissent than to see the Church break apart, and it was his hope that when things calmed down, the Church could get back to normalcy. George Weigel brands this the "Truce of 1968".[15] What was learned from the truce, Weigel says, "were two lessons that would shape an entire era of United States Catholic history". One lesson was that the

---

[14]Kenneth Whitehead, "Dissent", in *Encyclopedia of Catholic Social Thought, Social Science, and Social Policy*, vol. 1, ed. Michael Coulter, Stephen Krason, Richard Myers, and Joseph Varacalli (Lanham, Md.: Scarecrow Press, 2007), 311.

[15]George Weigel, *The Courage to Be Catholic: Crisis, Reform, and the Future of the Church* (New York: Basic Books, 2002), 68–72.

Holy See would retreat in the face of dissent, and the other is that bishops like O'Boyle would not receive the support they needed from Rome.[16]

Weigel notes that these lessons were not lost on what some called at the time the "Bernardin Machine", a reference to the team of progressive bishops led by Archbishop Joseph Bernardin.[17] In 1968, the future cardinal and archbishop of Chicago became the first general secretary of the National Conference of Catholic Bishops. Bernardin and Cardinal John Dearden of Detroit exercised tremendous influence in shaping the Catholic Church in the United States in the closing decades of the twentieth century, much to the applause of dissidents. (See chapter 12 for a discussion of Dearden's dissidence.)

Bernardin also worked with Belgian archbishop Jean Jadot, the person most responsible for appointing many progressive bishops, some of whom quietly dissented from Catholic sexual ethics. It is not a coincidence that clergy sexual abuse was peaking at the same time.

With no pushback, progressive Catholics seized the day, promoting dissent in the name of "the spirit of Vatican II". This vague term was given much elasticity, so much so that virtually any departure from traditional moral theology could find cover by simply invoking "the spirit of Vatican II". It got so crazy that one priest, speaking from the pulpit, smashed the rosary, scattering the beads on the floor, telling the faithful, "You don't have to say this anymore."[18]

Adding to this turbulence was a massive wave of homosexuals entering the priesthood. "Alongside the attrition rate of thousands of priests who left to marry," writes Jason Berry, "the numbers of homosexuals entering clerical life began to escalate. Dozens of priests over age fifty, in every region of the country, told me that in the 1970s homosexuals began pouring into seminaries and order houses."[19] Many of them were openly rebelling against the Church's teachings on sexuality, and few were reprimanded for doing so.

---

[16] George Weigel, "The End of the Bernardin Era", *First Things* (February 2011), http://www.firstthings.com/article/2011/02/the-end-of-the-bernardin-era.

[17] Ibid.

[18] Joseph A. Komonchak, "Interpreting the Council: Catholic Attitudes toward Vatican II", in Mary Jo Weaver and R. Scott Appleby, eds., *Being Right: Conservative Catholics in America* (Bloomington, Ind.: Indiana University Press), 21.

[19] Jason Berry, *Lead Us Not into Temptation* (New York: Doubleday, 1992), 183.

There is a lesson for the Church in all of this chaos: don't raise expectations of reform too high. Political scientist James Davies posited what he called the "J-curve" theory of revolutions, and it has application to what Pope John XXIII did in establishing a committee of priests and laypeople to advise him on the wisdom of the Church's teaching on artificial birth control.

Davies argued that revolutions do not occur when people are most oppressed. Rather, they occur when a period of dramatic social and economic improvements is followed by a quick and sharp reversal. Applied to the Catholic Church, had there been no commission, or had the commission not recommended a change in the Church's teaching, there may have been some discontent but the convulsions that followed would have been avoided.

Sexual Deviance Taught to Seminarians

In 1990, I appeared on the *Phil Donahue Show*, debating the propriety of some human sexuality classes on college campuses, especially courses that assigned the text *Our Sexuality* by Robert Crooks and Karla Bauer (new editions are still being used). The authors positively rejected the idea that there is any such thing as "deviant sex". Whether the subject is sex with the dead (necrophilia), incest, bestiality, or a fetish like smelling someone's dirty underwear for sexual excitement, all of this can be understood as merely "atypical sex". Little did I know that this book was required reading for some seminarians at the time.[20] Sabotage is the only way to describe this.

What effect would such a book have on seminarians? For those who were normal and were not suffering from some disorder, probably confusion. They were surely invited to be skeptical of Catholic sexual ethics, and perhaps some took the bait. But to the sexually confused, and to those who inclined toward deviance, this was clearly a statement of affirmation, one that ratified their worst impulses. The leap from dissent to sexual experimentation—including, for some, sexual abuse—was certainly made easier.

[20]Rose, *Goodbye, Good Men*, 100.

There was another book used in the seminaries that was certainly damaging to young men studying for the priesthood. *Human Sexuality: New Directions in American Catholic Thought* was written by Father Anthony Kosnik and four associates. Kosnik was a member of the Catholic Coalition for Gay Civil Rights and an avid dissenter from Church teachings on sexuality. He maintained that when it comes to judging the morality of homosexual acts, we cannot reflexively accept what the Church teaches. "We cannot simply appeal for answers to tradition or to revelation, as if the question had been decided once and for all by divine decree on the shores of the Dead Sea."[21]

Seminarians were taught to reject the notion that homosexual acts were intrinsically evil and instead to consider them to be morally neutral. "Homosexual acts are to be evaluated in terms of their relational significance", Kosnik wrote.[22] He rejected Catholic sexual ethics as it had been understood throughout the ages. Indeed, he went so far as to question the validity of condemning bestiality, never mind homosexuality.[23] Human sexuality, he said, should be "self-liberating" and "joyous". He was as blunt as anything found in *Playboy*. "The importance of the erotic element, that is, instinctual desire for pleasure and gratification deserves to be affirmed and encouraged."[24]

If this were just a book written by a marginalized priest, that would be one thing. In fact, it was commissioned by the Catholic Theological Society and was given a first-place award by the Catholic Press Association. The bishops' conference issued a critical statement in November 1977, and two years later the Sacred Congregation for the Doctrine of the Faith weighed in, saying the book gave "broad distribution to the erroneous principles and conclusions", thus becoming "a source of confusion among the people of God".[25] This meant nothing to the dissidents. The book continued to be used in many

[21] Anthony Kosnik et al., *Human Sexuality: New Directions in American Catholic Thought* (New York: Paulist Press, 1977), 200.

[22] Ibid., 200, 202, 208.

[23] Ibid., 88.

[24] Ibid., 92, 95.

[25] Sacred Congregation for the Doctrine of the Faith, *Letter to Archbishop John R. Quinn, President of the National Conference of Catholic Bishops in the U.S.A.* (July 13, 1979), https://www.vatican.va/roman_curia/congregations/cfaith/documents/rc_con_cfaith_doc_19790713_mons-quinn_en.html.

seminaries throughout the 1980s and 1990s.[26] To this day, the book is applauded by the *National Catholic Reporter*, which portrays Kosnik as a victim; he says he is a victim of "oppression".[27]

The Catholic Theological Society has a long history of dissidence. In 1969 it elected Charles Curran president, and in 1997, it endorsed women priests.[28] Professor James Hitchcock blames it for ostracizing conservative Catholics. "People have been denied tenure, lost their jobs, were never hired in the first place, or were otherwise penalized for upholding Church teaching, not only in academia but even in official Church agencies."[29]

The academics in the Catholic Theological Society deny that books like the Kosnik volume they commissioned could ever be blamed for the clergy sexual abuse scandal. By itself, of course, Kosnik's book cannot be blamed, but to say it is without effect is nonsense. Books are written to influence the reader's thought and behavior, and this is especially true of assigned student texts.

As I mentioned in an earlier chapter, in 2020 a scandal erupted in France about Gabriel Matzneff, the writer who for decades bragged about having sex with boys as young as eight, as well as scores of teenage girls and boys. French intellectuals adored him. But when times changed, he lost his glamour. A lawyer who works to combat pedophilia commented on his influence: "We know of emotionally troubled men who justified pedophilia after reading Matzneff's books."[30] Might there likewise be troubled seminarians and priests who justified their sexual abuse of minors after reading Kosnik's book?

[26]Father Matthew Habiger, O.S.B., "Reluctance among Catholic Clergy to Speak about the Catholic Sexual Ethic", Catholic News Agency, August 2007, https://www.catholicnewsagency.com/resources/life-and-family/sexuality-contraception/reluctance-among-clergy-to-speak-about-the-catholic-sexual-ethic.

[27]See Arthur Jones, "Theologians See, Experience Downside to John Paul II's Papacy", *National Catholic Reporter*, April 2, 2005, http://www.nationalcatholicreporter.org/update/conclave/arthurjones.htm; Regina Schulte, "On Sexuality, the Hierarchy Has Usurped the Entire Teaching Office", *National Catholic Reporter*, October 15, 2010, https://www.ncronline.org/news/parish/sexuality-hierarchy-has-usurped-entire-teaching-office.

[28]Robert L. Fastiggi, "Catholic Theological Society of America", in Michael Coulter et al., *Encyclopedia of Catholic Social Thought, Social Science, and Social Policy*, 1:156.

[29]James Hitchcock, "The Failure of Liberal Catholicism", *Catholic World Report*, May 15, 2011, http://www.catholicworldreport.com/2011/05/15/the-failure-of-liberal-catholicism.

[30]Norimitsu Onishi, "A Pedophile Writer Is on Trial. So Is the French Elite", *New York Times*, February 12, 2020, A1.

Paul Shanley

If there is a classic case of a molesting priest who took his cues from dissident texts, it was Paul Shanley. In 1968, when he was having sex with one of his young men, he became a strong proponent of situational ethics. "Every behavior, every so-called sin, he said, had to be dealt with separately and anew, within its own framework. That was the job of the priest, measuring and weighing, the work of the philosopher."[31] It was also the work of the molester. Shanley's justification for his predatory behavior is exactly what Kosnik taught in *Human Sexuality*. Kosnik's book did not teach Shanley to think this way; rather, it ratified his thoughts, giving them affirmation.

Boston's archbishop, Cardinal Medeiros, may have meant well by making Shanley his "minister to alienated youth on the streets" (Shanley, and the media, preferred the term "minister to sexual minorities"), but it was a bad decision. Shanley's idea of ministering to youth was to rape them.

According to David France, Shanley believed that authority was "an elemental evil".[32] Why would a man like this pay any attention to what his bishop said, or what the Church taught? Monogamy, Shanley said, was simply unnatural and had to be disregarded.[33] Predictably, he condemned the Church's teaching on homosexuality. "I do not think sexual activity among members of the same sex is so much the problem. It's what society says and does about it."[34] This explains how he rationalized his molesting behavior.

In 1970, Shanley was very open about this, writing newsletter dispatches on the Church's war on homosexuals. And what did Cardinal Medeiros do about it? In 1973, after fielding many complaints about Shanley's heretical views, he wrote him a letter saying, "I must express deep concern and disapproval."[35] A lot of good that did.

In that same year, Shanley ratcheted it up a notch. Here is what he told a young man in one of his "therapeutic" sessions: "I don't care

---

[31] David France, *Our Fathers: The Secret Life of the Catholic Church* (New York: Broadway Books, 2004), 48.
[32] Ibid., 5.
[33] Ibid., 76.
[34] Ibid., 93.
[35] Ibid.

what your parents told you. I don't care what your pastor told you. Forget everything you've learned, or thought was true. *Gay is good"* (italics in the original).[36] The boy was confused and told Shanley he had never had sex with a guy before. Shanley advised him to go to a gay porn theater, but the boy said he could not do that. Shanley then invited the boy to have sex with him.[37]

Bold as ever, Shanley started making cassette tapes about his lectures on the virtues of homosexuality.[38] In 1977, the same year Kosnik's work was published, Shanley could have been taking a page out of Kosnik's book when he said there was no sexual activity that causes psychic damage, "not even incest or bestiality".[39] In that same speech in Rochester, New York, he gave his infamous pro-pedophilia speech, claiming that the adult is not the seducer: "The kid is the seducer."

What did Medeiros do when a woman complained to him? He pitched the complaint to auxiliary bishop Thomas Daily. And what did he do? He blew her off. "The position of the Archdiocese of Boston is that while Father Shanley enjoys the faculties of the Archdiocese of Boston, he alone must be held responsible for any statements regarding homosexuality."[40]

In 1989, Shanley publicly criticized the revision of two new oaths issued by the Vatican: the Profession of Faith and the Oath of Fidelity. And what did the Archdiocese of Boston do about it? It excused him from taking the oath.[41] Shanley was in command, and he knew it. Bishop Daily was not alone in giving Shanley a pass. Bishop John McCormack, who vacationed with Shanley, knew of Shanley's infidelities but, as far as we know, did nothing about it. He also allowed Shanley to go wherever he wanted, even when it meant missing his assignments.[42] About the only person to stand up to Shanley was New York archbishop John O'Connor. In the mid-1990s, when Shanley, who was acting director of Leo House, a guest home in New York,

[36] Ibid., 101.
[37] Ibid., 102.
[38] Ibid., 118.
[39] Matthew L. Lamb, "Theological Malpractice", *National Review*, October 3, 2002, www.nationalreview.com.
[40] France, *Our Fathers*, 119–21.
[41] Podles, *Sacrilege*, 129.
[42] Ibid., 166.

sought to become the director, O'Connor told Boston archbishop Cardinal Law he would not accept him.[43]

Though Shanley disgraced himself and the Catholic Church, many times over, there were still those who exculpated him, blaming the Church's teachings on sexuality for his serial rapes. Brian McNaught was a homosexual activist who was thrown out of the priesthood in 1974; he was known to the *New York Times* as "the godfather of gay diversity training". Even after he was tossed, he exercised influence among homosexual priests. In 2015, he rallied to Shanley's side, saying the Church is responsible for turning its people into "molesters, deviants and repressed, immature, ignorant and sexually non-functioning individuals".

McNaught blamed his "sexually repressed, Irish Catholic family", and his sixteen years in Catholic schools, for his condition. He described that condition as "damaged".[44] Apparently, he never questioned why *almost all* Catholic young men never end up like him or Shanley, including those who (like myself) were raised in Irish-Catholic families and attended Catholic schools. But not taking responsibility for one's behavior is hardly an anomaly among people like Shanley and McNaught.

Rembert Weakland

No bishop demonstrated the link between dissent and homosexual behavior better than Milwaukee archbishop Rembert Weakland. He took over the archdiocese in 1977, and four years later, he attended a meeting of the National Gay Task Force.[45] It was conducting a gay rights "public education" campaign to mobilize religious and secular leaders to promote its agenda.

In the 1980s, under Weakland's tutelage, the archdiocese embarked on a series of courses on sex education that were more salacious than

---

[43] The Investigative Staff of the *Boston Globe, Betrayal: The Crisis in the Catholic Church* (Boston: Little, Brown, and Company, 2002), 71.

[44] Brian McNaught, "Who's to Blame for Sexually Deformed People?", Between the Lines, February 11, 2015, https://pridesource.com/article/75279-2/.

[45] Enrique Rueda, *The Homosexual Network: Private Lives and Public Policy* (Old Greenwich, Conn.: Devin Adair, 1982), 248.

scientific. Children were taught there is "no right and wrong" regarding sexuality, and adults were shown movies that featured naked men and women engaged in various sex acts. Regarding the latter, when a parishioner complained to Weakland, asking if he thought such a movie was tantamount to an occasion of sin, he said no. He did not answer when the woman asked, "Why then do we pray in the Our Father 'and lead us not into temptation'?" Also, Weakland received many complaints about a four-week course called "Homosexuality and Its Impact on the Family", which offered a "factual, nonjudmental presentation about homosexuality".[46]

Weakland allowed radical gay groups to hold meetings in parish halls and allowed Father James L. Arimond, who wrote for a homosexual magazine, to lecture about homosexuality at the archdiocesan Cousins Center. He taught that the Church's teaching on homosexuality was wrong and that homosexuality was, in fact, "God's holy gift". Weakland was critical of celibacy, supported women priests, and said it was okay for Catholics to be pro-abortion. When asked on television to describe his "brand of Catholicism", his reply was straightforward. "My brand of Catholicism? It's my brand of me."[47]

Weakland not only defended pro-homosexual priests; he punished whistleblowers. In July 1984, three lay teachers wrote to him about an assistant pastor who was inviting young boys to stay in his bedroom. They also complained about another priest who "signed an open document supporting homosexuality and has preached support of it from the pulpit". Weakland was angry, not at the heretical priests, but at the whistleblowers. On August 13, 1984, he put them on notice, warning that "any libelous material found in your letter will be scrutinized carefully by our lawyers." The three teachers resigned. Meanwhile the assistant pastor whom they complained about, Father Dennis Pecore, was molesting a teenage boy. On January 22, 1987, Pecore was charged with second-degree sexual assault.[48]

More serious still was Weakland's passivity in dealing with one of the worst predator priests in American history, Father Lawrence

[46] Art Moore, "Catholics Learning Sex from Kinsey's Disciples", *WorldNetDaily*, June 12, 2002, https://www.wnd.com/2002/06/14206/.

[47] Margaret Joughin, "The Weakland File", *Christian Order* (August/September and October 1996), http://www.christianorder.com/features/features_1996-08-09-10.html.

[48] Berry, *Lead Us Not into Temptation*, 306.

Murphy. He allegedly molested some two hundred deaf boys in Wisconsin in the 1950s. The civil authorities were not asked to investigate these crimes until the mid-1970s; following a probe, they dropped the case. Fast-forward to 1996, when the Vatican learned of the Murphy case for the first time. It immediately ordered a trial. Murphy died during the trial in 1998, but many questions remained.

Weakland was notified in 1980 about Murphy. Why did it take him sixteen years to contact the Vatican? Why did Weakland unjustly seek to blame Cardinal Ratzinger, saying he frustrated his attempts to help Murphy's victims?[49]

Why didn't Weakland pursue these cases of sexual abuse? Why did he routinely shred reports of sexual abuse by priests? He tore up the weekly reports. This is not a matter of dispute: he admitted doing so in a 1993 deposition.[50] Why did Weakland seek to deflect responsibility from his molesting priests by blaming the victims? He said, "We could easily give a false impression that any adolescent who becomes sexually involved with an older person does so without any degree of personal responsibility. Sometimes not all adolescent victims are so innocent; some can be sexually very active and aggressive and often quite street wise."[51] Surely his rejection of the Church's sexual ethics played a role in these decisions, demonstrating once again the nexus between dissent and sexual abuse.

Weakland's dissidence may also have played a role in his own case of alleged sexual abuse. Paul Marcoux, Weakland's lover, said the archbishop sexually assaulted him on several occasions. Weakland admitted to the homosexual relationship but insisted that it was consensual. After this was publicly revealed in 2002, Weakland retired. He admitted paying Marcoux $450,000 in hush money in 1998. Soon after he retired, he issued a strong apology to the faithful, describing his conduct as "sinfulness". Margaret O'Brien Steinfels, who lauded

---

[49] Father Raymond J. de Souza, "'Sign of Our Repentance': Weakland's Name Expunged from Milwaukee Church Building", *National Catholic Register*, April 2, 2019, https://www.ncregister.com/news/sign-of-our-repentance-weakland-s-name-expunged-from-milwaukee-church-building.

[50] Bruce Vielmetti, "Weakland Shredded Copies of Sex Abuse Reports, Documents Say", *Milwaukee Journal Sentinel*, December 3, 2009, http://archive.jsonline.com/news/milwaukee/78431087.html/.

[51] Michael D'Antonio, *Mortal Sins: Sex, Crime, and the Era of Catholic Scandal* (New York: St. Martin's Press, 2013), 122–23.

Weakland in the pages of *Commonweal*, was saddened by his need to retire, saying his "two-decade ago encounter" was "perhaps an indiscretion, perhaps a grave sin".[52] She wasn't sure.

As it turned out, Weakland had been involved in much more than just one encounter. In his memoir, published in 2009, he admitted to having a series of homosexual affairs.[53] He also said that when the Church teaches that the homosexual orientation is "intrinsically disordered", it is promoting language that is "unhelpful, even harmful".[54]

Father Richard McBrien, feminist nun Joan Chittister, and other "progressives" praised Weakland for writing his memoir.[55] Prior to its release, Weakland made two startling statements. He said he didn't know it was against the law to rape kids and that, in any event, they would "grow out of it". Yet he paid no price for this among his loyal followers. "We all considered sexual abuse of minors as a moral evil," he said, "but had no understanding of its criminal nature." He added that he "accepted naively the common view that it was not necessary to worry about the effects on the youngsters: either they would not remember or they would 'grow out of it'".[56] To say this was the "common view" is positively absurd. Weakland, like Shanley, was so enmeshed in dissent that he could not see, or admit, that his behavior was abusive.

[52] Margaret O'Brien Steinfels, "Rembert Weakland", *Commonweal*, June 14, 2002, 6.

[53] De Souza, "Sign of Our Repentance."

[54] William L. Portier, "Restrung", *Commonweal*, July 13, 2009, https://www.common wealmagazine.org/restrung.

[55] Hitchcock, "The Failure of Liberal Catholicism".

[56] "Archbishop Weakland: I Didn't Know Clerical Abuse of Children Was a Crime", Catholic Culture, May 19, 2009, https://www.catholicculture.org/news/headlines/index .cfm?storyid=2965&repos=4&subrepos=2&searchid=2077356.

12

The Role of Organized Dissent

Protestants who are unhappy with their denomination can switch and join another, which explains why there is comparatively little in the way of organized dissent in Protestant churches. But for discontented Catholics, many of whom stay put, there are any number of dissident organizations they can join. Of course, they could always quit the Church, and many do, but for priests and nuns who are dissatisfied, some would rather stay and fight than quit. They know where the power is, and it isn't down the block at the local mainline Protestant church.

In 1970, at the Catholic University of America, there was a conference on religion and homosexuality organized by Dr. John R. Cavanaugh, a Catholic psychologist. Dissidents and outside extremists interrupted the program, listing several demands. They concluded by holding "the Catholic Church and the institution of psychiatry responsible for political crimes committed against homosexuals". As an example, they said, "every gay suicide is political murder."[1] Supporting their agenda were New Ways Ministry and many organizations of dissident nuns, priests, and brothers, as well as the Catholic Theological Society of America and some Catholic hospitals and state chapters of Catholic Charities.[2]

The 1970s proved to be the most pivotal decade in the rise of homosexual activism in the Church. Not coincidentally, it was also the decade when predatory priests ran wild. In 1974, Dayton, Ohio, was home to the first-ever National Conference on Gay Ministry, attended by homosexual activist Brian McNaught, Father Paul

[1] Enrique Rueda, *The Homosexual Network: Private Lives and Public Policy* (Old Greeenwich, Conn.: Devin Adair, 1982), 325.
[2] Ibid., 326.

Shanley, Father John O'Neill, and Sister Jeannine Gramick. In that same year, the National Federation of Priests' Councils announced its support for gay rights and an end to laws that criminalized homosexuality.[3] Two years later, dozens of Catholic organizations, including many dioceses and orders of nuns, declared their support for Dignity, a Catholic homosexual group that rejects the Church's teachings on sexuality.[4]

No organization did more to rally Catholics against the Church's sexual ethics than Call to Action. It was founded in 1976 by Dan and Sheila Daley, who at the time were a priest and a nun. They fell in love, relinquished their respective roles, and married. They inspired a large following, many of whom were priests and nuns, and directed their efforts at exerting public pressure on the Church to adopt wideranging changes. They got a big boost from Detroit's Cardinal John Dearden and Chicago's Cardinal Joseph Bernardin, both of whom promoted their agenda. Dearden chaired the 1976 conference, and 64 percent of those in attendance were Church employees.[5] Dissidence was now mainstreamed in the Catholic Church.

In 1989, Call to Action ran advertisements in newspapers across the country seeking to obtain one hundred thousand signatures in support of their objections to Church teachings on ordination and sexuality and their demand for more lay involvement. Two years later, they could come up with only twenty-one thousand signatures,[6] but their impact far surpassed their numbers.

In 1996, Sister Maureen Fiedler was convinced she could do what Call to Action could not. Her petition campaign, "We Are Church", sought to get one million Catholics to sign a statement calling for radical changes in Church teachings on women and sexuality. The Ford Foundation sent her millions by way of Catholics for Choice. And Fiedler paid kids a dollar for every signature they could snatch. After a year, the tally was in: thirty-seven thousand signatures had been

[3] David France, *Our Fathers: The Secret Life of the Catholic Church in an Age of Scandal* (New York: Broadway Books, 2004), 111–13.

[4] Rueda, *The Homosexual Network*, 338–40.

[5] *Call to Action: 25 Years of Spirituality and Justice*, Call to Action anniversary edition newsletter, October 2001.

[6] Peter Steinfels, "Bishops and Liberals Split on Agendas", *New York Times*, November 11, 1991, A10.

garnered.[7] She was off by 96 percent. It was another monumental flop. Fiedler blamed the laity for not being smart enough to support her. She agreed with the assessment that progressives "overestimated Catholic theological maturity, and underestimated the pietism of the Catholic laity".[8]

Dignity and New Ways Ministry are the most well-known dissident organizations that champion the gay agenda. They claim to be Catholic although they openly rebel against Church teachings on sexuality. Like Call to Action, they are lavishly funded by outside sources, such as the Arcus Foundation, a left-wing philanthropy.[9]

Dignity had some early success gaining support inside the Catholic Church. In the late 1970s, a key employee at the Office of Public Affairs and Information of the bishops' conference was president of the Washington, D.C., chapter of Dignity.[10] In 1980, its leaders secured a meeting with Archbishop John Quinn of San Francisco and Bishop Roger Mahony of Stockton and announced their satisfaction with the outcome.[11] In the early 1980s, Dignity boasted that it had among their supporters 1,600 bishops, priests, nuns, and laypeople from the United States.[12] It should surprise no one that Father Paul Shanley was the chaplain of the Dignity chapter in New York, demonstrating the link between dissent and the clergy sexual abuse scandal. Today Dignity continues to call for changes in Catholic teachings on homosexuality and has taken up the cause of transgender persons, though it does not command the attention of the Catholic hierarchy the way it did in the 1970s and 1980s, two decades that saw clergy sexual abuse spike. The connection is not an accident.

New Ways Ministry was founded in 1977 by Father Robert Nugent and Sister Jeannine Gramick. From its beginning, according

---

[7] Jay McNally, " 'We Are the Church' Referendum Is Huge Failure, Sr. Fiedler Admits", *Wanderer*, November 27, 1997, 6.

[8] David Morrison, "We Are Church: 'It Seemed Like a Good Idea' ", *Our Sunday Visitor*, December 7, 1997, 21.

[9] Steve Warner, "Dissenting Catholic Charities: Changing the Unchangeable", Capital Research Center, December 12, 2017, https://capitalresearch.org/article/dissenting-catholic-charities-1/.

[10] Gabriele Kuby, "Abuse: 'Let Not Your Heart Be Troubled' ", LifeSiteNews, February 20, 2019, https://www.lifesitenews.com/images/local/files/PDFs/Abuse_by_Gabriele_Kuby.pdf.

[11] Rueda, *The Homosexual Network*, 323–24.

[12] Ibid., 330.

to a 2010 statement by Cardinal Francis George, then president of the United States Conference of Catholic Bishops, "serious questions have been raised about the group's adherence to Church teaching on homosexuality."[13] In that same year of 1977, Rembert Weakland was installed as archbishop of Milwaukee, and four years later, he was hosting a retreat for the organization.[14] Nugent had close ties with the bishops' conference in the early 1980s, and he exploited that relationship effectively: he cited it when giving pro-homosexual speeches.[15] New Ways also infiltrated the seminaries during this time, especially in the Washington, D.C., area, promoting dissidence in the classroom.[16]

This did not sit well with Washington archbishop James Hickey. He sent a letter to all Catholic bishops, alerting them that the group rejected Church teaching against homosexual acts. Dissident priests and nuns, however, sought to undermine him; they were the biggest supporters of New Ways and Dignity.[17] In 1984, Hickey denied New Ways any official authorization or approval of its activities and forbade Nugent and Gramick to continue their work in his archdiocese. At the same time, they were ordered by their superiors to cease and desist with their pro-homosexual agenda. They resigned from their leadership posts but defiantly continued to work for New Ways. In fact, in 1997, Nugent was a consultant to the United States Conference of Catholic Bishops on its pastoral document about homosexuality, *Always Our Children*.[18]

In 1999, the Congregation for the Doctrine of the Faith permanently prohibited Nugent and Gramick from any pastoral ministry with homosexuals, but they carried on with their advocacy work. It was when they publicly criticized the Church for defending the definition of marriage, as between one man and one woman, that

[13] "USCCB President Clarifies Status of New Ways Ministry", February 12, 2010, United States Conference of Catholic Bishops, https://www.usccb.org/news/2010/usccb -president-clarifies-status-new-ways-ministry.

[14] Rueda, *The Homosexual Network*, 353–54.

[15] Ibid., 308.

[16] Ibid., 293.

[17] Ibid., 359.

[18] Kevin Eckstrom, "Fr. Bob Nugent, Silenced for His Work with Gay Catholics, Dies at 76", *National Catholic Reporter*, January 3, 2014, https://www.ncronline.org/news/people /fr-bob-nugent-silenced-his-work-gay-catholics-dies-76.

Cardinal George issued his 2010 statement. It said that "New Ways Ministry has no approval or recognition from the Catholic Church" and that "they cannot speak on behalf of the Catholic faithful in the United States."[19] None of this was enough to stop New Ways from giving Father James Martin an award in 2016 for his work with homosexuals, and it certainly didn't stop Martin from accepting it.

National Catholic Reporter

Dissident nuns, priests, and laypeople rely on the National Catholic Reporter for their information. It influences and reinforces the opinions of left-wing faculty members at Catholic colleges and universities, as well as many who work for the Church. Many of its writers reject the Church's teachings on marriage, sexuality, ordination, and priestly celibacy and, in doing so, have inspired, however unwittingly, molesters who look to Catholic sources for legitimacy. When molesters blame their sexual problems on Catholic moral teaching—absurd as that is—they find support in the pages of the National Catholic Reporter.

Before the 2020 presidential election, the bishops put out a statement saying abortion was the preeminent issue for Catholics to consider. But the Reporter disagreed: "That kind of distortion of the Gospel message and the church's social justice teachings is an example of what Pope Francis describes as a 'harmful ideological error.'" It branded the bishops' statement "a thinly disguised endorsement not only of the Republican Party but also the Trump administration".[20] The abortion issue means so little to this newspaper that it awarded Representative Nancy Pelosi, a champion of abortion on demand, its 2019 Newsmaker of the Year award.[21]

[19] "USCCB President Clarifies Status of New Ways Ministry", United States Conference of Catholic Bishops, February 12, 2010, https://www.usccb.org/news/2010/usccb-president -clarifies-status-new-ways-ministry.

[20] "Editorial: The Failed Leadership of US Bishops is Clear", National Catholic Reporter, November 22, 2019, www.ncronline.org/news/opinion/editorial-failed-leadership-us-bishops -clear.

[21] "NCR's 2019 Newsmaker of the Year: Nancy Pelosi", National Catholic Reporter, December 20, 2019, www.ncronline.org/print/news/opinion/ncrs-2019-newsmaker-year-nancy -pelosi.

In 2020, Jamie Manson, who "spent over a decade challenging the hierarchy's teachings on women's ordination, contraceptive access, abortion, religious liberty and LGBTQ issues", was named the new president of Catholics for Choice.[22] That she had written a column for the *Reporter* for twelve years removes any doubt about the agenda of the newspaper. No wonder foes of the Catholic Church herald its "independence".

The *National Catholic Reporter* was founded in Kansas City, Missouri, in 1964. Even then, it was Catholic in name only. Bishop Charles Helmsing of Kansas City–St. Joseph wasted no time telling the editors to remove the word *Catholic* from its title. But they refused to do so. In 2002, I debated Tom Roberts, one of the top editors at the newspaper, on television. "Now guys like Roberts, the *National Catholic Reporter*, they don't believe in anything the Catholic Church says on sexuality anyhow," I said, "so of course he doesn't want to talk about homosexuality." The moderator, Mike Barnicle, interrupted me. "Wait, Bill, please. Tom, take it up. I mean, you just got whacked across the face. Take it up." To which Roberts replied, "I'm not going to take it up."[23] How could he? What I said was undeniably true.

According to Father Paul Shaughnessy, Roberts is one of those critics of the Church who attack the bishops with regularity, intimidating them from speaking out about the role homosexuality has played in the scandal.[24] "Liberals characteristically refuse to acknowledge their own role in creating the gay priest problem," he wrote, "and often attempt to transfer blame to others."

In 2008, the *National Catholic Reporter* proved its conservative critics right when it endorsed a book by two Catholic theologians, *The Sexual Person*. The book argued that the Church's teachings on homosexuality, and all other matters of sexuality, were wrong; one of the authors

[22] "CFC Announces New President, Catholic Thought Leader Jamie Manson", Catholics for Choice, September 29, 2020, www.catholicsforchoice.org/cfc-announces-new-president-jamie-manson.

[23] This episode is related in Bill Donohue, *Secular Sabotage: How Liberals Are Destroying Religion and Culture in America* (New York: FaithWords, 2009), 167.

[24] Paul Shaughnessy, "The Gay Priest Problem", *Catholic World Report* (November 2000), posted on Catholic Culture, https://www.catholicculture.org/culture/library/view.cfm?recnum=12047.

headed the theology department at Creighton University, a Jesuit school. The book was found "contrary to Catholic teaching" by the bishops' Committee on Doctrine,[25] yet Regina Schulte, writing in the *Reporter*, said the book was an attempt to "bring lay insights into the subject of human sexuality". It would have been more honest to say it was an attempt to sabotage the Church's sexual ethics. The title of Schulte's piece, "On Sexuality, the Hierarchy Has Usurped the Entire Teaching Office",[26] showcased the newspaper's dismissal of the Church's Magisterium.

The *National Catholic Reporter* does more than simply challenge Church teachings on sexuality; it acts as a conduit for dissenting nuns affiliated with the Leadership Conference of Women Religious (LCWR). After the Vatican announced in January 2009 that the Congregation for the Doctrine of the Faith was conducting a doctrinal assessment of the LCWR, the newspaper became home to dissident nuns and routinely leaked confidential information about the Vatican probe.[27] The Hilton Foundation worked against the Catholic Church by funding both the *Reporter* and the LCWR: it was reported in 2014 that it gave the newspaper $2.3 million to promote a positive picture of dissenting nuns.[28]

Dissident Nuns

The Vatican decision to assess doctrinal problems among women religious in the United States was not made impulsively. Quite frankly, dissent has been a central feature of many orders of nuns since the 1960s. Their role in undermining the Church's teachings on sexuality, and in creating the kind of milieu that was a breeding ground for troubled priests, is incontestable.

[25] Nancy Frazier O'Brien, "Doctrine Committee Says 2008 Book Errs in Views on Moral Issues", *Catholic News*, September 22, 2010, https://catholicnews.sg/2010/10/18/doctrine -committee-says-2008-book-errs-in-views-on-moral-issues/.
[26] Regina Schulte, "On Sexuality, the Hierarchy Has Usurped the Entire Teaching Office", *National Catholic Reporter*, October 15, 2010, http://www.ncronline.org/print/news/parish /sexuality-hierarchy-has-usurped-entire-teaching-office.
[27] Ann Carey, "How Is It Going?", *Catholic World Report* (January 2011): 18–21.
[28] Anne Hendershott, "When Members of the Catholic Press Fail the Church", *Crisis Magazine*, September 15, 2014, http://www.crisismagazine.com/2014/catholic-press-fails-church.

In 2001, the Vatican admonished the LCWR for its interpretation of Church teachings on many subjects, ranging from homosexuality to the salvific role of Jesus.[29] Naturally, the dissident nuns claimed victim status, accusing the Church of oppression. Yet when the keynote speaker at the LCWR assembly in 2007, Sister Laurie Brink, O.P., noted that some orders of nuns had moved "beyond Jesus" to become "post Christian", what was Rome expected to do?[30] When nuns make up their own liturgy, by substituting "Source of all being" for "Father" and replacing "Son" with "Eternal word", it is evident that they have decided to leave the Church.[31] But not really: even though they have moved "beyond Jesus", they park themselves comfortably within Catholic institutions.

The LCWR claims to have about 1,500 leaders who represent 80 percent of the nation's women religious. Most of the nuns simply ignored the Vatican questionnaire, and some found it to use the language of "violence".[32] When the report was released in 2012, serious doctrinal errors were found, as well as problematic statements made by members of the LCWR. It cited New Ways Ministry for promoting the gay agenda and took radical feminists to task for their pronouncements about Jesus.[33] Predictably, radical nuns said they were stunned, and the *National Catholic Reporter* branded the report an attempt at "thought control".[34] The *New York Times* weighed in, taking the side of the LCWR. It said that "much of the Catholic laity has registered outrage" about the Vatican probe.[35] This was total nonsense. Most Catholics hadn't a clue that there was such an investigation, and if they knew how many nuns had moved "beyond

[29] Carey, "How Is It Going?"

[30] Ann Carey, "In Denial", *Catholic World Report* (November 2009), posted at Catholic Culture, https://www.catholicculture.org/culture/library/view.cfm?recnum=9230.

[31] Ibid.

[32] Tom Fox, "Women Religious Not Complying with Vatican Study", *National Catholic Reporter*, November 24, 2009, https://www.ncronline.org/news/global-sisters-report /women-religious-not-complying-vatican-study.

[33] Congregation for the Doctrine of the Faith, "Doctrinal Assessment of the Leadership Conference of Women Religious", April 18, 2012, http://www.vatican.va/roman_curia /congregations/cfaith/documents/rc_con_cfaith_doc_20120418_assessment-lcwr_en.html.

[34] "Editorial: Consolation on LCWR Rings Hollow in Unhealthy Church", *National Catholic Reporter*, May 8, 2012, https://www.ncronline.org/news/opinion/editorial-consolation -lcwr-rings-hollow-unhealthy-church.

[35] "Speaking the Truth to the Vatican", *New York Times*, September 18, 2012, A24.

Jesus", they might have wondered why the Vatican didn't look into the matter sooner.

If Catholics in the pews knew more of what was going on with the LCWR, many would side with Raymond Arroyo. "Far from a crackdown," he said, "the Vatican is asking the LCWR to prayerfully return to their roots and to the reasons their religious institutes were founded. These monasteries were not founded 100 to 200 years ago to picket and contradict church teaching or the bishops. They were founded to faithfully serve brothers and sisters throughout the society in the spirit of Christ."[36]

Arroyo's comments are not an exercise in hyperbole. George Weigel has called attention to something that I have witnessed first-hand: "Some communities of LCWR sisters no longer participate regularly in the Eucharist, because they cannot abide the 'patriarchy' of a male priest-celebrant presiding at Mass. Thus faux Eucharists celebrated by a circle of women are not unknown in these communities." Weigel also took the LCWR to task for misrepresenting themselves as "just a modernized version of The Bells of St. Mary's".[37] Dissident nuns such as Elizabeth Johnson, who teaches at Fordham University, confess they "would not be at all adverse if we simply dropped the word 'Trinity'".[38]

It would be wrong, and wholly unfair, to say that there are not magnificent nuns who give of themselves selflessly, helping those in need and serving the Church with great devotion and effect. There are many outstanding orders of women religious that continue the grand tradition of nuns who have done so much yeoman's work in the United States and around the world. The good news is the orders that are heavily stocked with dissidents are crashing, while orthodox orders are holding their own, if not growing, and many are of recent vintage. According to one account, "Those doing well typically share some common characteristics, such as wearing the habit, living and

[36] Eric Marrapodi, "Nuns' Fight with Vatican Highlights Catholicism's Global Struggle", CNN, May 30, 2012, https://religion.blogs.cnn.com/2012/05/30/nuns-fight-with-vatican-highlights-catholicisms-global-struggle.

[37] George Weigel, "The Vatican and the Sisters", National Review, April 23, 2012, https://www.nationalreview.com/2012/04/vatican-and-sisters-george-weigel/.

[38] James Hitchcock, "The Failure of Liberal Catholicism", Catholic World Report (May 15, 2011), www.catholicworldreport.com/2011/05/15/the-failure-of-liberal-catholicism.

praying together in community, and fidelity to the teaching authority of the Church."[39]

Unfortunately, as I have seen more times than I care to think about, faithful nuns are often ridiculed and mocked by progressive nuns, some of whom have called them "deadwood". Similarly, I have encountered nuns in habit who take their vows seriously yet are forced to labor under criticism from sisters who have abandoned their Catholicism for pagan worship. Indeed, I know several women who left their order because the women they lived with made following their rule of life nearly impossible.

If progressive nuns were not corrupted by their radical brand of feminism, they would herald a woman who stood up to the bishops and who left her mark on communications throughout the world. But instead they loathe Mother Angelica. She was an orthodox nun, and there is no place for them in their pantheon of women religious. Similarly, while Saint Teresa of Calcutta was loved all over the world for her outreach to the dispossessed, some feminist nuns had no use for her. When I asked the owner of the Empire State Building to light the towers of the iconic building in blue and white in honor of Mother Teresa's centenary, the Women's Alliance for Theology, Ethics, and Ritual and the National Coalition of American Nuns signed a letter in support of the owner who turned me down (the same man honored mass murderer Mao Tse-tung).[40]

Dissident nuns have contributed to the clergy sexual abuse scandal by espousing a heterodox message on matters of sexuality, which has played right into the hands of sick priests. The nuns' complaints about the "oppressive patriarchy" give credence to those abusers who claim that Church authorities and Catholic morality have caused their sexual problems.

Before his crimes were known, Father Paul Shanley was the darling of many progressive Catholics who were pushing for Church acceptance of homosexual behavior. Sister Jeannine Gramick credited Shanley with having "motivated her to activism".[41] In 2005, after saying

[39]Jim Graves, "Orders That Are Running Out of Room", *Catholic Herald* (U.S. edition), January 18, 2019, 17.
[40]"Media Guide to Phony Catholic Groups", Catholic League, September 9, 2015, https://www.catholicleague.org/media-guide-to-phony-catholic-groups/.
[41]France, *Our Fathers*, 115.

how horrified she was by Shanley's sexual predation of minors, Gramick told the *National Catholic Reporter* that she "grieved for this man I had not seen in almost 20 years, but whose principles and whose advocacy for the downtrodden I had applauded for three decades".[42]

Journalist Maureen Orth responded to Gramick's embarrassing apologia, recounting that nine of Shanley's victims she interviewed explained how the hippie priest would instruct them to "use" his body. Gramick, Orth pointed out, never spoke to one of Shanley's victims.[43] Though many progressive Catholics distanced themselves from Gramick after this episode, Father James Martin not only embraced her but also announced in 2017 that he would like to "canonize" her.[44]

I have never heard a dissident connect the dots between dissent from Church teaching and the behavior of molesting priests. I have only heard dissidents blame conservative Catholics for defending traditional sexual morality. But the Shanleys of the Church did not take their cues from conservatives. No, they found them in the words of those challenging Church teaching, including those on the pages of the *National Catholic Reporter*, which praised Shanley at least three times for his advocacy even after his crimes were exposed.[45]

Catholic Education

In 1975, when I was teaching at St. Lucy's School in Spanish Harlem, the principal asked me to represent the school at a meeting of educators across the Archdiocese of New York. At the time I was teaching religion and social studies at the elementary school. There were sixty-nine educators at the meeting (I was one of only a few people), the purpose of which was to improve teaching Catholicism to students. I raised my hand, stood up, held a copy of a religion text

[42] Jeannine Gramick, "Finding Empathy for Shanley," *National Catholic Reporter*, January 14, 2005.
[43] Maureen Orth, "Gramick's Charity to Shanley Is More Than He Deserves", *National Catholic Reporter*, January 14, 2005.
[44] Jim Russell, "Fr. James Martin 'Canonizes' Sr. Jeannine Gramick", *Crisis Magazine*, June 27, 2017, http://www.crisismagazine.com/2017/fr-jim-martin-canonizes-sr-jeannine-gramick.
[45] Hitchcock, "The Failure of Liberal Catholicism".

in my hand, and said it was not easy to teach religion when there is no religion in the book. All it talks about is love and kindness, with pictures of hippies in garbage cans waving the peace sign. There is almost nothing in the book, I said, that wouldn't be acceptable to any atheist. The room exploded: roughly half were supportive, and half were not. I was then elected chairman of the religious-education committee for the archdiocese.

After I left St. Lucy's for a position at La Roche College, a liberal arts institution run by the Sisters of Divine Providence, I attended campus visit-day sessions; these were opportunities for prospective students and their parents to meet with faculty and administrators. I never heard the word "Catholic" mentioned more times than at these events (the feminist administrators wanted to appeal to parents who were holding their checkbooks). Indeed, when I sat on search committees to select a new faculty member, the president and the academic dean made it clear they did not want to hire someone who was "too Catholic". In fact, when the nun who was president announced she was leaving the college, I had to fight hard to secure a monsignor as her successor: she did not want to hire a priest, preferring a Presbyterian woman.

Father Joseph Fessio, S.J., founder and editor of Ignatius Press, said that 90 percent of theologians on Catholic campuses do not accept Catholic teachings on sexuality and the priesthood.[46] I would add that a large segment of the faculty and administrators at Catholic colleges and universities are hostile to Catholic teachings on marriage, the family, and sexuality. They get away with this because prospective administrators and faculty are more likely to be screened for their commitment to multiculturalism and the twin principles of inclusivity and diversity than they are for their fidelity to Catholic teachings.

Pope Benedict XVI observed that "Catholic moral theology suffered a collapse that rendered the Church defenseless" against changes in society with respect to sexuality.[47] Instead of resisting the most corrupt trends in the West, too many Catholic institutions of higher

---

[46]Richard Ostling, "U.S. Scholars Wonder Whether Pope Benedict XVI Will Take Further Actions Against Dissenters", Associated Press, May 12, 2005.

[47]Benedict XVI, "Full Text of Benedict XVI: The Church and the Scandal of Sexual Abuse", *Catholic World Report*, April 10, 2019, http://www.catholicworldreport.com/2019/04/10/full-text-of-benedict-xvi-the-church-and-the-scandal-of-sexual-abuse.

education embraced them, which provided excuses for molesting priests who sought to legitimize their behavior.

Catholic colleges and universities became increasingly less Catholic and more secular beginning in the mid-1960s. In 1965, the Higher Education Act provided significant new funding for institutions of higher learning, including religious institutions. Many Catholic administrators quickly concluded that in order to receive federal funding, they were obliged to secularize their schools. The truth is they came to this conclusion more out of desire than obligation.

The secular thrust of Catholic institutions received another bump in 1967, when twenty-six Catholic educators met in the town of Land O' Lakes, Wisconsin. Many presidents of major Catholic colleges and universities attended, committing themselves to major reforms while claiming that "to perform its teaching and research functions effectively, the Catholic university must have a true autonomy and academic freedom in the face of authority of whatever kind, lay or clerical, external to the academic community itself."[48]

The autonomy the universities prized most was independence from the Catholic Church. They certainly did not mind submitting themselves to the external accrediting institutions of higher education. Kenneth Whitehead, a noted Catholic scholar and government education official in the Reagan administration, summed up what happened: "The result was that most Catholic colleges and universities in America became effectively secularized institutions, Catholic in name only."[49]

As conditions worsened, the Church, ever slow to respond, issued a new *Code of Canon Law* in 1983. One of the eight new canons was a declaration that no university can claim to be a "Catholic university" without receiving the consent of the competent ecclesial authority and that those who teach theology must have a mandate (called a *mandatum*) to ensure fidelity to Church teachings. As expected, most Catholic universities pushed back, refusing to cooperate.

In 1990, Pope John Paul II issued *Ex Corde Ecclesiae*, a document that recognized the "institutional autonomy" and "academic

---

[48] Kenneth D. Whitehead, "Education, Catholic: Higher Education in the United States", in Michael Coulter et al., *Encyclopedia of Catholic Social Thought, Social Science, and Social Policy*, vol. 1 (Lanham, Md.: Scarecrow Press, 2007), 349–51.

[49] Ibid.

freedom" of Catholic schools, while insisting that these are not absolute principles and "must be preserved within the confines of truth
and the common good". It wasn't until 1999 that the United States
bishops finally approved this document.[50] By that time, it was too late
to have a real impact.

If there is one person in Catholic education who was more responsible for the secularization of Catholic schools, it was the long-time
president of the University of Notre Dame, Father Theodore Hesburgh. He made his mark early when he became the most influential
member of the Land O' Lakes community of educators. Father Hesburgh argued that Catholic schools would "lose a lot of government
assistance if we conformed to the dictates of the Church". He was
convinced that "institutional autonomy is essential to federal support." But, as Whitehead points out, this position was not dictated
by the government. Instead, it represented Hesburgh's interpretation
of the requirements for federal financial assistance.[51] No matter, Hesburgh's position was accepted and cited by the presidents of Catholic
colleges and universities throughout the nation.

Why did Hesburgh come to this conclusion? His biographer,
Notre Dame scholar Father Wilson "Bill" Miscamble, chalks it up
to a very common need on the part of Catholic leaders: the desire
for affirmation from secular elites. "The desire to be part of the elite
circles of power and influence colored how he led Notre Dame as
well as the causes he pursued", said Miscamble. He asked, "Might it
even be said of him that he did perhaps too much kneeling before
the world?"[52] In fairness, no one, including Miscamble, denies Hesburgh's role in making Notre Dame a first-class academic institution,
and it still employs some of the most committed Catholic scholars in
the nation.

If there is one cluster of Catholic colleges and universities that
is run by those eager to curry favor with secular elites, it is schools
run by Jesuits, which have become the most welcoming of dissident

[50] Ibid.

[51] Kenneth Whitehead, *Catholic Colleges and Federal Funding* (San Francisco: Ignatius Press, 1988), 17–18, 32–33.

[52] Heidi Schlumpf, "Author, Panel Debate Controversial Book about Notre Dame's Fr. Hesburgh", *National Catholic Reporter*, May 11, 2019, http://www.ncronline.org/print/news/people/author-panel-debate-controversial-book-about-notre-dames-fr-hesburgh.

faculty and administrators. It is also no secret that the Jesuits have been hit hard by the clergy sexual abuse scandal. These factors are not independent of each other. To cite one example, consider what a student at Berkeley's Jesuit School of Theology said of his experience: "The attitude of the Jesuits here is 'We need to affirm the gay life.'" The school made good on its promise by allowing credits to be earned for "gay spirituality" courses.[53] To a normal student, such exposure to these courses is not likely to generate deviant behavior, but to the already troubled young man, such experiences are likely to be more consequential.

Among the first Jesuit intellectual dissidents in the modern era was John J. McNeill, who received his Ph.D. from the Catholic University of Leuven in Belgium in 1964. A homosexual, he was integral to the founding of Dignity, the gay dissident-Catholic group. In 1976, he published *The Church and the Homosexual*, which rejected Catholic sexual morality, especially regarding homosexuality. The Vatican rescinded its approval of this book two years later. In 1986, Father McNeill challenged Cardinal Joseph Ratzinger's letter to the bishops on the pastoral care of homosexual persons, in which he labeled homosexuality "an objective disorder". Finally, in 1988, Rome directed McNeill to give up his ministry; he was subsequently expelled from the Jesuits.[54]

If McNeill were simply a renegade priest, it may not even be worth mentioning him in a discussion on the link between dissent and priestly sexual abuse. But such is not the case. After his 1976 book was released, wherein he said that "the most serious problem here is the call for priests to be chaste",[55] a statement defending him was made by prominent Catholic theologians, including Father Richard McBrien of Notre Dame, Daniel McGuire of Marquette, and Father Charles Curran of the Catholic University of America. They criticized the Vatican for cracking down, preferring to stick with the priest who said that Christ is exemplified by the homosexual movement.[56]

---

[53] Michael Rose, *Goodbye, Good Men* (Washington, D.C.: Regnery, 2002), 22.

[54] Tom Fox, "'Patron Saint' of LGBT Catholics, John J. McNeill, 90, Dies", *National Catholic Reporter*, September 24, 2015, http://www.ncronline.org/news/people/patron-saint-lgbt-catholics-john-j-mcneill-90-dies.

[55] France, *Our Fathers*, 385.

[56] Rueda, *The Homosexual Network*, 305.

THE ROLE OF ORGANIZED DISSENT

Think of how this plays out in reality. If it were unfair to contend that priests should be chaste and if it were true that Christ would be happy with the homosexual movement, then fidelity to Catholic sexual morality would not be a priestly imperative. Would this not give encouragement to priests who are sexually attracted to male adolescents?

Catholic educators who rail against the bishops for their role in the clergy sexual abuse scandal need to take a hard look at themselves. By tolerating, if not fomenting, dissent on campus, especially in sexual matters, they have made it easier for priests who reject these teachings to justify or excuse predatory behavior, in some cases their own. That may not be the intent of these dissident faculty members, but they cannot escape culpability for the signals they send to troubled priests.

The Role of Outside Activists

In 1953, Bella Dodd, an immigrant from Italy, testified before a congressional committee about her work with the Communist Party. She was no longer a member and had returned to the Catholic Church (Fulton Sheen, then a monsignor, played a key role in her return). Her efforts to undermine the United States, she said, were geared toward sabotaging the Catholic Church. During her time with the party, she told the committee, "more than eleven hundred men had been put into the priesthood to destroy the Church from within." It was hoped that some of the men would become monsignors, even bishops. She stunned the congressmen when she admitted that "right now they are in the highest places in the Church." A few years later, she confessed that there were four cardinals within the Vatican "who are working for the Communists".[57]

The Communists did not randomly choose to target the Catholic Church. They knew that if the economic and political freedoms intrinsic to American society were to be destroyed, they had to go after their pillars, and that certainly included the Catholic

[57]Eleonore Villarrubia, "Bella Dodd—From Communist to Catholic", *Catholicism.org*, August 31, 2010, https://catholicism.org/bella-dodd-%E2%80%94-from-communist-to-catholic .html. See also Dodd's book, *School of Darkness*.

Church—and the family. Even before the Communists, those who have sought to undermine Western civilization have always targeted its Judeo-Christian culture, and prime among their targets have been marriage and the Catholic Church.

Dodd is just one example of those who have penetrated the Catholic Church with the intent of destroying it. Their modus operandi is to foment dissent within the Church, proving that this is not wholly a matter of internal forces; outsiders have played a role in promoting it as well. Those outsiders are usually activists such as Dodd, but they are typically inspired by intellectuals who have embraced atheistic philosophies and ideologies. The latter have been working to sunder the Church for a long time, beginning in the Enlightenment, though contemporary activists are much more coordinated and sophisticated.

If there is one intellectual who is most responsible for igniting activists to attack the Church, it is the early-twentieth-century Italian Marxist Antonio Gramsci. Where Marx looked to the urban factory workers, the proletariat, to carry out the revolution that would displace capitalism, Gramsci favored a cultural approach. He maintained that only by taking control of the cultural command centers of education, the media, and religious institutions, could the overthrow of the existing order succeed. "In the new order," he wrote, "Socialism will triumph by first capturing the culture via infiltration of schools, universities, churches, and the media by transforming the consciousness of society."[58]

Gramsci contended that his goal of cultural hegemony would take place through a "long march" that penetrated every nook and cranny of society. He was convinced that to succeed the Catholic Church had to be radically transformed. He wanted to infiltrate the Church to disseminate ideas that undermined traditional Church teachings. He believed that by promoting dissent within the ranks of the clergy, he would set in motion the Church's ultimate demise.

In 2008, it was revealed by Vatican sources that Gramsci, who had founded the Communist Party in Italy, converted back to Catholicism

---

[58]Roger Kiska, "Antonio Gramsci's Long March through History", *Religion & Liberty*, December 12, 2019, https://www.acton.org/religion-liberty/volume-29-number-3/antonio-gramscis-long-march-through-history.

on his deathbed in 1937; he even received the sacraments before dying. His followers were undeterred, claiming that Gramsci's method of cultural hegemony had been taken up by feminists and used effectively to promote abortion rights and the homosexual agenda.[59]

In the United States, no outside activist had more influence on the Catholic Church than Saul Alinsky. Alinsky was born in Chicago in 1909 to Orthodox Jewish parents, and he became an agnostic in 1926. Widely regarded as Gramsci's disciple, he sought to change society radically from within its cultural institutions. The father of "community organizing", he spent his life forming "people's organizations" that could effectively make demands of employers, landlords, and government leaders.[60] Eventually people unhappy with Church teaching followed his example and formed similar groups to make demands of Church leaders.

Though he never joined the Communist Party, Alinsky worked with many Communists and spoke positively about their efforts among the downtrodden. Like many of them, Alinsky believed that "the end justifies almost any means." Similarly, he believed that "truth is relative and changing."[61]

Alinksy ingratiated himself to members of the Catholic clergy when he partnered with Joseph Meegan to create the Back of the Yards Neighborhood Council (BYNC) in 1939.[62] Meegan's brother was a priest and the secretary to the auxiliary bishop Bernard Sheil. Believing BYNC's mission was in line with Catholic social teaching, Sheil gave it his blessing and served as its honorary chairman. He described Alinsky's 1946 work, *Reveille for Radicals*, as "a life-saving handbook for the salvation of democracy".[63]

---

[59] "Founder of Italian Communist Party Converted before Death", Catholic News Agency, December 2, 2008, https://www.catholicnewsagency.com/news/founder_of_italian _communist_party_converted_before_death.

[60] Patrick J. Henry, "A Study of the Leadership of a 'People's Organization'", 4–7 (master's thesis, Loyola Univserity, 1959), https://ecommons.luc.edu/cgi/viewcontent.cgi?article =2586&context=luc_theses.

[61] See the EWTN video *A Wolf in Sheep's Clothing*, which was aired by the network in 2016. It is available from EWTN online.

[62] Lawrence J. Engel, "The Influence of Saul Alinsky on the Campaign for Human Development", *Theological Studies* 59, no. 47 (1998): 6, http://cdn.theologicalstudies.net/59 /59.4/59.4.3.pdf.

[63] Henry, "A Study", 9.

Another Chicago cleric Alinsky influenced was Monsignor John Egan, "whose work on issues of civil rights, changing neighborhoods and poverty shaped church efforts in those areas nationally".[64] Father Egan had been working in Catholic Action when a 1954 letter from Jacques Maritain introduced him to Alinsky.[65] Beginning in 1958, Father Egan directed the Chicago Archdiocese's Office of Urban Affairs, and he closely collaborated with Alinksy to organize groups that could address housing, integration, and other issues in the inner city. Their partnership "laid the groundwork for what is now a national pattern of community organizing projects based on interfaith coalitions of congregations".[66] Egan accessed diocesan funds to pay for Alinsky's three Chicago organizations in the 1960s and was "the first person to develop community-organizing as an official mission and function of diocesan life".[67] It was Egan who asked Alinsky to explain his community-organizing tactics in the book *Rules for Radicals*. In it, Alinsky acknowledges "the first radical known to man who rebelled against the establishment and did it so effectively that he at least won his own kingdom—Lucifer."[68]

By 1976, Alinsky-style activism had become mainstream in the Catholic Church. That year, the National Conference of Catholic Bishops convened a Call to Action Conference to help implement Vatican II's mandate for the laity to work for justice in the world, and Monsignor Egan cochaired the plenary sessions. On October 21–23, about 1,300 delegates, priests, religious, and laity from 152 dioceses, along with 1,100 observers from around the country, met in Detroit to discuss racism, sexism, and poverty in modern society. When the conference ended, the assembly declared that to deal with these issues "in a credible way the church must reevaluate its positions on issues like celibacy for priests, the male-only clergy, homosexuality, birth control, and the involvement of every level of the church in important decisions."[69]

[64] Peter Steinfels, "John J. Egan, Priest and Rights Advocate, Is Dead at 84", *New York Times*, May 20, 2001, https://www.nytimes.com/2001/05/22/us/john-j-egan-priest-and-rights-advocate-is-dead-at-84.html.

[65] Engel, "The Influence of Saul Alinsky", 7.

[66] Steinfels, "John J. Eagan".

[67] Engel, "Influence of Saul Alinsky", 8.

[68] Saul D. Alinsky, *Rules for Radicals* (New York: Vintage Books, 1989), 4.

[69] "History", Call to Action website, https://www.cta-usa.org/history.

Cardinal John Krol, the archbishop of Philadelphia, declared, "Rebels have taken over our conference."[70] It is startling to think that Alinsky could have penetrated the Church as much as he did. Most of his success took place in the 1970s, when the Church was in upheaval and clergy sexual abuse was skyrocketing. Alinsky died in 1972, one year after *Rules for Radicals* was published, so he did not live to see how effective he was in wreaking havoc.

---

[70] Vincent P. Miceli, "Detroit: A Call to Revolution in the Church", *Homiletic & Pastoral Review*, March 1977, reprinted in Catholic Culture, https://www.catholicculture.org/culture/library/view.cfm?recnum=4544.

CONCLUSION

Thanks to the Dallas reforms, and an awakening of concern for the victims of sexual abuse throughout society, Scandal I is largely behind us. We never had a monopoly on this problem in the first place, but a combination of media bias, rapacious lawyers, politically driven victims' advocates, dissident Catholics, and outside activists have made it seem as though nothing has changed. They don't want it to change. They have a vested interest—whether it be economic or ideological—in keeping the scandal going, at least in the mind of the public. This includes right-wing purist Catholic groups as well as left-wing reformist groups.

It would be helpful if the bishops became more aggressive and less defensive about this issue. For example, many Catholics, never mind the public, are under the impression that somehow the Church still owns this problem. The bishops have a moral obligation to tell them that's not true.

How many know of the "abusive boyfriend syndrome"? They need to know that child abuse in the home is a major underreported crime and that nonbiological live-in partners are the most likely to molest children, not members of the clergy or teachers. They should further note that when states allow for a suspension of the statute of limitations, few lawyers are interested in small cases. Most lawyers go after the deep pockets. Indeed, in some instances where we have data, 95 percent of the cases accepted by attorneys involve suing institutions—that's where the money is. As one victims' advocate admitted, "They'll gladly take a case to sue the church."[1] Moreover, for many people, suing the Church satisfies an ideological need as well as an economic one. It has cost the Church over $3 billion to settle these claims.

[1] Jay Tokasz, "Few Abusers Are Sued as Child Victims Act Lawsuits Target Institutions", *Buffalo News*, February 16, 2020, https://buffalonews.com/news/local/crime-and-courts/few -abusers-are-sued-as-child-victims-act-lawsuits-target-institutions/article_e106c644-7b28 -5055-be2d-436d9a4c020d.html.

The faithful and the public need to be told that the reforms are, in fact, working and that more is being done by the Church, with its independent compensation programs to reach out to victims, than by any other institution in society. Importantly, everyone needs to know that the Church is virtually alone in not tolerating confidential nondisclosure agreements. When the former head of human resources for Bloomberg L.P. from 2008 to 2013, Melinda Wolfe, says, "I don't know of a company that provides severance that doesn't ask for those people who are subject to that severance to sign a nondisclosure agreement", Catholics need to hear this from their dioceses.[2]

Without doubt, among the greatest victims of this contrived drama are accused priests. They are deserving of the same treatment under the law as given to every other segment of society, and this should not even have to be said. But it must. When we have people like Illinois Supreme Court Justice Anne Burke, who used to advise the bishops, arguing that priests should be removed from ministry after only one unsubstantiated accusation—she does not say her dictum should apply to anyone other than a priest—we have all the proof we need that the animus against priests' rights has been mainstreamed.[3] No wonder I get calls, letters, faxes, and e-mails from priests who are grateful for the Catholic League's efforts to stand up for their rights, both in the courts and in the court of public opinion. Too many feel abandoned.

Despite the progress, we can do better. In particular, all of us, especially those who work with the clergy, need to beware of red flags, signs that a priest is troubled and may act out. Not every priest who has an alcohol problem is likely to be an abuser, but if that priest also congregates frequently with young men, especially in his quarters, that should do more than raise eyebrows: the bishop should be told, and the priest must be confronted.

Lack of accountability is a serious issue in the Catholic Church, and not simply in relation to clergy sexual abuse. For all the talk about the Church being a punitive institution, it is, in fact, just the

[2] Jessica Silver-Greenberg and Natalie Kitroeff, "How Bloomberg Buys the Silence of Unhappy Employees", New York Times, updated March 4, 2020, https://www.nytimes.com /2020/03/02/business/michael-bloomberg-nda.html.

[3] Cathleen Falsani and Stefano Esposito, "Cops Wanted to Charge Priest Sooner", Chicago Sun-Times, January 25, 2006, 3.

opposite: there is a very relaxed culture in the dioceses, so much so that it is a wonder there aren't more problems. While cracking the whip is not the optimal sanction—certainly not on a regular basis—there are times when it is needed. If the most irresponsible Church employees are not punished, it sends a message to everyone else that compliance with norms is not important. Conversely, if serious violators are held accountable, everyone gets the message.

Here's an example. In 2018, two nuns in the Archdiocese of Los Angeles were accused of embezzling $500,000 from a Catholic school; as much as $3 million may have been taken over a period of twenty years. The nuns subsequently admitted bilking the school of tuition, fees, and donation money. And what did the school administrators do about it? They refused to file charges against the nuns. It took the police to do that.[4] The in-group favoritism shown the nuns is understandable, and it is what many bishops did when dealing with offending priests, but it is still unacceptable. This kind of reaction is born of myopia: What about the parents who paid the salaries of school employees? Sentimentalism should have no role in making tough decisions, yet too often it does in the Catholic Church.

On the subject of homosexuality, it would be helpful if the bishops could get on the same page. That page is the one in the *Catechism of the Catholic Church*. When we have the archbishop of Newark, Cardinal Joseph Tobin, going on television to tell the public that he disagrees with the *Catechism*'s description of homosexual acts as "intrinsically disordered", we have a real problem. He dubbed it "very unfortunate language".[5] Similarly, a priest who represents Pope Francis' point man on sexual abuse, Maltese archbishop Charles Scicluna, told a radio audience that "a relationship of love" between homosexuals is as "good" as relationships of "love between heterosexual couples".[6] Though he did not address the issue of homosexuality

[4] Veronica Miracle, "Parents Say Torrance Catholic School Nuns Embezzled Millions over 20 Years", ABC7, December 18, 2018, abc7.com/parents-say-torrance-nuns-embezzled-millions-over-20-years.

[5] "Cardinal Tobin: Catechism Language 'Very Unfortunate' on Homosexuality", Catholic News Agency, April 18, 2019, https://www.catholicnewsagency.com/news/cardinal-tobin-catechism-language-very-unfortunate-on-homosexuality-45966.

[6] Edward Pentin, "Maltese Catholics Criticize Archbishop Scicluna's Leadership on 'LGBT' Issues", *National Catholic Register*, March 17, 2019, http://www.ncregister.com/daily-news/maltese-catholics-criticize-archbishop-sciclunas-leadership-on-lgbt-issues.

being "intrinsically disordered", it seems plain that he also rejects the Church's teaching.

Many in the Church wrestle with the issue of having homosexuals in the priesthood. As we have seen, while most homosexual priests are not abusers, most of the abusers have been homosexuals. Therefore, while a homosexual orientation does not cause one to be a molester, it can in some cases make it more likely to become one. This is due primarily to sexual and emotional immaturity, a condition related to being sexually attracted to minors.

This raises the question: Should homosexuals be admitted to the priesthood? In an ideal world, all men would be welcome to the priesthood, *provided they have the internal discipline necessary to accept a vow of celibacy*. Regrettably, it appears that criterion is more difficult for many homosexuals to practice.

Between the time the *Boston Globe* published its stories on the clergy sexual abuse scandal in 2002 and the Dallas conference of bishops, Cardinal Anthony Bevilacqua told reporters something that other bishops believed but were not comfortable saying in public: "We feel that a person who is homosexually oriented is not a suitable candidate for the priesthood, even if he did not commit an act [of gay sex]." What was the source of his reservation? "It is possible we have homosexuals who are very chaste. But the risk is much higher, that he will fail on celibacy. The risk is higher, that's all we are saying."[7]

Distinguished theologian Germain Grisez came to the same conclusion: "Sexuality profoundly shapes the lives of human persons, and a homosexual orientation, albeit less bizarre than the commonly recognized *paraphilias*, is a grave disorder. Homosexual men no doubt can be perfectly continent, but the charism of celibacy involves more; peaceful chastity and the sublimation of sexual energy into priestly service for the kingdom's sake" (his italics).[8] This dovetails with what many homosexual men have confessed: their sex drive is stronger than that of heterosexual men. Dutch psychologist Gerard J. M. van den Aardweg agrees. "Homosexual inclinations tend to be obsessive", and for this reason, he says, "no man with homosexual

[7]Ron Goldwyn, "Bevilacqua: Gays Can't Be Priests; at Meeting of Cardinals, He Says Homosexuals Aren't 'Suitable' Candidates", *Philadelphia Daily News*, April 27, 2002, 3–4.

[8]Thomas J. Gumbleton, "Yes, Gay Men Should Be Ordained", *America*, September 30, 2002, http://www.americamagazine.org/issue/403/article/yes-gay-men-should-be-ordained.

or pedophile inclinations must be ordained to the priesthood, nor admitted as a seminarian."[9]

Even if the sex drive of homosexual men were not any different from that of heterosexuals, how much sense does it make to put them in all-male environments where temptations are bound to flare up? Father Robert Altier raises some thoughtful issues. "We don't allow men into women's convents because it's not going to be long before somebody's going to be having problems." Isn't this just common sense? He also related a conversation he had with a homosexual friend he knew in the seminary. His friend asked him, "Would you ever consider taking a shower in the women's locker room?" He replied, "Certainly not." Then his friend explained, "Now you know what I have to go through when I go into a men's locker room."[10]

Monsignor Andrew R. Baker shares this perspective: "In such a clearly male environment as the seminary and the priesthood, the temptation is ever-present for those with the [homosexual] disorder." It is because the temptation "could make their efforts to live chastely or to be healed of their disorder very difficult" that he recommends against allowing homosexuals to enter the priesthood.[11]

These are practical concerns. No one is saying that homosexuals cannot be good Catholics or that their service to the Church is not welcome. It's just that the seminary and the priesthood, being all-male environments, are not practical for men with strong same-sex attractions. At the very least, those with "deep-seated homosexual tendencies" should not be admitted to the priesthood.

This rule, which is current practice, is common sense. There is a reason why adult young men who are camp counselors are not permitted to chaperone girls on overnight camping trips. Regrettably, young homosexual men became camp counselors and chaperones in the Boy Scouts, and we know what happened there. It does no

[9] Gerard J. M. van den Aardweg, "Psychologist Explains Why Catholic Church Is Right to Exclude Homosexuals from Priesthood", LifeSiteNews, March 12, 2019, http://www.lifesitenews.com/opinion/psychologist-explains-why-catholic-church-is-right-to-exclude-homosexuals-from-priesthood.

[10] Robert Altier, "The Enemy Within," *Catalyst* (October 2018), https://www.catholicleague.org/the-enemy-within/.

[11] Andrew R. Baker, "Ordination and Same Sex Attraction", *America*, September 30, 2002, http://www.americamagazine.org/issue/403/article/ordination-and-same-sex-attraction.

one any good to pretend that the weakness of human nature doesn't count. It always counts.

The role of dissent in the Church functions to legitimize the behavior of molesting priests. When homosexual priests who are drawn to sexual contact with minors learn how acceptable it is in some quarters to disagree with—even to denounce—Church teachings on sexual ethics, what are we to expect? The dissent does not cause troubled priests to abuse, but it does provide cover, making it easier for them to rationalize their behavior. If a teacher told his students that it is okay to disregard what they deem to be unfair parental directives, would we not hold the teacher accountable when the children misbehave?

Bishops understandably find it difficult to discipline dissident priests; superiors of religious orders are in the same boat. They can begin by starting with the most egregious examples. If that is done, others less insubordinate will get the message. To do nothing is just as judgmental as it is to do something; both have consequences, not only for the guilty party but for everyone else as well.

It is more difficult to deal with activists and organizations not subject to Church authority that promote dissidence among Catholics. At the very least, bishops need to be more observant about the way some activists work to undermine Catholic sexual morality through groups that claim to advocate for the social teaching of the Church in the public square. This requires doing a better job of evaluating their platforms, goals, and political allies, as well as their sources of funding.

Here is a case in point. In 2005 Alexia Kelley and Chris Korzen founded Catholics in Alliance for the Common Good, which received funding from the atheist George Soros through his philanthropies: $100,000 through the Foundation to Promote Open Society (2009) and $300,000 through his Open Society Institute (since 2007).[12] Kelley had worked for ten years at the bishops' Catholic Campaign for Human Development (CCHD). In 2004 she was the religious outreach director for the Democratic National Committee during the John Kerry presidential campaign. In the Obama administration, she headed the Center for Faith-Based and Neighborhood Partnerships under Health and Human Services secretary Kathleen Sebelius. Before working as a union organizer and an activist for Pax

---

[12] Patrick J. Reilly, "Rallying the Catholic Left", Capital Research Center, July 4, 2012, https://capitalresearch.org/article/rallying-the-catholic-left/.

Christi, Korzen had cofounded and directed Catholics United, and in 2004 and 2005 directed the Catholic Voting Project, aimed at persuading Catholic voters to select Democrats running for office on the basis of their support for programs for the poor.[13]

But this is just scratching the surface. In 2016, we learned from 2012 WikiLeaks documents how John Podesta, former chief of staff for President Bill Clinton and chairman of Hillary Clinton's presidential campaign, claimed credit for creating Catholics in Alliance for the Common Good in an e-mail to Sandy Newman, president of Voices for Progress. Newman had e-mailed Podesta about the need for a "Catholic Spring" in the Church (an allusion to the "Arab Spring" freedom movements in the Middle East) in order to counter the American bishops who were resisting the Health and Human Services mandate that Catholic organizations provide their employees with health insurance coverage for contraceptives and abortifacients. Newman wrote:

This whole controversy with the bishops opposing contraceptive coverage even though 98% of Catholic women (and their conjugal partners) have used contraception has me thinking ... There needs to be a Catholic Spring, in which Catholics themselves demand the end of a middle ages dictatorship and the beginning of a little democracy and respect for gender equality in the Catholic church. Is contraceptive coverage an issue around which that could happen. The Bishops will undoubtedly continue the fight. Does the Catholic Hospital Association support of the Administration's new policy, together with "the 98%" create an opportunity?

Podesta replied, "We created Catholics in Alliance for the Common Good to organize for a moment like this."[14]

Where Do We Go from Here?

The answer to all of these challenges is a commitment to authentic Catholic teaching and the pursuit of the truth. Doing this not only

---

[13] See Chris Korzen's bio at https://www.huffpost.com/author/chris-korzen, accessed April 16, 2021.
[14] "Re: Opening for a Catholic Spring? Just musing ...", WikiLeaks, February 11, 2012, https://wikileaks.org/podesta-emails.

requires courage; it demands that all bishops and priests resist appeals of affirmation from secular elites. I recall one day when Cardinal John O'Connor called me into his office to discuss some matter but, seeing that I was agitated, he asked me what was wrong. I expressed my exasperation at priests who were more interested in currying favor with parishioners than they were in defending the truth. He said, "Bill, they want to be liked." I replied, "I want to be liked, too, but I also want to be respected." He completely understood.

This is not just a priestly problem. I have witnessed firsthand how the organizers of the Saint Patrick's Day Parade in New York City will do anything, even to the point of overthrowing tradition, to gain the applause of the secular elites. Even after a unanimous decision of the U.S. Supreme Court in 1995 held that parade organizers did not have to allow homosexuals the right to march under their own banner—it was a private event—two decades later, the officials caved in to elite pressure and changed their norms.

For twenty years, I was the unofficial spokesman for the Saint Patrick's Day Parade in New York City, and I always told the media that the parade was no more anti-gay than it was anti-life (gay Catholics and pro-life Catholics could march but not under their own banners). So, when discussions about allowing gays to march as a separate unit took place in 2014, I was approached by parade officials asking if I objected. I was not happy about the concession, but I said I would not publicly object as long as pro-life groups could march under their own banner as well. I was assured they could. It turned out to be a lie: pro-life groups were barred from marching. I then pulled the Catholic League contingent from the parade.[15]

The need to be liked is strong in all of us, but there is a big price to be paid when it becomes controlling, and this is especially true of Catholic leaders, secular as well as religious. Cardinal Sarah understands this problem as well as anyone. "The Church is dying because her pastors are afraid to speak in all truth and clarity. We are afraid of the media, afraid of public opinion, afraid of our own brethren!"[16] All priests should follow his advice: "I am not here to be popular or to increase the numbers in the churches or on the social networks."[17]

[15]Bill Donohue, "We Will Not March; NYC Parade Debacle Grows", *Catalyst* (October 2014), http://www.catholicleague.org/will-march-nyc-parade-debacle-grows.

[16]Robert Cardinal Sarah, *The Day Is Now Far Spent* (San Francisco: Ignatius Press, 2019), 15.

[17]Ibid., 160.

The Church is always in need of reform, but what we don't need is a *new* Church. This was strongly driven home by Pope Emeritus Benedict XVI. Indeed, he calls such appeals the work of the devil. "Yes, there is sin in the Church and evil. But even today there is the Holy Church, which is indestructible."[18] Or, as Cardinal Sarah says, "Despite the violence of the attacks that she may suffer, the Church will not die. This is the Lord's promise, and his word is infallible."[19]

This, of course, is not a recipe for passivity. Just the opposite. We are called as Catholics to put into action the Word of God, and to do that, we need to practice fidelity to the Church's teachings and to have the courage to defend them. That is the surest way to stop scandals from arising in the first place.

---

[18] Benedict XVI, "Full Text of Benedict XVI: The Church and the Scandal of Sexual Abuse", *Catholic World Report*, April 10, 2019, http://www.catholicworldreport.com /2019/04/10/full-text-of-benedict-xvi-the-church-and-the-scandal-of-sexual-abuse.

[19] Sarah, *The Day Is Now Far Spent*, 13–14.

ACKNOWLEDGMENTS

In one way this has not been an easy book to write. After all, those of us who love the Catholic Church have been taxed by the scandal. On the other hand, writing this book gave me the opportunity to clear the air, dispelling many myths; the conventional wisdom has been wrong almost every step of the way. The fact is that almost all priests have never been tagged with accusations of wrongdoing, and indeed they are very good men, deserving of our admiration. Moreover, the progress that has been made is undeniable.

I would like to thank Father Joseph Fessio, S.J., and Mark Brumley of Ignatius Press for having the courage to publish this book. Vivian Dudro, my editor, worked hard to make it better.

The members of the Catholic League—they are the best—are the most loyal supporters in the world. "Be Not Afraid" is written all over their faces.

The same is true of the Catholic League's board of directors, ably led by Walter Knysz. I would also like to give a special shout-out to Mary Ann Glendon of our board of advisors; more than anyone, she inspired me to write this book.

Many of the ideas that shaped this book were influenced by my daily interactions with the Catholic League's policy staff. The exchanges I've had with Bernadette Brady-Egan, Michael McDonald, Donald Lauer, and Nicholas Palczewski helped enormously.

Valerie, Caryn, Paul, Caitlin, and Jay have always been in my corner, and their goodwill has been enhanced by my grandchildren, Grant and Nina. Also deserving of thanks are my good friends Maggie and Mike Mansfield, Linda and Tom Boyle, the McGetricks, and the rowdy ones at Doc's. I toast them all, many times over.

INDEX

Goldberg, Whoopi, 63, 198
Gomez, José, Archbishop, 69
good/goodness
    Catholic Church as force for, 36
    common good, 173, 231
    good priests as majority, 8
    See also virtues
Goodstein, Laurie, 16n24, 40n13,
    43n21, 47n33, 73n60, 77–78, 124
    "sociological rationalization", 181–82
grace, divine, 135
Graham, Billy, 14
Gramick, Jeannine, Sister, 219–20,
    227–28
Gramsci, Antonio, 234–35
grand jury, Pennsylvania, 64–69
Greeley, Andrew, Father, 44, 47–48,
    87–88, 127–28, 147, 151, 184
Gregory, Wilton, Bishop, 147
Griffin, Carter, Father, 150
Grisez, Germain, 242
Guarino, Thomas G., Father, 44–45
guilt
    and denial systems of abusers, 86–87,
        125–26
    sin and, 125, 203
"guilty until proven innocent", 45
    See also due-process rights
Gumbleton, Thomas, Bishop, 162

Halperin, Mark, 25
Hamilton, Marci, 182
Hammond, Gretchen Rachel, 78–80, 82
harassment, sexual. *See* sexual
    harassment
Hasselbeck, Elisabeth, 63
Hawley, Caroline, 30
Hay, Harry, 197
Helmsing, Charles, Bishop, 223
Hendershott, Anne, 195
heresy, 212, 215
Herman, Pee-wee, 199
Herranz, Julián Cardinal, 86
Hesburgh, Theodore, Father, 231
heterosexual men, 90
Hickey, James Cardinal, 118, 221

hierarchy, Church, 142–45
    See also bishops
higher education. *See* colleges and
    universities
Higher Education Act, 230
Hill, Jerry, 69
Hill, Stephen, 60
Hinshaw, Rick, 80
Hinton, Jimmy, 13–14
Hitchcock, James, 127, 131–32, 193, 211
Hitler, Adolf, 11
HIV infections, 154
    See also AIDS
Hoatson, Robert (former priest), 81–83,
    131
Hobbes, Michael, 168
Hollywood
    role in public perception, 61–64
    sexual abuse in, 23, 42, 198–99
homophobia, 93–94
homosexual acts/behavior, 90, 135,
    143–46, 149, 157, 159–60, 210, 221,
    227, 241
    as different from sexual orientation/
        attractions, 108, 144
    dissent and, 214
homosexual crisis, 159, 184
homosexual pedophiles, 141
homosexuality, 136n41, 144, 232
    attractions *vs.* acts, 108, 144
    in the Church, 108, 144, 243
    gay rights, 92, 104, 167–68, 187, 198,
        214, 219
    gay subculture, 145–49
    gift, described as, 135–37
    marriage, same-sex, 189
    most gay priests as not abusers, 128
    in the priesthood, 128, 139–40, 156,
        242
    See also homosexual acts/behavior;
        sexual orientation
homosexuality, role in sexual abuse
    scandal, 128, 164–80
    admitting the obvious, 138–52
    denying the obvious, 127–37
    John Jay thesis, analysis of, 153–63